WITHDRAWN
NDSU

Date Loaned

The
CHRIST
at the Peace Table

OTHER BOOKS BY THE AUTHOR:

LINKS IN CHRISTIANITY'S CHAIN

THE BIBLE: BEACON LIGHT OF HISTORY

YES, 'TIS ROUND!

EAST AND WEST OF JORDAN

FELLOWSHIP: THE STORY OF A MAN AND HIS BUSINESS

WHO WAS THIS NAZARENE?

The
CHRIST
at the Peace Table

BY

Albert Field Gilmore, Litt.D.

1943

PRENTICE-HALL, INC.
New York

112086

Copyright, 1943, by
PRENTICE-HALL, INC.
70 Fifth Avenue, New York

All rights reserved. No part of this book may be reproduced in any form, by mimeograph or any other means without permission in writing from the publishers.

First Printing ....March 1943
Second Printing ....September 1943

PRINTED IN THE UNITED STATES OF AMERICA

To those everywhere who are inspired with the high purpose of bringing into actuality a just and permanent peace for all the peoples of earth—a peace that will insure to every person the opportunity to develop to that degree of freedom and dignity which belongs to the children of God—this volume is dedicated.

And the King shall answer and say unto them, Verily I say unto you, Inasmuch as ye have done it unto one of the least of these my brethren, ye have done it unto me.

MATT. 25:40

Preface

IT IS not the purpose of the author of this book to furnish a complete plan, a blueprint for the New World Order which will be formulated at the Peace Table. Rather is it his purpose to state, repeat, and emphasize the fact that peace, lasting because just, can be accomplished only upon the basis of divine justice as taught, demonstrated and applied by Christ Jesus during his brief ministry in Galilee and Judea. Foreseeing his departure from their midst, he assured his disciples that he would pray the Father who would send them another Comforter (Helper) even "the Spirit of truth," [1] and this Comforter would teach them all things. Thus did Jesus assure his followers that the same agency, the Christ, Truth, which had enabled him to do all that he had done, would be with them, potent and available, to solve their problems, to meet their needs in every direction.

The author is convinced that since this "Spirit of truth," this Christ-Comforter, has never departed beyond the reach of humanity it is everpresent, everywhere, as potent and available to meet the needs of mankind today as during the first century. The necessity is to understand and utilize this divine agency, for by this means only will be gained the lasting peace for which the Allied Nations are so valiantly striving.

It cannot be gainsaid that the present crisis is due to the failure to understand and apply this spiritual power, this "Spirit of truth," which is ever at hand and ever available. The Treaty of Versailles with its basis of idealism was far from bringing this power into operation. Extreme nationalism expressed

---

[1] John 14:17.

Preface

in greed and love of dominion dominated the situation to the exclusion of the Christ expressed in terms of true humanitarianism. It was not the Good Samaritan but self-interest, the lust for power and prestige, that in a large degree finally had its way.

The result is a crisis which has brought the whole world into a conflict unprecedented in its savagery and unparalleled in its extent. So dangerous to civilization does it appear, that many are convinced that a repetition of this frightful devastation would turn humanity backward to the darkness and primeval chaos.

In view of this prospect, it seems incredible that there are still currents of thought that would take the chances again of basing a peace treaty upon selfish aims, nationalism and greed, a policy of isolation for the United States and of commercial imperialism for it and other nations. Apparently the lesson has not been learned that only as the inter-relationship of nations and peoples is based upon the brotherhood of man will a just and durable peace be established.

The situation, however, is not hopeless. Far from it. The remedy is at hand. And the purpose of this volume is to awaken its readers to the understanding that through the utilization of this "Spirit of truth," the world may be saved from its present chaos and a Christian civilization be assured for future generations. No situation of such vital import has ever before faced humanity. Never during the Christian era has evil seemed so dominant. Consequently no such opportunity for service to mankind has ever been placed in the hands of a group as will confront the makers of the New World Order at the Peace Table.

During the last war the Indian poet, Tagore, inquired of a Christian friend, the last Charles F. Andrews, "What are you Christians doing? You have the clearest moral precepts in the Sermon on the Mount! Why do you not act up to them?" Why, indeed! The answer is obvious. Because the spirit of

Preface

this incomparable sermon had not become dominant among the world leaders. Self-interest, nationalism and greed were still in the saddle. The result requires no explication.

Christian civilization is fighting for its very existence. War never makes peace. It never spiritually transforms the human consciousness. It can only halt certain evil passions and thus enable "the Spirit of truth" to enter. It seems incredible that the same old evils will be permitted to control in the next peace effort. Insistence that the spirit of righteousness and justice shall dominate in the deliberations upon which the future welfare of mankind will so largely depend, is the bounden duty of Christendom. There is no other way to the greatly desired goal than the way made so plain by the Founder of Christianity that none need miss it. "This is the way, walk ye in it" [2] has a tremendous urge at this time of world crisis.

The term "Comforter," "the Spirit of truth," as used in this book signifies Divine Science revealed by Mary Baker Eddy. She writes on page 55 of *Science and Health with Key to the Scriptures,* the Christian Science textbook: "In the words of St. John: 'He shall give you another Comforter that He may abide with you *forever.*' This Comforter I understand to be Divine Science." My understanding of the "Comforter," "the Spirit of truth," has inspired the religious sentiments expressed in this book. This understanding has been gained wholly through my many years' study of Christian Science, as set forth in the writings of its Discoverer and Founder, Mary Baker Eddy.

Certain of the material appearing in Part Two in somewhat changed form first appeared in the Magazine Section of *The Christian Science Monitor* and is published by permission.

THE AUTHOR

[2] Isa. 30:21.

Contents

PREFACE vii

Part I

I. THE CHRIST EVER PRESENT 3
II. HAS CHRISTIANITY FAILED? 10
III. JESUS REVEALED GOD 18
IV. THE CHRIST METHOD 27
V. JESUS AS EVANGELIST AND REFORMER 34
VI. THE CHRIST, THE REDEEMER OF MEN AND NATIONS . 46
VII. HEALING MINISTRY OF THE CHRIST 54
VIII. THE KINGDOM: WHAT, WHENCE, WHERE? 63
IX. THE CHRIST AS UNIVERSAL TRUTH 69
X. CHRISTIANITY AND NATURAL SCIENCE 80
XI. SUMMARY 84

Part II

XII. A BROAD VIEW 109
XIII. TOTAL WAR, TOTAL PEACE 120
XIV. WHAT OF DEMOCRACY? 136
XV. PATTERN OF THE NEW WORLD ORDER 150
XVI. LABOR AND INDUSTRIAL PEACE 165
XVII. "AND ALL THE NATIONS SHALL FLOW UNTO IT" . . . 183
XVIII. GOOD NEIGHBORS 199
XIX. PEACE AND THE ATLANTIC CHARTER 217

Contents

XX.	Religious Revolution	226
XXI.	Citizens of the World	240
XXII.	The Christ at the Peace Table	249
	Index	261

PART I

I

The Christ Ever Present

MANY an earnest Christian, troubled, discouraged, disheartened, distraught by the chaos of the times, asks himself, What would the Man of Nazareth do if he were present? Would he out of his demonstrated spiritual authority be able to heal humanity of its many conflicts, of the hatred and malicious racial egotism which has brought on the terrible conflict in which the world is now engulfed? Would he be able to stop the conflict, establishing in its place the peace characterized as passing all understanding?

Behind these queries is the hope and some measure of conviction that, were there present the one whom they are wont to describe as Lord and Saviour, he would be able to correct the evil ways of the world, bringing the reign of peace and good will in place of discord and devastating strife. This conviction is based upon faith and some degree of understanding of the mission of the Master and of the unparalleled accomplishment of this man of marvels. It is apparent to all followers of Jesus that he possessed and exercised a power in degree unlike that of any other who has appeared on earth, although many of his works have been and are being in impressive measure repeated today.

The acknowledgment of this fact inevitably raises a vital question with every thoughtful Christian. What power did Jesus possess that enabled him to annul the laws commonly accepted by humanity as final and inexorable, thereby not only healing sickness, reforming the sinful out of hand, as it were, overcoming distance, stilling the tempest, restoring to life those who had died, walking on the water; in short, reversing laws and conditions thought to be permanent and unchangeable? How did he do it?

These queries involve the character and mission of the Man of Nazareth, and his relation to the source of the power he possessed, which enabled him to perform these and many other "mighty works."[1] How did he feed the multitude; how did he take the boat with him when he was immediately at the other side of the lake; where did he obtain the bread and fish prepared by him for that memorable morning meal on the shore of Galilee? Did he alone possess some transcendental power which enabled him to do all these things; or was this power something which others may possess and utilize if they follow his teachings, walk in his footsteps, live the life he exemplified as the true way of life?

Accepting the Bible narrative as true, we learn that Jesus was born of a Virgin, Mary by name, a resident of Nazareth, an unimportant town nestled among the hills of Galilee, near the edge of the plains of Esdraelon. This spiritually minded maiden gained so clear a concept of God as the Father of all, that she was enabled to bear the Christ child, the Babe of Bethlehem, born in a stable and cradled in a manger.

This Babe developed so spiritual a mentality that he became surpassingly conscious of the divine presence and the availability of this supreme power to overcome, to annul, laws of the flesh, in fact, all material laws. Prepared for his holy ministry by a series of compelling experiences, he taught and demonstrated his position as the Messiah and, because of his teaching, character, and works, acquired the title The Christ, or Anointed One.

Jesus, crucified by his enemies, who feared his growing popularity as threatening to their rule and way of life, was resurrected, appeared again and again to his disciples and friends,

---

[1] Matt. 11:20.

The Christ Ever Present

and later disappeared from mortal vision. Before his final departure, known as the Ascension, he promised the coming of a Comforter, "Even the Spirit of truth," [2] who should reveal all things.

Jesus, the Babe of Bethlehem grown to the stature of manhood, more completely expressed the divine nature than any other who has ever appeared on the earth. He was supremely conscious of his relation to God, his Father; he was fully aware of the divine omnipotence and omnipresence, and it was this knowledge of God, of His Christ as the Truth about all things, and of His likeness, man, that Jesus so authoritatively possessed and exercised. And it was this consciousness of the Truth, the Christ, that enabled him to do all his incomparable works. Moreover, the Comforter, this same Christ, never departed, and hence is available here and now to repeat the works of the Master. But this Comforter must be regarded as ever-present and utilized to correct the false beliefs which so grievously beset mankind.

To answer the queries posited at the outset of this chapter: Would Jesus, were he present here and now, be able to heal the terrific wounds which the world is suffering in punishment of its sins; would he establish a just and permanent peace? The only logical answer derives from an examination of his works, his teachings, and the impress he made upon humanity in his own day, through the agency of the Christ, "the Spirit of truth."

Notwithstanding all he did, manifested, and taught, he was crucified by his enemies, the enemies of the Truth he expressed and proved as divine. An unknown number of believers in addition to his immediate disciples took up the ministry he exemplified, and carried Christianity to neighboring regions. But strife did not cease. The carnal mind had not lost its lust and its cruelty; and in a few decades following his disappearance,

---

[2] John 14:17.

Jerusalem was razed, great numbers of its inhabitants destroyed, and chaos reigned. Jesus brought peace and good will only to those who were receptive to his teachings, willing to adopt them as the way of life, to accept him as the Way-shower, and to consecrate their lives to the ministry he so valiantly set forth. And yet these were unable to bring to humanity lasting peace.

Is not, then, the conclusion justifiable that if Jesus were present today, if he were here in person, he could scarcely establish a mental attitude of peace and good will except with those who were willing to accept his way of life and to follow in his footsteps? In other words, peace would follow only upon the acceptance of the Christ-way of life by the general masses of the people. Then is it not indisputably patent that the work to be done now is to evangelize humanity, to spiritualize the thoughts of the masses to the degree that they who are now selfish and sinful will be ready to transform their thinking, and to exchange their evil ways for the ways of Truth, righteousness, and good will? This is inevitably the problem confronting Christianity, and this means the problem facing the Church of Christ as the instrument having the holy purpose of disseminating the Christ-message.

That many Christians are fully aware of the problem in its many aspects, there is convincing evidence. That the manner of its solution is little understood is equally patent.

It is the purpose of the author in succeeding chapters to discuss first what Jesus actually taught and some results of the applications of those teachings, and to attempt to apply the Christ-remedy to the problems confronting the world at present. And the healing of these erroneous conditions must of necessity be preliminary to the finding and establishing of that peace for which Christendom so poignantly longs and so earnestly prays. It is with a deep sense of humility that the task is undertaken, but the needs, of themselves, compel the effort.

In the incomparable fourteenth chapter of John's Gospel,

The Christ Ever Present

we are told that Jesus promised the coming of another Comforter, sent of God in answer to the Master's prayer. This Comforter was to abide forever, "the Spirit of truth." This Comforter cannot be materially perceived or received. Only through spiritual sense can the Comforter be understood; only through spiritually enlightened consciousness can it be understood and received.

This declaration by the Master was followed by another of specific import, "I will not leave you comfortless; I will come to you." [3] Thus did Christ Jesus assure his faithful students that although he, the human Jesus, would leave them, that is, physically disappear, the Comforter, "the Spirit of truth," would remain, would be with them to meet their needs, if they but held to the vision of the Father received through him.

His rebuke to Philip (John 14:8) plainly indicates that Jesus had revealed God the Father to those who were spiritually prepared to receive the vision. Those who, while companioning with the Master, had seen that he was the Messiah or Christ had seen the Father. For what was the Christ but the Son of God, the deific nature made manifest! It was this "Spirit of truth," this Christ, that would never depart from them, but would be everpresent everywhere, for the omnipresence of Divinity makes inevitable the omnipresence of the manifestation of Deity, the Christ, which Jesus had so convincingly expressed.

In a later verse of the same chapter we read another statement specifically defining the nature of the Comforter as "the Holy Ghost, whom the Father will send in my name," [4] that is, as the Christ. This Christ-Comforter would teach them all things, that is to say, all spiritual truth, the truth about God, His universe, and man, the truth regarding all reality. This would be the same truth which he, as the Christ, had taught them and exemplified through his many demonstrations of the ability of

---

[3] John 14:18.
[4] John 14:26.

the Christ, Truth, to destroy the clamor of evil of whatever nature; in short, to overcome material law at every point.

In the following chapter of the Fourth Gospel again Jesus refers to the coming of the Comforter, this Holy Ghost, or "Spirit of truth," declaring that "he shall testify of me." [5] And he plainly states that his followers would bear witness to what they had seen and heard. They who had seen the manifestation of the Christ in overcoming the laws of the material universe were to bear witness of what they had seen. They, too, must become doers of the works as well as preachers of the word.

Moffatt's rendition of the Greek word for Comforter, "Helper," indicates something of the character of the benefit to be received from the presence of the Holy Ghost when thought should be receptive to its approach.

Jesus as the Babe of Bethlehem was not the Christ, this "Spirit of truth"; but through his progressive and unparalleled expression or manifestation of the divine nature, he became known as the Christ. Peter, with keen insight into what he had seen and heard, voiced the fact precisely when he declared Jesus to be "the Christ, the Son of the living God." [6] Not God, not "very God of very God" [7] in substance, but the Son, the manifestation or expression of Divinity.

Jesus revealed to humanity the divine nature, and this understanding which he possessed enabled him to do his many extremely important works. Leaving the ken of mortals, he did not remove or take away that which had always been present, the divine nature, the Holy Ghost and Comforter. But the withdrawal of the personality of Jesus beyond the mental reach of the disciples turned them of necessity to dependence upon his revelation for their comfort and well being.

---

[5] John 15:26.
[6] Matt. 16:16.
[7] Nicene Creed.

The Christ Ever Present

When Jesus declared, "I am the way, the truth, and the life," [8] manifestly he was not speaking of his material personality. Rather was he asserting that the Christ, his spiritual selfhood, was the only approach to the Kingdom of God. This Christ, was the truth about God, and his understanding of the divine nature made Jesus known as the Messiah, the Christ.

As this "Spirit of truth" is infinite, is everpresent, it is as available to meet the needs of humanity now as when the Nazarene was present in person. This, it was promised, will teach all things; that is, this Comforter was the Truth which would invariably solve humanity's problems of whatever nature. It would heal as Jesus healed; it would reform the sinner; it would raise the dead; it would still the tempest; it would heal the political and social ills of society; it would feed the multitude, solve economic problems; in short, it would do, when understood and applied, all that Jesus had exemplified. It would lift all the burdens with which mortals have bound themselves and, transforming consciousness, it would lead straight into the Kingdom of Heaven. It was and is the way of salvation for all mankind.

There are, however, preliminaries to this state of complete freedom: "If ye love me, keep my commandments." [9] And it is through loving God and His Christ, through loving good and striving to demonstrate it in the daily life, that is furnished proof of our mental status. This Comforter, this Holy Ghost, this "Spirit of truth," sets forth the teachings of Jesus and what he accomplished through the application of his spiritual understanding. And the contents of this volume state my understanding of this "Spirit of truth" in its application to the problems of humanity.

---

[8] John 14:6.
[9] John 14:15.

II

Has Christianity Failed?

IF OFT repeated statements of the day were to be accepted without question, one would conclude that Christianity had egregiously failed because it had not in twenty centuries succeeded in evangelizing humanity to the degree that makes war impossible. Were one to judge solely from the present terrific struggle now encompassing the whole earth, the conclusion would be inevitable—Christianity has failed. And many prominent Christians openly express that view.

Christianity in Peril[1] is the title of a current book, by an eminent clergyman, in which a chapter bears the ominous heading, "Protestantism Is Sick." Similar statements from prominent Christians could be repeated *ad lib* to the purport that Christianity has not accomplished what the Founder and the followers of the Master in the early centuries conceived that it would accomplish.

Many thoughtful people who consider the world chaos from a religious point of view are raising the pertinent query, Has Christianity really failed, that is, has it been proved to be inadequate to develop an orderly society in which nations live in peace and brotherliness? Or have the teachings of Christ Jesus been misinterpreted, and in consequence what is commonly termed Christianity, that is, the corpus of Christian doctrine, as applied does not represent the true teachings of Jesus, the most potent man who has appeared on the earth because he was most conscious of the divine presence?

---

[1] Andrew R. Osborn, Oxford University Press.

Has Christianity Failed?

The query is just and should be answered fairly and openly. If the Master's teachings have been properly applied, then the conclusion is inevitable that he was not the Messiah whose mission was to point the way to the Kingdom of God, that his teachings were not true, and the proof is that they have not done what his immediate followers were led to believe they could do.

Not many followers of the Nazarene are prepared to accept this version of the situation. Many more, and the number is growing, are convinced that not in the numerous precepts of the Master, so frequently buttressed by works, but in the application of those teachings lies the difficulty; that the truth uttered in such simple language, often in impressive metaphor and parable, has been perverted, clothed in garments which have in the centuries hidden their spiritual import, darkening with shadows where only the light of Love should shine forth.

This conclusion is justified and the fundamentals are being examined with care and intelligence. Convictions are being arrived at that are wholly revolutionary toward the generally prevailing concept and ethic of Christian practice.

While Christians are convinced of the fundamental facts regarding the mission of the Master, to point the way to the Kingdom, to make perfectly plain the path to salvation for the individual, many believe that there has developed in the Christian Church a serious diversion from the simple teachings of the Founder, and a marked disparity as to the form and method of worship. Manifestly, to know God as He is, is of primary importance. For surely worship of a false concept of Deity could never bring the salvation which Jesus has promised and to which he has so definitely pointed the way.

God's Kingdom can never be understood and gained except through a clear knowledge of God Himself. Equally sure it is that in order to profit by the coming of Christ Jesus, this messenger of God, His interpreter and revelator must be understood as to his Source, mission and method, if the salvation for

Has Christianity Failed?

humanity which he came to declare and provide is to be generally gained. The need, then, is for re-examination of the Gospels apart from the various creeds and doctrines that have been evolved from them through the centuries. His concept of the Father is beyond question the true concept of Deity. His expression of the Christ, the emanation from the Father, plainly revealed the potency of Truth in redeeming and reforming humanity. Jesus went the whole way. Nothing was left undone. He even proved that death does not conquer Life, and that the real man, in God's likeness, is above control by material beliefs and conditions.

Why has not the freedom which Jesus promised been gained? There can be but one answer, and that answer has more often been felt than uttered by the earnest Christians who have lost their way amid the maze of intellectual arguments to which attention has commonly been given. Intellectualism as such will never solve the world's problems, will never *per se* win for humanity its freedom and salvation. A return to the type of Christianity so plainly set forth by the Master, devoid of dogma, wholly apart from creed and ritual which but hide the sun of salvation, will redress and restore the true concept of God and bring to actuality the redemption, promised in the message, when grasped in the fullness of its possibilities.

It seems that conditions have conspired to develop and perpetuate a wrong concept of God. The old Hebraic idea, the Lord God, Jehovah, borrowed from the second chapter of Genesis, has been held to and expanded even in the face of Jesus' declaration in plainest language at Jacob's well. How can God as Spirit be an anthropomorphic Being, sitting apart from His own creation, bestowing rewards and punishments according to human standards of right and justice?

Limitation of language has often added to this mistaken concept of Deity. Use of "He" and "His," figures of speech which personalize God, "walking with God," "His outstretched hand," "His arm not shortened"—these and many other terms but confirm the manlike concept of God. The tendency to accept mortals as God's children, matter as the likeness of Spirit, has been the major source of the tendency to personalize God.

Plainly, this type of belief regarding the Creator of the only real universe has not brought peace and redemption to the world. And it never can. Only by gaining a true idea of the Almighty can the course of salvation be accurately determined. Nothing is of more importance to humanity than this. Nothing is so fundamental to the salvation of Christianity from the enemy which now strives to destroy it than the firm laying of this stone in the platform of Christian building. It is indeed a cornerstone all too long neglected, a stone which true builders of the structure of Christianity must accept and firmly set in its foundation.

It is little wonder that the student in college or university, reared in the orthodox point of view, or with no religious predilections, finds in his study of physical science that which appears utterly to repudiate the Scriptures. And, instead of presenting the true concept of Deity, the Church all too often has added to the confusion by adhering to and setting forth a materialistic idea of the Creator and of His creation.

In the light of this fact, there can be pointed out but one remedy, namely, a return to the story of the Nazarene's life and teachings as presented in the Four Gospels; and acceptance of that which is plainly expressed in words and directly implied in his works. From this course there evolves the true concept of Deity.

If a mortal is God's likeness, then surely God is not Spirit. Jesus never uttered a more concise statement, or one of more signal importance, than when he declared that God is Spirit. And this makes impossible the creation by Spirit of a material universe including mortals. Whatever explanation may be given for the appearance of mortals upon the earth, or of the phenomenon of the earth itself, many find in the theory of evolution the most satisfactory explanation of that appearance. But this by no means explains the man of God's creating, the man in His likeness, the man of whom Jesus saw God to be the Father. Whether one accepts Darwin's thesis set forth in the "Descent of Man" or Henry Drummond's theory in the "Ascent of Man," explanation of the real man, his Source and nature still awaited the clear revelation.

How manifest it is that the problem of healing mortals, of redeeming the world from the darkness of chaos is not solved by intellectualism. Standing in the midst of the library of the British Museum, amid the millions of the Bibliothéque Nationale, or the huge Library of Congress, one can scarcely fail to be impressed by the immense scope of the human intellect which has produced such a tremendous output. The great intellects of the ages are here represented in all their fullness of knowledge. The great philosophers from the Greek school to the present are here represented. Poets, historians, scientists, mathematicians, in short, representatives of the whole great galaxy of notables here stand in impressive array.

Pause for a moment amidst this plethora of intellectualism and ask yourself, Why, after such immeasurable expenditure of mental effort, is the world immersed in such a terrible calamity as now confronts humanity? Why all this, if the wisdom of the ages is the healing agency for the ills of mankind? And the answer is plain. Humanity has backed the wrong remedy. It has applauded the intellectual when it should in due humility have stood for the spiritual.

It was a little child whom the Master set in the midst of those inquiring as to who would be greatest. The receptivity of the child intelligence, its humility, its trust, its positive faith, its simple honesty—all these are the mental qualities which make thought receptive to the healing touch of the Christ. How very little have these qualities been manifested in those whose impressive tomes crowd the library shelves of the world! How great a part has human pride, plain egotism, played in establishing these as intellectual masters of the world! What has led poor humanity into the most terrific struggle the world has ever known?

There is a reason for this world chaos. There has been a cause for the present situation. Much has been done to precipitate it. Still more has been left undone. The simple humility of the Master has been forgotten. Pride and love of prominence have mounted the ladder of human endeavor, instead of submission—humble, grateful and obedient—to the admonitions of the meekest, the most humble, yet the mightiest man who has ever appeared on earth. "I can of mine own self do nothing;" [2] and "the Father that dwelleth in me, he doeth the works." [3] These sublime expressions of humility have found little recognition and less exemplification even among the spiritual leaders of the times.

This writer does by no means fail to recognize the utmost degree of devotion, the unending sacrifice put forth by uncounted millions of lofty characters during the Christian era. But when the simple spiritual teachings of the Master, supported by his many marvelous accomplishments, were early superseded by philosophical dissertations, when dogma and creed supplanted "seek ye first the kingdom of God," [4] then the door was closed to the light of the glorious Christ, and opened wide to the reception of that which has overshadowed the direct, simple, priceless and effective teachings of the Nazarene.

Diversity of opinion early appeared in the development of doctrine and dogma. These diversities widened into disparate groups, each intent upon its own interpretation of the records

---

[2] John 5:30.
[3] John 14:10.
[4] Matt. 6:33.

Has Christianity Failed?

of the life, words and work of the Master as recorded in the Gospels. Through the centuries these divergent dogmas grew in number, and their proponents stiffened in their adherence to some specific creed until Christendom was divided and subdivided into many denominations, each contending for its own interpretation of the fundamentals.

In large measure the true teachings have been lost sight of in the ardor of denominational defense. The spiritual meaning of the Master's words has been drained off, spiritual healing abandoned, and the support of the Church given to the medical fraternity in the healing of mankind's rapidly increasing types of disease. And God has been proclaimed as the creator of the material remedies in common use, with the result that the Great Physician, whom Jesus proclaimed as the only true Physician, was abandoned as the true healing agency. Thus was the Christly garment divided.

Examination of the present situation and of its background leads to the inescapable conclusion that the clergy, the men of God who have assumed to carry on the Christian ministry—the ministry which has the holy purpose to redeem and save mankind—have failed in one of its most essential features, healing of sickness of every type. Of this, specifically, more will be said in succeeding chapters.

After all the evidence has been examined, evidence merely touched upon here, after present world conditions have been explored and the causes determined, it seems inevitable that there must be an acknowledgment that Christianity as applied, as taught and generally practiced, has fallen far short of the Master's purpose in his Messianic mission. Humanity is not redeemed. Salvation for the human race is yet to be won. The time is late and the need is urgent. Is the Church ready to face the issue, give up its dogmatic and ritualistic methods, turn to the Bible for instruction and inspiration, gain the spiritual import of its priceless message; and, understanding of God and His Christ gained, to apply that knowledge with humility and renewed consecration to the solution of the problems so poignantly demanding solution?

The time is now, and the means are at hand. But these means must be gained and applied in order to produce the desired results. When Jesus admonished his disciples that if they would persist in the use of his teachings, the spiritual truth, not only were they true disciples but he assured them that they would gain the Truth that makes men free. Can there be the slightest semblance of doubt as to the character of that Truth? It is the Truth about God and His Christ; the Truth about the universe, and man. In brief, it is the Holy Ghost, the Comforter—spiritual understanding.

III

Jesus Revealed God

THERE had long lain in the heart of Jewry the firm conviction that the golden age which had come to flower in the reigns of David and Solomon would be again restored; that the yoke of the foreigner would be lifted and the ancient prestige reestablished. This was to be brought about through the coming of the Messiah, the earthly representative of the Jehovah whom they had, as they believed, so worthily worshiped.

That Jesus failed to fulfill their dreams, that he brought an entirely different message than the anticipated one, that his promised Kingdom was far from their concept of the glory to which Israel was to be restored, that he overthrew and disregarded many of their sacred and ancient rituals, their customs and convictions, stirred the opposition which finally led to his crucifixion. His ways were not their ways, his teachings did not conform to their concepts of religion and worship, his outlook upon life and its purpose was so far from theirs that there could be no conciliation between them. One or the other must give way, and the belief of the hierarchy—that, with the one whom they regarded as the chief malefactor removed, they could continue in their accustomed ways—determined their course of action.

What was the new doctrine that was regarded as completely revolutionary to their social, political, and religious ways? What it was and what impact it made upon society will be the purpose of succeeding chapters.

Jesus came in fulfillment of the divine Law, which is ever

operative in human consciousness whenever that consciousness becomes susceptible to its influence. Not because the spiritually illumined prophets had foretold his coming did he come, but because inexorable spiritual Law, forever operative through the activity of Christ, progressively illuminated human consciousness until it produced a mentality so devoid of the material concept of generation that it beheld God as the only Father, and man in God's likeness as a grand brotherhood.

Then did Jesus appear; and that he fulfilled prophecy in nowise made his advent the result of the prophetic vision. Rather did the spiritually illumined, sages and seers, through their exalted perception, foresee the coming of a Way-shower and Saviour as the sure result of the operation of this divine Law, leavening, exalting, preparing a human consciousness for an unprecedented experience. Thus appeared the Messiah, the Christ-Comforter and herald of salvation, forerunner of the advent of the Kingdom for all prepared for the perfect type of citizenship in the only true Democracy, that which is God-established and divinely maintained.

To understand the teachings of Jesus and their impact on the times, it is necessary to examine somewhat the social conditions of that period. Palestine was an overcrowded region whose inhabitants ranged in material possessions from extreme poverty, the condition of the masses, to great wealth, possessed by the few. The dominant, ruling class, made rich through trade and exploitation of the people, and especially through the administration of the religious orders, was small in numbers but powerful in influence. The masses, ignorant and in poverty, were conscious of a dominance of the rulers which had reduced them to a type of servitude, if not to actual slavery. Since Palestine was a province of Rome, taxes were wrested from the people and sent to the Imperial City. Other taxes were collected for the support of the religious orders of the day. In local affairs Rome was only partially dominant, although its military authority was final in keeping the people in subjection.

Under the Roman yoke were the local rulers, established by the religious hierarchy. These officers exercised authority over the masses, authority, however, not in conflict with or inimical to the interests of the Caesars. The people had few political rights or important status as citizens of Palestine. But those who were citizens of Rome were entitled to certain privileges which accompanied such citizenship, as, for example, the right of trial when charged with misdemeanor. It was Paul's assertion of the rights of Roman citizenship which took him to Rome for trial. When accused of crime, sedition, or the lesser felonies common to humanity, the culprit was commonly hailed before the Sanhedrin for hearing and judgment. In this respect the local government was a type of theocracy.

Briefly, it was a time of depression and discouragement on the part of the people. Burdened, in poverty, under a domination by the religious hierarchy that was almost intolerable, the masses were near to despair. Worship of Jehovah, God of rewards and punishments, had evolved into rules and dogmas, creeds and formalism that left little liberty whereby the individual might work out his salvation. The times were harsh, cruel, intolerant. The individual was of little value in the sight of the constituted authority. In many respects the situation was a parallel of the conditions in Greece when democracy was first given birth. The upper stratum of society, the aristocracy—the rulers, Pharisees, and scribes—rested upon the shoulders of a disturbed, unhappy, discontented proletariat. Such was the social situation when Jesus appeared.

* * * *

Jesus came for the most exalted purpose, to bring the Gospel to heavily-laden humanity—the Good News of salvation, of freedom from every constricting condition—even to show the way to eternal life. He came to establish a state of consciousness which was and is the Kingdom of God. This Kingdom in which God reigns supreme is the realm of Truth and Love, the spiritual state into which there can enter nothing that "defileth . . . or maketh a lie."[1] It is the state of supreme good, of perfect being, of holiness and sanctity. It is the spiritualized consciousness wholly devoid of material beliefs or conditions.

Contrary to the common belief that the Kingdom of God was related only to some future state, Jesus declared its present presence. It was not a state to be gained through the gateway of death; rather was it a present state to be attained by all ready to make the effort to gain it. And its attainment would bring freedom from every sense of lack, from all that defeats right human endeavor. It would bring joy and peace and plenty in place of grief, of burden, of misery, of want. In the Kingdom is plentitude; lack is unknown. Moreover, Jesus gave the precise, the exact method, for winning this most precious of all prizes, this Kingdom of God wherein all are blessed and free.

Unlike the great philosophers who had preceded him, Jesus came not to expound and develop a carefully defined theory to satisfy the intellect. His message was wholly unlike the philosophy of the great Greek intellectuals and the methods of the Hebrew theologians. He came, as we have seen, to establish the way of salvation, the state of consciousness termed the Kingdom of Heaven, and to prove it possible of present attainment. He did not immediately make plain his own relation to this heavenly state, did not at once declare himself in his majestic role. Rather did he prepare the way, through his teaching and his deeds, to be accepted as the Messiah, as sent of God, when his followers had been impressed to the point of conviction.

John Baptist had in a measure prepared for the advent of the Master. He had struck out boldly against the methods of the Pharisees and the scribes, who were accredited adherents of the

---

[1] Rev. 21:27.

Jesus Revealed God

Jewish religion. Thus heralded, Jesus immediately demanded a new Israel, a regenerated body politic, shorn of its false authority and claim to racial superiority. He called for a moral awakening, for a spiritual upsurge, a recognition of the spiritual needs of the masses.

This was not to be limited to the "educated," to the Scribes and Pharisees, to those who had been taught the orthodoxy of the Jewish religion, but for all ready to accept the new evangel, the good news of freedom and regeneration. He taught as none had ever taught before, by parable and proverb, exemplified by acts of mercy, by the healing of sickness and forgiveness—the regeneration which would bring freedom from every type of bondage.

Before entering deeply into the quality and effectiveness of Jesus' teachings, let us look for a moment at his physical surroundings, the theatre of his revolutionary drama. Galilee was the scene of the Nazarene's youth and young manhood. This province was not, as is commonly believed, an isolated and sparsely settled region. On the other hand, it was, in a sense, a land of plenty. Its numerous cities were populous and with much wealth, held for the most part by the aristocracy and a prominent merchant class. Manufacturing, as that term is now used, was practically unknown. Small hand crafts were numerous, but the machine age was far in the future.

Nazareth was a straggling village set in an elongated basin with surrounding hills that bordered the plain of Esdraelon. This level plain reached from the sea at Joppa eastward to the Jordan. Across it from east to west ran the road connecting the Mediterranean with the valley of the Jordan and the populous cities of the Decapolis beyond. Across it also ran in a general northern-and-southern direction the great highway that connected Egypt with Syria and the Great East, with Mesopotamia, and led on even to India.

Jesus Revealed God

Over these roads flowed a constant stream of commerce, borne by camel and donkey trains, exchanging the products of Europe and Africa for the treasures of the East. It was a cosmopolitan crowd that traversed these highways, which may well at that period have been described as the crossroads of the world. Along these rough ways soldiers bore the Roman Eagles to and from the Imperial City, symbol of the greatest empire of ancient history. Against the hills to the northwest the considerable city of Sepphoris rested on the plain.

In the midst of these surroundings the youth of the young Nazarene was passed. Can one imagine a more cosmopolitan tide of humanity than that which passed before his young eyes? No more can we believe that this mentally alert youth, with a constantly growing vision of spiritual values, was not learning lessons of the complex problems of humanity, exemplified in the ebb and flow of this restless tide.

The notion that Jesus was constricted in his years of preparation, that he was merely a rustic lad, that he lacked contact with humanity in its varied aspects, is wholly dispelled when the true picture of his environment is envisioned. He was gaining an understanding of humanity and its needs that would be invaluable to him in the great work that lay ahead. Not in Rome, not in Alexandria, not in Athens, but here on the edge of the great plain was he observing humanity in its varied aspects, its needs, its aspirations, its worth, its failures and its triumphs. Surely, nothing was lacking in the experiences he was undergoing, experiences that gave him both a broad and an intimate outlook upon life.

Other influences beside the geographical and physically environmental bore in upon Jesus' youth. Coupled with the glamour of the Roman authority exercised by Pontius Pilate and other officials of the Empire, living in splendor regarded as in keeping with their positions, was the insidious infiltration of the Greek culture. The language of their forefathers, the ancient Hebrew, was gradually giving place to the liquid cadences of the Greek tongue.

With the Greek language came not only the Greek philosophy, but Greek manners and Greek forms of worship as well. The old formal ritual of worship, dating far back in Hebrew history, was being shaken to its very foundations by this incursion of a new philosophy and a new type of religion through the vehicle of a language euphonious and appealing. It was a period of change, a situation favorable to the reception of the revolutionary doctrine about to be set before the people of Palestine. Even the Hebrew Bible had been translated into Greek: both the Septuagint and the Apocrypha appeared in this imported tongue.

It was to the upper stratum of society that this new culture, brilliant, easy in its morals, made its first and chief appeal. Herodians and Sadducees, powerful sectors of Palestinian society, were first to come under its subtle influence. The tendency of this Greek culture was greatly to change the social conditions that the youthful Jesus was to challenge. Like the aristocratic classes today, these ancient autocrats were intensely desirous of maintaining the *status quo*. Of course, they desired to continue their luxurious manner of living; and their mode of life reflected in no small measure the glamorous extravagance of the Roman ruling class throughout the Empire.

What chance had an unknown young carpenter of Nazareth to overthrow these conditions, to change the trends and meanings of the social order, to the extent that justice and righteousness should supersede class and special privilege, that mercy and kindness and the message of the Golden Rule should supplant cruelty and domination, greed and covetousness? It was, indeed, a difficult task that faced this indomitable crusader; one, however, from which he never flinched, even though he foresaw the Cross, with all its terrible significance.

[24]

Jesus Revealed God

It was the resentment engendered by the overturning of the social status, no less than the resistance of the Pharisees, that led to his persecution. Whenever cherished habits, vested interests, and established social customs are strongly challenged, immediately there follows resistance with such combined forces as the disturbed can bring to hand. In the case of the Master it was the combined authority of Rome and the religious hierarchy in the form of the Sanhedrin that undertook to cross and barricade the path of this revolutionist. They could betray and crucify him, but the Truth he brought to mankind is universal and eternal, and hence beyond possibility of destruction. Its operation has never ceased, since Truth universal and eternal is everoperative.

Jesus well knew the limitations of life under the heavy hand of a dominant power. Rome had long held Palestine in a firm grasp, tightened whenever internal discord in the shape of rebellion dared to show its hand. To be sure, the Caesars were wise enough to leave local government to the local authority; but the hand of Rome was ever ready to quench any uprising against the Empire. The symbols of Roman authority were never absent. Widespread about the country were Roman garrisons, and the Roman Eagles even hovered over the entrance to the Temple.

In this atmosphere Jesus was reared. It was a period of tension. The restless spirit of the masses was for the time held in suspense. But it was the calm before the storm. Jerusalem itself was in the path of the mighty tornado of imperial might that in a few decades swept it into ruin and, its destroyers believed, into oblivion.

The flow of commerce along the great highways, together with the enterprise of Roman merchants, had brought extensive wealth to the upper classes. And this flow of wealth reached beyond the secular group, into the pockets of the priestly class. An intricate system of taxes for various phases of worship, together with the exorbitant prices charged for the creatures gathered for sacrifice at the great festivals, aggregated a vast sum, for the most part extracted falsely from the people. This was another condition that Jesus confronted when he began his ministry. It was not new to him, for, reared in the very midst of it, he was thoroughly familiar with the hypocrisy and dishonesty involved.

One can hardly wonder at the vehemence with which Jesus denounced these evils. Thoroughly imbued with the spirit of honesty, of justice and mercy, he was deeply stirred; and with him witness of a wrong was the signal to attack it, not in the spirit of hatred and malevolence, but rather to heal it, to remove its weight from the shoulders of the people. No man was ever so courageous in attacking evil; no man was ever so little afraid of consequences. He sought no worldly honor. He served no purpose but service to God, to establish a Kingdom of good, or righteousness, in which every mortal could become a citizen and a beneficiary of its blessings by fulfilling the conditions of citizenship, exchanging material beliefs for spiritual understanding, for knowledge of God and His universe; that is, by forsaking the god of mammon, of materiality, for the Christ, the Comforter, the everpresent Truth. This was the price, the only cost of admission to citizenship in the city of the Great King, which Jesus came to offer to every mortal.

IV

The Christ Method

To be sure, Jesus began no frontal attack upon the evils that he saw all about him in the environment in which he had been reared. His method was neither that of the usual revolutionary nor that of the rebel. It was even more powerful, more effective than either method, as commonly used, could possibly have been. It was the introduction into human consciousness of the fundamental facts of existence: the truth about God the Father, the brotherhood of man forever existent in the Father's Kingdom, and the blessedness and peace abiding there. And he represented this spiritual state as everpresent and immediately available for all who would undergo the needed change of mentality, the transformation by the renewing of the mind, which Paul later so effectually set forth. He well knew that this type of transformation would be slow, for cherished beliefs do not yield rapidly. The determination to change may be made instantly, but the retracing of one's steps is a longer process. He was presenting to his fellows the beauty and loveliness of the Christ, his spiritual nature.

The proof of the effectiveness of Jesus' method is found in the degree of alarm felt by the rulers, an alarm mild at first but developing into a determined effort to destroy this disturber of their highly satisfactory system of extortion and government. Hence he was denounced as a stirrer-up of the people, a person manifestly dangerous to the accepted order. Therefore he must be removed.

Jesus' methods were the very essence of simplicity. His de-

The Christ Method

mand was for a moral awakening, for a change of mental habit from self-seeking to a desire to serve Him whose Kingdom was to be established. This change was to be accomplished by special "learning," that is, by gaining knowledge of God the Father, which leads to change of desire, of purpose, of heart. And in all this his approach was that of a humble Galilean, a carpenter's son who had companioned with the class of people he was now striving to awaken to the possibilities of a new and happier state of existence, wholly within their grasp if they would but accept his message as genuine, sent of the Father.

And all this was presented in their own language, the simple Aramaic tongue, the colloquial form of speech. He made no discrimination against those who were regarded as wicked and sinful, as low and degraded. But when he chose his intimates, those whom he was to instruct in preparation for the great mission of spreading his gospel to the whole world, he selected those of a different type—the sturdy and responsible sons of the better class, those who would be regarded with respect when they, as apostles, would enter upon their significant ministry.

How patent it is that this man, who was to become founder of the religion accepted by all Christendom, was divinely guided, was directed by God, his Father; that he was the greatest exponent of the indisputable fact that there is a Divinity presiding over the affairs of mortals, in fact, over the entire universe of reality! At first, it was mostly the simple people, humble peasantry, who listened with rapt interest to this preacher of a new order. Here were set forth teachings at once so plain as to be easily understood, which promised vastly more than they had ever expected to attain, a state of happiness, of permanent joy, the like of which they had never dreamed.

But there were conditions that this new experience demanded, radical, even complete change of thought and of the whole mental attitude. It gradually dawned upon his intent listeners that a tremendous demand was being made upon them,

The Christ Method

a demand, it seems, that was far more than many were ready to concede.

While this Father of all is surpassingly benevolent, yet He is inexorably exacting, His demands are imperative; they are definite and are to be strictly obeyed, both in the letter and in the spirit. Moreover, the reward will be in exact proportion to the degree of the obedience rendered, nothing more, nothing less. And there are to be no favorites, no special privileges bestowed upon the high and mighty. All are to be treated with strict impartiality, and all will receive the full reward for their obedience and selfless service. No distinction is drawn between classes of society. Even the publicans and harlots will gain the Kingdom of God before the self-seekers (Matt. 21:31).

But these blessings are not cheaply bought. For this Kingdom, this sacred experience, a great price must be paid, even complete self-surrender—that is, surrender of the things the carnal mind had held so firmly, had prized so highly. But this surrender entails no sacrifice of true value, that is, of things of the Spirit.

These revolutionary teachings that promised such rewards, plus Jesus' many merciful works, inevitably, it seems, attracted great crowds. The people, smarting under the many depressing conditions, sought surcease from want and misery. They were eager for what he promised them, until they learned the price. They were quite willing to be fed when they were hungry, were grateful to be healed of their many diseases, to be relieved of their constricting infirmities. Yet for many the price was too high. To lay off and renounce their habitual and cherished beliefs regarding life, regarding substance and existence, was more than they were then prepared to pay, even for the limitless blessings of the Kingdom.

It is easily understood why so many left him, turned away from his exacting messages. To gain the sense of ease in matter, they were willing to be healed. But to exchange material conditions that seemed so real for spiritual realities quite beyond cognizance of the material senses was too much for the majority of those depressed multitudes. How perfect a parallel to conditions today. Many desire the loaves and fishes, if they can be obtained by slight effort and with no loss of cherished beliefs. It is a longer step than they are prepared to take. While it is evident that Jesus was ever ready to heal the masses who crowded him whenever opportunity offered, yet there is evidence that he did not attempt to develop a following, except of those who gained some insight into the true significance of his message.

Frequently Jesus withdrew from the crowd, undoubtedly to refresh himself at the fountainhead of his spiritual nature, to commune with his Father. To accomplish this it became a necessity to gain the solitude that the presence of the masses precluded. It is convincingly apparent throughout the Gospels that Jesus relied much upon these periods of communion with the Father to sustain him in his works of leading his hearers, many or few, into the way of the Kingdom. Once convinced of his mission, he faltered not. The one purpose, to establish for all ready to receive the message the glories of the Kingdom, was paramount with him throughout the period of his ministry. His was a definite purpose. His was the eye single to the accomplishment of that purpose.

It is also apparent that it was not his purpose immediately to gather a great multitude of converts. He was not a political exhorter seeking support and suffrage of the people. He was the great reformer, sent of God to reveal the glories of the Kingdom, through revealing the nature of God Himself. How far removed was his purpose from that of the self-seeker, coveting political or social prestige! There could scarcely be a greater distance between two mental states than between those of this humble young Nazarene and the political autocrats of the time. One has endured; the others have long since passed into oblivion

The Christ Method

so far as the personalities of that day are concerned. But their mental outlook, sometimes in even aggravated form, is found to be distressingly manifest when the present world conditions are even casually explored.

To ensure the spreading of the gospel that he came to bring, Jesus selected and trained a body of men who became his faithful apostles. To fill the role he desired of them, it became necessary for them to detach themselves from their former environment in order to give full attention to his teachings and to the work of spreading them throughout the known world. Of both the Twelve and the Seventy he demanded the highest type of ministry. Not only did he require that they accept his teachings as the way to the Kingdom, but he demanded of them works to prove their understanding and their consecration to the mission set before them.

The world's greatest Teacher, fired by the Spirit, was not satisfied with half-way devotion. It was only the sacrifice of all material desires and possessions that satisfied this master-Christian. No half-way consecration would ever succeed in the evangelization of humanity, which Jesus desired and for which he was prepared on his own part to make every sacrifice.

Without a home, utterly devoid of those things which seem necessary for personal comfort and pleasure, Jesus bore the hardships that his incessant labors demanded without a murmur, for he knew he was in the service of the Father, a service in which he would not only be sustained but for which he would be bountifully rewarded. For was he not to sit at the right hand of the Father; that is, was he not through his sacrifice of all material possessions and pleasures to gain full understanding of the joys of the Kingdom, the joys which are permanent because expressive of the eternal state of consciousness that characterizes the Kingdom, the Heaven of perfect Being?

Nothing short of wholehearted faith and consecration did this Man of God demand of those who were to have the inesti-

The Christ Method

mable privilege of receiving his most intimate messages, the most precious teachings ever to reach human ears. The cause was of too great moment, of too deep significance to humanity to be trusted to any not prepared to lay all on the altar of sacrifice. An absolute faith based upon spiritual understanding was the standard he set as preparation for this ministry.

Jesus' method of teaching was both practical and impressive. Its pedagogy is perfect. His use of simile, of metaphor, of parable cannot be excelled in effectiveness. Constantly he used maxims and proverbs, each containing a truth vital to salvation from carnal modes of thought. His effort was to reach the various types of mentalities, to reach each by some impressive saying. Only those were prepared to receive and spread his message who were willing to make loyalty to the Father the chief and ruling motive of their lives.

The teachings of Jesus have two general aspects, those relating primarily to the individual and those that more definitely pertain to the social order. No strict line of division can be drawn between the two, for the one blends into the other as the first gleam of morning light merges into the fullness of day. Individual regeneration and reform logically lead to an improved social order. In fact, since the stream can rise no higher than its source, the social order can never rise above the spiritual status of its constituent members. The difficulty has been that the spiritual attainment of many individuals has not been carried into the halls of government. Self-interests that would be regarded as utterly abhorrent in individuals have often characterized the policies and acts of states and nations.

It was manifest that Jesus taught and expected that the reformation, the spiritual insight of the individual, would be carried into the social order, not alone into worship and education, into business methods, but into national policies and governments. The New Order to be established, the Kingdom of God, was the model for such organization and government as seemed

The Christ Method

necessary to meet humanity's needs. He rendered to Caesar the things that were due Caesar. He obeyed the law, paid his taxes, and met the demands upon him as a citizen.

Fundamental in the preparation of the individual for citizenship in the Kingdom was faith, whole-hearted, unshakeable, and constant faith in God and in His relation to His universe. It was the type of assurance in the goodness and presence of the Father that could pray, "Thy will be done," [1] in perfect assurance that God's will for His children would invariably bring blessings and joy. This faith in its fullness would enable one to move mountains. The right attitude of the prayer of faith would ask only for that which was necessary for the daily needs, not to satisfy the lust for possessions for their own sake.

It is palpable to the close student that Jesus regarded the Father as constantly bestowing upon His children much more than they are prepared to ask for. Because of their limited vision, they had scarcely glimpsed the glories that were to be theirs when they became willing and obedient citizens of the Kingdom.

---

[1] Matt. 6:10.

V

Jesus as Evangelist and Reformer

WHILE we have spoken of Jesus as the skillful teacher, he was also evangelist and reformer. His teaching was repetitious to a degree, for he well knew the tenacity of mortal mind, its tendency to hold fast to its own concepts of life and substance. Accordingly, he repeated again and again; "precept upon precept, precept upon precept; line upon line, line upon line; here a little, and there a little" [1] was his constant method. His precepts must be so thoroughly assimilated that his intimately instructed students would never lose their vision of spiritual truth which he was so impressively unfolding to them. If this foundation work were not well and permanently laid, the work of evangelization and reform that his disciples were to do would not stabilize and perpetuate the spiritual import of his message.

Jesus well knew the difficulties of the task ahead, for he was fully aware of the resistance with which the carnal mind invariably attempts to defend and preserve its own concepts. The true disciple, made steadfast through repetitious teaching, will stand in the face of the enemy, however threatening and powerful it may seem to be.

In addition to his public addresses, made when the multitude crowded about him, Jesus privately taught his chosen students to whom he looked for the carrying on of his work of reformation. And reformation of human thought, transformation

---
[1] Isa. 28:13.

from a material to a spiritual basis, was the end and purpose of his teaching. Only through this reformation could citizenship in the Kingdom be gained. So effective was his method that he was declared to be a "teacher come from God." [2] What more impressive proof could there be of the success of his teaching than that! His words did reach his students, for they saw his mission as God-ordained and divinely executed.

If we were to examine only the Sermon on the Mount, the very essence of Jesus' comprehensive teaching, and the experience with Nicodemus, we should be convinced of his consummate success as instructor in the most vital truth ever presented to mortals. Nicodemus was a Pharisee, one of that influential group which held to strict obedience to the law and observance of all its rites. He was a member of the Sanhedrin, yet that he was in some measure of open mind is seen in his coming to Jesus to inquire regarding his teaching and the authority which the Master had exhibited in his merciful works.

Nicodemus declared at the outset of the interview his faith in the Nazarene, that he had truly come from God. "Rabbi, we know you have come from God to teach us, for no one could perform these Signs of yours unless God were with him." [3] The answer was most significant and adroit in disclaiming special powers or ability inherent in himself. "Truly, truly I tell you, no one can see God's Realm unless he is born from above." [4] God was the source of his authority, to be gained by others only through a new birth.

This to Nicodemus was a new, a strange idea. To be born again, how could this be? And it is very apparent that the Pharisee was thinking wholly in material terms of a second, material birth. Jesus, consummate teacher, replied in direct

---

[2] John 3:2.
[3] Moffatt's translation, John 3:1–2.
[4] Moffatt's translation, John 3:3.

and forceful terms. One must be born spiritually, that is, "of water and of the Spirit"; [5] of water as a symbol of purity; of the Spirit, for only spiritual existence is real and permanent. And he follows with a statement as profound as it is simple: "That which is born of the flesh is flesh; and that which is born of the Spirit is spirit." [6]

How complete a presentation of the facts of existence, of Truth and its expression! The flesh and its offspring can never enter the Kingdom, the Realm of Spirit. The spiritual never derives from the flesh, that is, from matter; no more does material existence emanate from Spirit. Consequently, the only means whereby mortals can enter the Kingdom is through the process of regeneration, of transformation of one's concept of life from matter to Spirit as the actual and final condition of man, of God and His Kingdom. This spiritual existence is cognized through material sense no more than is the source of the wind.

The query of Jesus that follows is incisive in that it implies among the Pharisees a lack of understanding of things of the Spirit. Strange that a master in Israel, that is, a member of the Sanhedrin, should not be versed in these ultimate truths. And he reverts to the authority of his teachings, for has he not come down from Heaven? And no man can reach Heaven except he recognize that his true selfhood is in Heaven, God's Kingdom, from which His son, man's spiritual selfhood, has never departed.

In Cowden's *St. John's Christ* [7] the author points out the specific qualities that confirm Jesus as the highly successful teacher. He was approachable, even at night, divinely inspired, profound in his simplicity, natural though mystical to the material mentality, understanding and sympathetic, true to his

---

[5] John 3:5.
[6] John 3:6.
[7] F. L. Rowe, Publisher.

Jesus as Evangelist and Reformer

precepts even when approached by a man of the ruling class. He possessed and utilized the qualities of the perfect teacher, inspired and inspiring.

In the use of parable and metaphor, of symbol and sermon, Jesus was both artist and teacher. He oftenest drew his figures from the objects about him, objects with which his auditors were wholly familiar. The lilies of the field, the birds of the air, the wild creatures of the region, the vineyard and the wheat fields, the shepherd and husbandman—all furnished this inspired mentality with the material with which to drive home profound truths in simple terms.

Jesus' purpose was not "to call the righteous, but sinners to repentance," [8] to heal the morally and physically sick. And surely on more than one occasion the implication was that physical disorder resulted from sin, from false beliefs held to as reality. The injunction, "go, and sin no more," [9] is capable of no other interpretation.

As we have seen, the importance of the individual was a supreme thought with Jesus. Always was he providing for the salvation of the person, that each might become aware of man's spiritual selfhood, of the man God created. And this awareness was his passport to the Kingdom, the divine Principle. "It is your Father's good pleasure to give you the Kingdom" [10] contains a definite assertion of God's purpose toward His children, and an equally certain declaration of man's present, and of each person's, ultimate relation to that Kingdom.

When the friends of a paralytic, because of the multitude, could not enter the door of a house where Jesus was preaching, they took him to the roof, and, removing the tiles, let him down into the presence of the Master. Immediately Jesus suspended his sermon, turned to the sick man, and healed him

---

[8] Matt. 9:13.
[9] John 8:11.
[10] Luke 12:32.

so completely that he arose and walked away. The importance of the individual was paramount in his thought, even when addressing a multitude.

Salvation was for every mortal. None were to be excluded. "Though your sins be as scarlet, they shall be as white as snow" [11] was a definite promise of the forgiveness of sin when it was forsaken; and that every mortal transformed in consciousness should be entitled to the true citizenship.

If not even a sparrow shall fall to the ground without the Father's knowledge, how much more does the Father care for His son! Even "the very hairs of your head are all numbered," [12] a metaphysical assurance that man, as the child of God, is forever in the Father's care. None were forever lost. The infinite God who is Love forever holds in His bosom His own offspring. However far from the Father's house—spiritual consciousness—the wanderer may have roamed, the return of the prodigal is always hailed with joy and forgiveness.

The crux of the Master's teaching was always for salvation to the penitent. The abandonment of sin, of material belief as reality, was inevitably followed by realization of the great fact that man in God's likeness had never sinned; that man had never departed from the state in which infinite Love had created him. It would have been quite impossible for a sinning and wicked mortal to be the likeness of God, who is infinite good, eternally perfect. Imperfection, mortality, in no respect resembles or is the likeness of infinite Spirit, the Spirit that is Life eternal.

That Jesus recognized God as Life, eternal and omnipresent, is borne out by his emphatic words, "And this is life eternal, that they might know thee the only true God, and Jesus Christ,

---

[11] Isa. 1:18.
[12] Matt. 10:30.

whom thou has sent." [13] Surely these words could not have been uttered in the sincerity that invariably characterized the sayings of the Nazarene, had God Himself not been the Life, knowledge of which would reveal to mortals that the real life of man is eternal, indestructible.

No teaching of the Master is clearer or more emphatic than the continuity of existence. The individual as the child of God is forever in the bosom of the Father, forever held in the divine consciousness, the only Creator, forever in Heaven. The son is never separate from the Father.

To the rich young man who came to Jesus seeking how to be assured of continuous existence, the way was clearly pointed out. He was to keep the Commandments, to relinquish his too great love for material possessions, and, following the Master, to accept his teachings, to lay all his material desires upon the altar of spiritual consecration, thus gaining the Kingdom. For it is this Kingdom wherein Life is permanent, is eternal.

The young man, however, was not prepared to pay the price. His sense of substance was material. He believed that the things of which he was so abundantly possessed were valuable, were indispensable to his comfort and joy. With what compassion did Jesus witness his turning away from the gates of Paradise! How hardly, indeed, could the rich enter the Kingdom.

Materiality in whatever form, as houses, lands, any form of material possessions, can never enter the Kingdom. Its possession hinders the seeker for spiritual values, if it be held as true substance. Flesh and blood, the belief that mortals are made in God's likeness, have no place in a wholly spiritual realm. The rich man who pulled down his barns to make room for more material possessions was not prepared for the change which came to him, for he was still convinced that matter is true substance. He was self-righteous and proud.

---
[13] John 17:3.

The teachings of the Master wholly refute this idea. Spirit, God, being infinite, there can be in reality no substance-matter that is real, is permanent. Even the physical scientists today, men like Eddington, Jeans, Millikan, and others are reducing matter to mental phenomena, objectified belief. Still others reduce it to force, the basis of which is electricity. But neither of these theses in any degree meets the fundamental fact of God's allness, that is, the allness of infinite Spirit, a fact which precludes another and opposite existence, the phenomena of the material universe.

While electricity is the most common and subtle form of physical force, it is but a form of materiality that has no relation to the omnipotence of God. As divine power was not in the earthquake or the hurricane, no more is it in any form of materiality.

It is the righteous who inherit the Kingdom, who gain eternal life. Nicodemus was told on that memorable evening visit to the Master that whoever should believe on the son of man, that is, whoever should gain the true understanding of the Messiah, of Jesus as the Christ, that very believing would bring eternal life.

No teaching of the Master controverts these definite rules for gaining that continuous existence for which every mortal so poignantly longs. No longing of the human heart is deeper-seated, no desire has its roots so deeply planted. And yet how reluctant are mortals to accept the teachings of him who proved his words beyond possibility of refutation. Did not this great Exemplar by his own resurrection prove beyond possibility of refutation that Life is indestructible, permanent? After his wicked persecutors had done their worst to his poor mutilated body, he reproduced it in positive proof of Life as immortal.

The grasp upon material existence seems so firm that mortals often lack the courage and mental stamina to combat it. Yet the rewards of such struggle, when material beliefs are overcome, are precious beyond words. The best news ever brought to mortals, that mortality is not reality, is rejected as too good to be true. And poor humanity in its lethargy refuses to make the effort to gain the Kingdom. Yet there is comfort in the understanding that mortals will be saved in spite of themselves, for salvation is universal. None are excluded, none are shut off from this blessed experience. For every mortal is destined to awaken from his false sense of existence to the realization of his forever existence as the child of God, of the Father who is in fact the only Life.

Jesus was ever conscious of the Source of his existence. He knew himself, his spiritual selfhood, veritably to be the Son of God. His firm conviction that God was not only His Father but the Father of all is evident from his frequent use of the terms "our" and "your" in referring to the common fatherhood of God.

Equal assurance, also, he had regarding his mission and the Source of his teachings. "For I have not spoken of myself; but the Father which sent me, he gave me a commandment, what I should say, and what I should speak." [14] This conviction brought with it the sense of authority with which he spoke and acted. It made use of the power of the Word, a power exactly commensurate in extent with the conviction that it is the Word of God, hence expressive of omnipotence.

It is little wonder that many who heard his words and witnessed his works, works which completely revolutionized human experience, should have exclaimed that he spoke "as one having authority." [15] It was, indeed, the highest authority, for it came from on High, from that Source which "spake, and it was done," which "commanded, and it stood fast." [16]

The chief priests and elders, blind to the spiritual import

---

[14] John 12:49.
[15] Matt. 7:29.
[16] Ps. 33:9.

Jesus as Evangelist and Reformer

of the Master's message and purpose, were naturally, perhaps, incredulous as to the validity of his teachings, and in consequence mistrustful of his authority. "By what authority doest thou these things? and who gave thee this authority?" [17] they asked him as he was teaching in the Temple. Too wise to be caught in their trap, for he well knew that they were wholly ignorant of the true Source of his authority, he confused his questioners by propounding to them two questions, neither of which they were willing to answer. And he refused to disclose to unwilling ears the true Source and import of his words.

The authority which Jesus so successfully utilized did indeed come from on High. It sprang from God, the Source of all true authority. It was possessed by the Master in proportion to his understanding of God, of the divine omnipotence and omnipresence. It was the power of the Word of Him who "spake, and it was done." [18] He knew that this all-power was his to exercise exactly in proportion to his understanding of it, and to his conviction as to its everpresence and availability. As God's expression or manifestation, His image and likeness, he possessed that which God possessed. It was his through his knowledge of God and of himself as the Son of God.

It should not be overlooked that language fails in many respects to convey spiritual truth. The term Father as applied to God connotes a human relationship which, however, represents the relation of God to his universe incompletely and incorrectly. Even in its highest and best sense the term Father must fall far short of the true relationship which omnipotent God, who is Life, is Truth, is Love, holds to His own image and likeness. Human language is wholly inadequate to represent

---

[17] Matt. 21:23.
[18] Ps. 33:9.

Jesus as Evangelist and Reformer

the love, the solicitude, the mercy which this all-loving Father God has for His own offspring. Mortals can only glimpse the Truth, but even that scanty vision brings salvation, surcease from all burden, misery, sorrow, and lack.

With the Founder of Christianity, who visualized this as none other has, how poignant must have been his grief when he saw suffering, enslaved humanity turning away from the way of salvation, of eternal life and lasting bliss! Yet his example, his teachings—which are as potent today as ever, for they stem from the eternal Truth, the same yesterday and today and forever—are still ignored by the great majority of earth's population.

In substantiation of his precepts, many of his works are being repeated today in the healing of sickness, the regeneration of the sinful, the renouncing of the self-imposed burdens of humanity. What more convincing proof could be adduced than that the Christ, the spiritual truth about God, the Holy Ghost and Comforter, is available here and now to correct not alone personal ills, but the infirmities of society, in whatever form manifested!

Today the excuse for failure to accept the teachings of Jesus and to make practical use of them is that they were related to conditions very unlike present-day conditions and the present organization of society; that while they may have "worked" in that distant day, today they are visionary and impractical. Both these arguments are based upon ignorance and the resistance of the carnal mind to the transforming Christ.

Jesus varied his teachings to meet the need of the group or individual he was addressing. But this variation was the adaptation of the fundamental truth to the immediate needs. While he told the rich young man to sell his property and give the proceeds to the poor, he commended Zaccheus when the latter proposed to give half of his possessions to the poor, retaining the balance for himself. The Master so accurately read the carnal mind, so clearly sensed material conditions that he was able instantly to determine the best course of procedure to bring healing and regeneration to each individual.

What among his teachings may at times seem antagonistic is due to the peculiar conditions to which his understanding was applied. "But I say unto you, That ye resist not evil" [19] does not seem in accord with his frequent declarations regarding the necessity of overcoming every phase of evil with the power of Truth. He who would "take away thy coat, let him have thy cloak also" [20] does not seem logical until its spiritual meaning is gained. Be not fearful to give beyond what is exacted, for the Father's bounty is never withheld from those who understand the divine Source of all being.

Although the gentlest of men, yet at times Jesus used violence in correcting grievous abasement of the purpose and provisions for true worship. Deeply did his resentment stir over the signs of desecration he found in the Temple, which should have been held in sacred respect by all who frequented its holy halls. That, in excluding the violators of the sacred Temple, he used material means as well as vocal denunciation but emphasizes the deep significance that this center of Jewish worship held for him.

A significant phase of the Nazarene's character is displayed in his act of cleansing the Temple of its debasers. While disagreeing with many of the doctrines of the Jewish religion, yet it was to the Temple that he went to preach, to bring the "good tidings of great joy" [21] of which the people were in such dire need.

Christendom, it seems, has consistently refused to develop from these instances general laws for Christians to follow. Is this failure due to lack of grasp of the fundamental truth that

---

[19] Matt. 5:39.
[20] Matt. 5:40.
[21] Luke 2:10.

prompted Jesus at the moment of utterance and demonstration? It can scarcely be denied that the Christian Church in some measure has founded itself upon the shifting sands of materiality because of misinterpretation of the nature and purpose of its Founder.

VI

The Christ, the Redeemer of Men and Nations

THE second chapter of Genesis relates the story of the creation of a mortal from sheer materiality, of the provision of a wife made from Adam's own rib, and calls this combination the dual progenitor of the human race. And yet we are informed that God created man in His own likeness, "male and female created he them."[1] From this illogical reasoning has evolved an anthropomorphic creator, a manlike god, very far from the God whom Jesus declared to be Spirit, and the Life and the Love, the Mind and Soul that stand out in deific proportions throughout the New Testament.

Moreover, Jesus declared himself to be the Son of God, not "very God of very God," as the Nicene creed declares, but the Son, the likeness and representative of the infinite Father of all. Jesus by no means regarded himself as the only Son of God. He knew God to be the Father of all; hence the brotherhood of man, the united family of all God's children. But this does not imply that mortals are God's creatures. How could sinning mortality be made in God's likeness, the offspring of Spirit? Logic itself refutes such an assumption. Surely, logic and reason should be and are reconciled with revelation when the spiritual import of the Scriptures is gained.

That the Christian Church recognizes its failure to evangelize humanity is, as we have seen, generally acknowledged among the most prominent clergy and prelates today. This conclusion is borne out by the frightful chaos into which the world has

---

[1] Gen. 1:27.

been plunged. How could the Church, based upon a material aspect of creation and claiming for its Founder a condition which he never accepted for himself, expect to succeed in the spiritual ministry to which the Church of Christ should be committed? This is a very pertinent query when the acknowledged failure of the Church passes under review. If the concept of God held by the Church is not the true concept, in fact misrepresents the God who is infinite, everpresent Life and Love, how, pray, could true worship be established?

Jesus' words uttered at the well of Sychar specify the type of true worship. His words are teeming with meaning: "But the hour cometh, and now is, when the true worshippers shall worship the Father in spirit and in truth." [2] Could words be more definite? "In spirit and in truth." Surely, then, effective worship must be in truth, based upon the true concept of God, and of God as Spirit.

How completely did the Master refute the manlike concept of God! Moreover, he indicated the everpresence of Deity, not a manlike God on a throne in Heaven, but Spirit everpresent, whose worship was not confined either to the Samaritan's shrine on Mt. Gerizim or to the Temple of the orthodox Jew in Jerusalem. How complete are the words of the Nazarene in their revelation not only of the nature of Deity but of the priceless importance to humanity of accurate knowledge of God, and of the manner of true worship!

The teachings of Jesus in parable, in simile, cover a wide range of human experience. They invariably have the purpose to bring out some phase of Truth to correct false beliefs of the carnal mind. They represent experiences that may be regarded as analogous to the true experience of the real man, God's likeness, in the divine economy. They are never frivolous, never lightly presented, but always with a seriousness of purpose

---

[2] John 4:23.

that is unmistakable, the sacred purpose of correcting carnal beliefs and habits by reference to the status of the son of God in the Kingdom of which every child of God is of necessity a citizen.

Some are stories, imaginative, to be sure, like the narrative of Lazarus and the rich man, but invariably do they pertain to and correct false views and unseemly conduct of mortals. They cover a wide range of human experience. The king and his courtiers, in various roles in wars, in treaties, in his feasts and worship; the man hailed before the judge, the criminal at the bar of justice; the landlord and his steward and workmen; the merchant whose journeys afar call for wise disposition to insure the safe conduct of affairs during his absence; the various types of laborers, fishermen, farmers, keepers of vineyard, the shepherd, the banker with his pearls, the innkeeper in his inn, the priest and the Levite, the wounded man by the wayside, the wastrel returning to his father's house, the marriage and its attendant feast—all pass under the keen eye and analytical mind of this Master Metaphysician.

It is appealingly patent that his one purpose in this variety of precepts was to demonstrate the practical nature of Truth, of the Christ, which he so successfully represented, as the one effective healing agency for all that is erroneous in human experience. His was the universal remedy. And the results of his teachings were healed and regenerated masses, individual problems solved, and burdens removed by the application of his inescapable logic.

That he spoke with authority was invariably manifest, not only to those who benefited from his ministry but even from those who challenged his authority. These were aware that if they accepted his ministry and acknowledged his authority, it would necessitate the relinquishment of cherished beliefs. The rich, the socially and politically powerful, would scarcely accept, at least without a struggle, a gospel that would exalt poverty and decry wealth, that would disrobe the king and remove political and social prestige. Only those became his disciples whose purpose was to gain the Kingdom themselves and to aid others in gaining the salvation of which mankind was in such dire need.

Amid all this, the Master kept himself above every temptation to acquire material possessions, to accept worldly honor. His wilderness experience, which went far in preparing him for the tasks ahead, had raised him far above the lure of material things and of worldly praise. The humblest man upon earth, he was by far the mightiest. And his humility was not from any sense of powerlessness or lack of authority. It sprang from an absolute conviction, based upon actual knowledge, that the Father was the Source of all capability and strength, even of his very life.

"I and my Father are one,"[3] and "the Father that dwelleth in me, he doeth the works"[4] were acknowledgments which lifted him far above the egotism that so often accompanies and characterizes human accomplishments. His humility was the handmaiden of his supreme authority.

The Christian, whatever the color of his ecclesiastical garments, believes in God as the Source of the authority Jesus so impressively expressed. The title "Christian" connotes the fact. The division of belief among the various denominations arises from the varying concepts of the Christ and Jesus, their interrelation and unity.

As we have seen, the Christ, the "Spirit of truth," the Comforter, has always existed. It is as eternal as God Himself. For God has not been God unexpressed and unrepresented; and since the Christ is that representation, the fullness of the deific expression, the Christ is co-existent and co-eternal with God. Spiritual truth, the Holy Ghost or Comforter, has

---
[3] John 10:30.
[4] John 14:10.

appeared to mortals whenever human consciousness has sufficiently yielded to the divine influence to become in some degree its channel.

It was this "Spirit of truth" that illumined the mentality of the many prophets and seers of the Hebrew race until it brought forth one who became known as the Christ, a title bestowed, as we have seen, because of his incomparable and unparalleled manifestation or expression of the Truth. His life perfectly illustrates the promise told so appealingly by the Revelator.

"Behold, I stand at the door and knock: if any man hear my voice, and open the door, I will come in to him, and will sup with him, and he with me." [5] This promise is both perpetual and universal. How perfect its intimacy! Not as a stranger does the Christ enter, but as a friend, a cherished and personal friend, who if entertained and accepted will transform human consciousness, will dissolve the shadows with ineffable Light, the Light which the Nazarene himself declared to be the Light, which is the life of men.

Recognition that this Christ but awaited a clear transparency whereby to illumine the whole earth, the light, the way of salvation for all humanity, brings its importance into new perspective. It strengthens faith through presenting that which is eternal. The affairs of mortals are so ephemeral, so constantly hastening in and out of human experience, that exaltation springs as the eternal Christ is envisioned. And the healing of the nations, the coming of the Kingdom, but awaits the reception of this great Physician who, through spiritual ministry, heals all, individuals and society, of their false and hence burdensome beliefs.

The fact of the carnal mind's resistance alters no element of Truth, either of its availability or of its potency in this Christ-like ministry. None can doubt the need for this trans-

---

[5] Rev. 3:20.

The Christ, the Redeemer of Men and Nations

formation that constitutes entrance upon the Kingdom. None can deny its possibility as a practical and immediate experience. To be sure, resistance to the admittance of the Christ-Comforter stems from fear of loss of some cherished belief or object. In the transforming Christ inheres the deadly enemy of fear, for inevitably when Truth enters human consciousness, the shadows of evil, of all materiality, however dense, however dark, flee before this evangel of light.

None other has presented this healing and redemptive Christ so conclusively, hence so successfully, as did this Man of Nazareth. His was the mission to light the way for mortals into the Heavenly City. He could not drive or push them in. He was rather the Good Shepherd who leads his flock—all who accept him as the Way—into the Heavenly Fold, where all earthly burdens are laid down for the freedom of the children of God. It is the work of the Good Shepherd that devolves upon all who name the name of Christ and claim fellowship with him.

Not because Jesus was crucified are mortals redeemed from sin, relinquished of their false beliefs based upon a material existence. Rather is redemption won through the understanding of God, of man as the child of God made in His image, and of the regenerating Christ ever at hand to lead all who are willing and obedient into the haven of perfect being. This is the way of salvation.

To show this way to salvation by preaching the simple truths uttered by Jesus as he journeyed about the hills of Judea and Galilee, and by exemplifying the results of the acceptance of these teachings as the way of life, by doing the works he did, this is the mission of the Church of Christ. This way is not trod through a wilderness of creeds and dogmas; it is not paved with ritualisms and formalism. It is the way of life perfectly illumined by the life and teachings of him who is accepted by Christians as the Way-shower, even by those who have either not found the way, or, having found it, have adjudged it to be too straight and narrow. None can deny the tragedy of the present world situation. None can gainsay that Jesus revealed a better, a holier, and a happier way for mortals to tread.

A unique but important phase of the Master's teaching was that the lesson conveyed was learned only by those who had ears to hear; that is, whose spiritual perception enabled them to peer through the material terms in which it was expressed to find the rare pearls of truth which it conveyed. The dull of hearing, still deep in the mire of materiality, missed the pearl and consequently failed of the blessings offered them.

Jesus was far too wise to cast his precious truths before the swinish elements of the carnal mind, which would only become enraged over the facts glimpsed. His use of parable and metaphor often obviated this difficulty, of which he was wholly aware. He knew that the spiritually thoughtful would gain the lesson he conveyed.

Too often, it seems, commentators have looked upon the parables as riddles to be guessed, rather than as the skillful presentation of fundamental truths to be understood by those prepared to receive the Truth. In this again did the Master manifest his perfect understanding of the ways of the carnal mind no less than of the operation of the infinite Mind, whose agency he knew himself to be.

A most impressive method of expression is found in the use of antithesis where one clause is set against the other. "For a good tree bringeth not forth corrupt fruit; neither doth a corrupt tree bring forth good fruit." [6] No fountain can bring forth sweet water and bitter.

In another figure of speech frequently used, the second clause explains the first. "Call no man your father upon the earth: for one is your Father, which is in heaven." [7] Thus adroitly

---
[6] Luke 6:43.
[7] Matt. 23:9.

The Christ, the Redeemer of Men and Nations

did this teacher of men place before the disciples and frequently before the multitude these surpassing lessons of deepest import.

That humanity has not more fully profited from them is no reflection upon the accuracy of the messages conveyed nor the method of their presentation, but rather casts reproach upon the dullness of mortals, their unwillingness to lay off the "old man," [8] their accustomed ways of thinking, and to exchange them for spiritual truths which are indeed the very bread of life. This old man, the sum total of material belief of life injected into matter, and dying out of it, clings with the strength of despair, for it sees in the Christ, the true Light of life, the nemesis of all materiality.

---
[8] Eph. 4:22.

VII

Healing Ministry of the Christ

Two aspects of the Nazarene's ministry of paramount importance are the healing of sickness and redemption from sin, and the two are closely associated, as we shall see; the one merges into the other. That the cause of disease is mental Jesus fully demonstrated. When he said to the man, who after thirty-eight years of invalidism was instantly healed, "sin no more, lest a worse thing come unto thee," [1] he plainly implied that it was sin, that is, false and sinful thinking, that had caused the man's disability, and thus it was only through changing his thought that healing could be gained.

As a man "thinketh in his heart, so is he" [2] is a true axiom, and the belief in the reality of discord, which invariably springs from the belief that man is a mortal, must be changed through understanding man as he is—spiritual and perfect, God's likeness, who has never ceased to be perfect as the likeness of perfect God must be.

The healing of sin was after the same manner. To the woman taken in adultery, whom her accusers were so ready to condemn, he said, "Go, and sin no more." [3] And the evidence of complete redemption from her former evil ways is unmistakable. Thus Jesus' mission was to heal and redeem those ready for healing and redemption.

The nearly twoscore statements in the Gospels of the healing

---

[1] John 5:14.
[2] Prov. 23:7.
[3] John 8:11.

of disease constitute irrefutable proof of the ability of the Master to meet and destroy every type of discord manifested in the human anatomy, regardless of its aspects. To this Man of God no form of error was impervious to the healing touch of the Christ. He healed the ten lepers with the same facility as he restored the nobleman's son. The maniac in the tombs of Gadara was no more of a problem to this great metaphysician than was the palsied man let down through the roof when the crowd prevented his friends from taking him through the door. Error was error, false belief was false belief, to this exponent of the Christ, "the Spirit of truth," and removal of the mental cause through establishing the truth about man in the place of the false belief was the immediate and perfect remedy.

Christians generally accept the view that true ministers of the Gospels are true followers of Jesus. They accept his teachings as representing the way of life, opening the door to the Kingdom. But they have parted the garment of true fellowship. For the most part they confine their ministry to the redemption from sin, leaving to material methods and means the healing of the sick. This position is wholly devoid of logic. The assertion that God through His Christ heals sin but not disease springs from the belief that God, Spirit, has created material remedies for healing man of the one type of error but not of the other—of sinful thoughts *per se* but not of the results of the sinful, false beliefs about man that invariably cause disease. Poor logic, it must be admitted!

The true ministry is one and complete. It is the destruction of evil in its every aspect through the power of Truth. It is the redemption of the race from the manifold types of error that have pursued mortals from their first appearance upon the earth. Was it not the false, material, sinful aspect of man that Jesus so violently condemned, as related in the Fourth Gospel? Not as sons of God, but as the offspring of evil did

Healing Ministry of the Christ

he characterize the contentious Jews, who claimed Abraham as their Father.

Jesus knew the sons of God to be spiritual and enjoined upon his hearers to claim the perfection that belongs to all by divine right. The offspring of the evil one, either of the Adam dream, or through the modern theory of evolution, was not important. The sons of God have never entered upon or passed through a material experience, else man would have literally fallen from his original high estate.

The situation is clear regarding Jesus' desire to perpetuate his ministry in its completeness. He preached the gospel, told the world the good news, that God the Father forever cares for His children; that since man made in the divine image was never mortal, material, and sinful, the contrary belief that man is a mortal, subject to innumerable limitations and various types of discord is wholly false and can be extirpated only by application of the spiritual truth. And he proved the accuracy of his claims by his works, even restoring a sense of life to those who were believed to have passed the gates of death.

Indeed, Jesus proved Life to be beyond the possibility of death, and the grave not an end to existence. The restoration of Lazarus, four days dead, the raising of Jairus' daughter, the revival of the son of the widow of Nain—all were examples of the Master's ability to prove for himself and others that life is deathless; that the real life of man, which expressed God who is infinite and eternal Life, is indestructible. And the climax of this teaching was the resurrection and ascension of him who had so successfully proclaimed and exemplified this mighty Truth. He who asserted, "Ye shall know the truth, and the truth shall make you free," [4] went far beyond the utterance of the words. He proved his theses completely, irrefutably. Revolutionary statements may arrest attention, but

---

[4] John 8:32.

Healing Ministry of the Christ

they are proved to be irrefutable truth, only through demonstration.

Instructions to the disciples, sent out by the Master to spread the good news, also contained emphatic admonitions to heal the sick. This consummate teacher knew that the mere preaching of his faithful students would not carry conviction to their auditors. Their words must be accompanied by proof—positive proof—not only that their words were true, but that the divine power through the Christ was present and available to heal mortals of their burdens, of sickness, fear, and misery. His was a complete salvation, a perfect preparation for entrance into the Kingdom, God's great Democracy, where all His children forever enjoy the blessings of perfect existence, with no unfulfilled desires, no unsatisfied wants, no lack of any factor that makes for perfect living, for lasting bliss.

The contention that the healing ministry proclaimed so eloquently by Jesus was for his time only, and was not to be continuous is no more logical than to attach the same limitation to the redemption of sin. In fact this claim repudiates a most important and clearly defined aspect of the Messianic mission. To repudiate it through confining it to a given period is to stultify the genuineness of Jesus' words and works. It is a matter of record that the disciples took seriously the healing ministry, proving their convictions by their works.

Furthermore, the early Christians accepted the healing of disease as a valid part of the Christian ministry and carried their works on for nearly three centuries. It was only when the intellectual supplanted in some measure the spiritual import of the Master's words, that the ability to heal seems to have disappeared. Philosophical discussion, intellectual capability, as such, is no substitute for the healing animus of the Christ. Had healing through intellectualism been a possibility, humanity would long ago have been relieved of its burden of sickness and misery, of lack and want. That this result has not been obtained is no proof of the inability of the Christ to lift mankind out of its limitations. The Christ as the perfect physician has not been generally accepted.

The inescapable conclusion is that the Truth has not been accepted and applied in either the spirit or the letter. Had humanity been willing to become as the little child, Christendom would long ago have symbolized the heavenly Kingdom. Here upon earth would have prevailed the peace that can only be gained and established by men of good will. The way has been shown and the signals are all open. Every highway of the Lord is marked with green lights, and there are no barriers except those created by the stubborn, carnal mind.

The argument is sometimes raised that Jesus did not heal every case, nor in all communities. To be sure, it was those who believed on him who received the instant healing and redemption. It was in his own city that he did no healing works, because of their unbelief. To those hard-headed religionists accustomed to the stern and rigid rules of Judaism it seemed quite impossible that one who had been reared in their midst, a carpenter's son, could have so spiritually attained as to be able to perform such miracles of healing, reports of which were being brought to their ears. To disbelieve and deny is often far easier than to investigate and accept upon the basis of the evidence adduced.

That feature of the Nazarene's experience that pertained to overcoming the sense of death was one of the most difficult to accept on the part of the multitude of his own day. The change called death seemed so inevitable, the grave yawned so poignantly, that the belief that death could be overcome and denied seemed more than mortals were prepared to accept. As life was born into matter and was sustained by matter, it must eventually pass out of matter, was the argument, an argument that has persisted throughout the centuries.

Healing Ministry of the Christ

Material sense utterly refuses to accept the fact of continuous life; yet Jesus emphatically declared that "whosoever liveth and believeth in me shall never die." [5] This obviously means that he who has gained the true sense of life will never pass through the experience called death. Since Life is God, man in God's likeness expresses that Life which is permanent and perfect, continuous, eternal. This, of necessity, relates to the real man, who is never born of the flesh, but of the Spirit, the selfhood of the child of God.

The only fair method of determination of the value and practicability of the Master's teachings is an examination of the entire corpus of those teachings. And when these teachings are so examined, the conclusion regarding the life of man as permanent and perfect is inescapable. Man *is* because God *is*. "Because Thou art, I am," is a logical and compelling conclusion when all the facts are examined.

No teaching of Jesus is more conducive to human satisfaction than that which removes the belief in death as reality, an experience that all must undergo. Yet Jesus' words have an import precisely contrary to this common conclusion. When he declared that "he that loseth his life for my sake shall find it," [6] he expressed two important facts. He asserted that life, that is, continuous existence, is to be obtained, gained, by the individual; and the means of gaining it was and is through understanding that God is Life, thus losing the false sense of life.

To gain truth, error and false belief must be discarded, laid off. So long as mortals cling to the conviction that life inheres in matter, the belief of death will persist. But when the true sense of Life is gained, that man's life is the expression of the Life which is God, then will the fact be grasped that man is

[5] John 11:26.
[6] Matt. 10:39.

immortal. These may be classed as the things hard to believe, as Paul asserted, but nonetheless are they true; and they open the way to the Kingdom.

Let none believe that, because the way marked out by the Nazarene was straight and narrow, it must of necessity be hard and joyless. On the contrary, rejoicing—constant and overflowing joy—characterizes the pilgrim who plants his feet firmly in the path and persists in this course, for progress is accompanied by the lessening of the burdens of life until the freedom of the sons of God is glimpsed and won. Can one doubt the value of the prize, the quality of this priceless pearl?

Beyond doubt, as we have seen, the most intense fear that haunts human experience is the fear of death. To many it is a haunting, constant, nagging dread. Surely relief from its toils would bring a rebound that would change the whole aspect of life. Individual life has been likened to a rubber ball, in its primal state, symmetrical, round, a perfect sphere. But under the pressure of fear and limitations, of sin and its consequences, it becomes distorted, loses its symmetry, is deformed in exact proportion to the intensity of these constricting beliefs. Remove these one by one, and the natural resiliency of life appears and the true life, spiritual and perfect, becomes manifest. The ball has regained its natural beauty. Mortals have the ability and the privilege to choose between the roads that open before them.

Jesus broke with what is commonly termed respectability. He had no more regard for the upper stratum of society than for the lowest. He was the friend of all, but not to condone sins, among high or low. His friendship was of the highest and purest, to heal and to save, to regenerate and redeem.

When rebuked for associating with those of the lower class, with sinners, Jesus declared that it was the sick who were in need of a physician. No respecter of the personally exalted, of kings and rulers, no more did he refuse to aid and heal the

Healing Ministry of the Christ

humblest. Was not God the Father of all, regardless of their social position and standing? His call was universal, to all humanity, to come and partake of the living waters; and those who partook of these waters would never thirst again.

In his work of reformation Jesus accepted no compromise. While he took humanity as he found it, nevertheless he stood absolutely foursquare for the Kingdom. He provided no half-way-houses in which to rest during the journey from matter to Spirit. Time was no factor in the process of transformation. It could be instantaneous in his healing works, as he more than once proved.

Many of the world's great reformers, taking the world as they have found it, have undertaken a gradual reformation. Not so this ardent Galilean. There was nothing conciliatory in his approach. Radical acceptance of the Gospel of the Father and of His Kingdom was the necessity, and when one put his hand to the plough there was to be no looking back. Wholehearted loyalty or radical stand for Truth was the only sure way to the Father's house.

Jesus called men from the world of tradition and set standards of righteousness for them which demanded acceptance of the grace and truth he was teaching. He was making God manifest in his unfamiliar deeds of mercy and kindness. Going with the sinner the first mile might not be sufficient to meet the need. If not, go the second mile—indeed, so far as seemed necessary to reform the sinner.

Forgiveness, not condemnation, was the burden of his theme. And forgiveness was complete when the last trace of belief in the reality of sinful thoughts and acts had been overcome. Not seven times, but "seventy times seven," [7] if necessary, he told Peter in answer to the query as to how many times he should forgive his brother who sinned against him.

---

[7] Matt. 18:22.

The servant who went to the king for lightening of his debt was forgiven in answer to the servant's prayer. But when the latter met a fellow-servant who was his debtor, despite the man's earnest plea that he would pay all, the unforgiving servant had him cast into prison. This news got to the lord, who called the servant to whom a great debt had been forgiven, and sent him to the court to be punished.

And this master of parables drew the conclusion from the narrative: "So likewise shall my heavenly Father do also unto you, if ye from your hearts forgive not every one his brother their trespasses."[8] In other words, there is no hypocrisy in the Kingdom of Heaven. For there can enter in nothing unlike spiritual truth, truth devoid of all pretense, all show, all deceit. This Kingdom is the dwelling place of only the good, the true, the perfect.

---

[8] Matt. 18:35.

VIII

The Kingdom: What, Whence, Where?

To MAKE practical use of the Master's teachings regarding the nature of the Kingdom, there is need of definite knowledge of it; of its character, what it is like; of its origin, whence came it; and of its locale, in what specific place it may be found: where is it? The whole trend of Jesus' teaching, its specific trend, its implication and its summation, indicate that the Kingdom is a state of consciousness, a mental state in which is no sense of materiality, a wholly spiritual state into which has never entered aught but spiritual perfection. It is the primal and eternal state of Spirit, of God, of the infinite Mind that is Life and Love, of God who is unchanging Principle. This is the natural and native state of consciousness in which the sons of God have always existed, the state from which the real man has never departed.

The query, Whence came it? that is, Where does it come from, and what is its source? is perfectly answered in Jesus' assertion that the Christ, his true selfhood, came from God, its true Source, and to which it, the Christ, would return. He came from Heaven and would return to Heaven, for as reality the Christ as the spiritual truth—forever dwells in that divine state which is spiritual consciousness; that is, in fact, the Kingdom of Heaven. Its locale Jesus definitely fixed: "Neither shall they say, Lo here! or, lo there! for, behold, the Kingdom of God is within you." [1]

This state of consciousness is man's true state, "within you,"

---
[1] Luke 17:21.

[63]

The Kingdom: What, Whence, Where?

the real man. It has no place, that is, it has no specific location, either in time or space. It is an everpresent, universal, eternal and infinite, spiritually mental state into which can never enter that which "defileth . . . or maketh a lie." [2] It is the state to which mortals attain when they have completely transformed their thinking from a material basis to spiritual understanding. It is the atmosphere of divinity, the abiding place of all reality, to be gained only through dropping off the "old man," [3] and gaining the "new," the spiritual state. It is the state in which the true selfhood of every mortal has forever existed, the secret place of the most High, wherein the dweller is forever safe "under the shadow of the Almighty." [4]

Another query may be added: When is this exalted state to be brought into realization? The answer is complete: It is the real man's present state. And it will be gained by mortals whenever they lay off their false sense of life and substance, exchanging the old man for the new. This saying might well be reversed, for the new man, man's real selfhood has always existed, in fact, is co-existent with the Father, with the Source of all existence; while the old man, that is, the mortal whose existence extends only from the cradle to the grave, could better be described as new, since his seeming existence has both a definite beginning and ending within the limits of time. The child of God, co-existent with the Father, has never left the Heavenly state into which he was created and from which he can never depart. In other words, he has never ceased to be the Son of God.

The eschatologists and the anti-eschatologists have long waged combat over the problem of the relation of death and the future life to the gaining of the Kingdom. It seems that close examination of the Master's teachings resolves the problem by

---
[2] Rev. 21:27.
[3] Eph. 4:22, 24.
[4] Ps. 91:1.

The Kingdom: What, Whence, Where?

eliminating it. There is no longer a problem when it is realized that the Kingdom is gained solely through the attainment of a spiritualized state of consciousness. Neither "Lo here! or, lo there!" but "within you," [5] within consciousness, is the Heavenly state.

That death will hasten this experience no one can surely aver. That death is not an experience necessary to gaining the Kingdom, Jesus plainly stated. He who believes on, that is, accepts and understands, the Christ, gains the Kingdom; and this attainment overcomes the necessity of passing the gates of death. In other words, mortals do not *die* into the Kingdom. Rather do they *live* into it, through gaining the true understanding of Life. It is not death, but the gaining of the knowledge of Life, that ushers man into immortality.

Thus is the problem of gaining the Kingdom placed squarely before every mortal. And furthermore, every mortal sometime has to face it. None can escape it; there are no side doors, no back entrances to the Father's house. Through the doorway of spiritualized thinking is salvation won. The Truth that sets men free is this gateway. There is none other, and unlimited blessedness is the reward.

Many misconceptions have developed in the established forms of Christianity, sprung from the teachings of its Founder. The statement sometimes heard that many of the accepted forms of Christianity are *about* the teachings of Jesus rather than the teachings *of* Jesus is an averment worthy of careful examination. The fact that Christianity, on the word of numerous of its exponents, has failed to evangelize humanity may be due to this fact. And a return to the simple teachings of the Master apart from dogma and ritualism, and a general revival of their application will bring a renewal of the tremendous impetus which characterized Christianity during those early centuries.

---

[5] Luke 17:21.

The Kingdom: What, Whence, Where?

It is plainly patent that something has happened to draw off the power of the stalwart faith of the early Christians who, without flinching, faced torture and death rather than renounce that which they had accepted as eternal truth. Christianity has become institutionalized to a degree, and to the institution rather than to the divine Author of the universe has allegiance been paid. In some instances this has been carried to the extent of disclaiming the possibility of gaining salvation except through the Church. This theory would eliminate the possibility of individual communion with the Father, the Source of one's being, except through the instrumentality of the Church. To many this seems to shut off the very means of salvation to him who, like the Master, goes apart from the multitude to pray, to affirm his unity with the Father and through this realization of that unity gain heartening and refreshment. When Jesus declared his oneness with the Father, he showed the way, to all who have gained the true vision, to proclaim their natural, divine relationship. The Lord's Prayer, the perfect medium of unity between God and man, requires no institution in order to gain its blessings.

The Kingdom of God does not have to come, for it is ever-present, to be revealed to all mentally prepared to receive it. Accepted, it is to be demonstrated—that is, brought into actual experience. The demand is for something more than mere declarations. The teachings of the Master must be so deeply embodied in consciousness that they have become the way of life. They divest dark thoughts of their seeming potency.

To the true worshipper it becomes the chief purpose of the daily experience to demonstrate the divine presence as a practical guide to all the affairs of life. And to serve God, to glorify and praise Him, becomes not only the chief desire but the deepest joy of life. Under the stimulation of this holy purpose what may have seemed like burdens, heavy and often meaningless, suddenly are transformed into glorious oppor-

The Kingdom: What, Whence, Where?

tunities for recognition of the divine Source of all good. The words of James are pertinent: "Every good gift and every perfect gift is from above, and cometh down from the Father of lights, with whom is no variableness, neither shadow of turning." [6] And these perfect gifts are possessed only through righteous prayer. For the true seeker, the way that often seemed dark and uncertain suddenly becomes illumined by Heavenly light, spiritual illumination, and the burdened heart breaks forth in hymns of praise.

The Kingdom presents limitless opportunities for joyous unfoldment, has unlimited resources upon which all may draw. Since evil has no abiding place in Truth, it is unknown in the Kingdom. Reality alone has its abiding place there, for evil and sorrow have fled away. The consciousness spiritually illumined is not the abiding place of any slightest trace of materiality. Love alone characterizes this divine state, and Love knows neither pain nor sorrow.

Jesus revealed God to mortals. He interpreted the divine character in terms that made it understandable to those prepared for such revelation. Not even all of those who constantly companioned with him so intimately understood the meaning of his message. It was Philip who, apparently confused and uncertain, urged, "Shew us the Father." [7] Somewhat taken aback that one of his chosen ones should not have grasped the significance of his teachings and works, had not seen in the Christ-presence as demonstrated by the Master a revelation straight from God, the Master queried, "Have I been so long time with you, and yet hast thou not known me, Philip? he that hath seen me hath seen the Father." [8]

There follow words of unmistakable proof that as Jesus was expressing the Christ, the divine nature, he was surprised and

---
[6] James 1:17.
[7] John 14:8.
[8] John 14:9.

The Kingdom: What, Whence, Where?

troubled that the disciples had not recognized the true Source of his demonstrated authority over material beliefs, over every type of so-called material law. There follows also the promise that those who believed on him should not only do the works he did, but would do even greater works, perhaps because of the superior facilities for disseminating his message in the centuries to come.

Furthermore, they were assured that whatever they should ask of the Father in his name would be granted. Surely no more definite or comprehensive promise could one make of the blessings to follow, to those who would believe that he, Jesus, was God's representative, His revelator to tired humanity.

IX

The Christ as Universal Truth

WHILE it is plainly evident that Jesus' first concern was for salvation of the individual, it by no means follows that he had no regard for the masses as such. He fed and healed the multitude whenever they were in need of food and healing. But this was something apart from mass manipulation. The truth spoken with understanding heals those who are receptive of the message. And these go away healed and grateful, if they recognize the significance of the experience. To be sure, when the Master healed the ten lepers, the record states that but one returned to give thanks, and he was a Samaritan, a member of a people usually held in extreme disfavor by the Jews. It is altogether likely that the nine were grateful even though they did not voice it.

That Jesus made no discrimination of race or religious belief in his healing ministry is of more than passing importance. He regarded all men as brothers, the earthly representation of the true brotherhood, the sons of God, made in His likeness, a state of perfection from which the real man, God's son, has never departed.

Corroboration of the attitude of the disciples toward many races and peoples, an attitude derived directly from the Master's teaching, is found in the experience on the day of Pentecost. "Parthians, and Medes, and Elamites, and the dwellers in Mesopotamia, and in Judea, and Cappadocia, in Pontus, and Asia, Phrygia, and Pamphylia, in Egypt, and in the parts of Libya about Cyrene, and strangers of Rome, Jews and proselytes, Cretes and Arabians, we do hear them speak in our tongues the wonderful works of God." [1] What greater, what more convincing proof of the universality of Truth could be adduced than was presented on that memorable day of Pentecost! And all these races, with many and varied dialects and modes of speech, heard the message of Truth in terms which they understood.

Then as now, however, the doubting Thomases were present. They always are. To the materially minded, spiritual demonstration in whatever type of manifestation is absurd, ridiculous, mere make-believe. On that day of Pentecost the unbelievers standing by said, "These people are drunk." Peter, the ever-ready defender of the faith derived from the Master, would have none of this. He knew whence came this miracle; and, knowing, he declared that the experience they were undergoing was not due to drunkenness, but in fulfillment of the prophecy of Joel. And Peter followed with one of the most effective sermons ever preached.

How significant were these events! This man, fresh from witnessing the last great act in the drama which had been so impressively portrayed by his Master and Teacher, his Lord and Saviour, out of the depth of his heart declared in unmistakable terms the mission of the Man of Nazareth, his earthly experience, crucifixion, resurrection, and ascension, and a final appeal to receive him as their Lord and Saviour, their Wayshower into the Kingdom where all abide in a true brotherhood. It is little wonder that the hearts of those who heard were "pricked," [2] their thought awakened by the witness and words of him who had beheld what no mortal before or since has had the privilege of witnessing. When the significance of this experience is grasped, the wonder is why humanity today is so reluctant to accept the Christ-way of lifting their burdens and of solving all their problems.

---
[1] Acts 2:9–11.
[2] Acts 2:37.

The Christ as Universal Truth

Truth is universal. Under whatsoever circumstances presented, however large or small the group of auditors—one or a million—it is universal Truth. It is without time or space. It is everywhere present and everywhere available to meet the needs of humanity, to lift the self-imposed burdens which mortals have so heavily borne. It is the Comforter, or Helper, as Moffatt puts it. The qualities included in universal Truth were more completely and more successfully set forth by Christ Jesus than by any other, and this fact makes him both Way-shower and Saviour. Not by his suffering are we saved, but by accepting his teachings in the fullness of their significance in both the spirit and the letter, by making him the great Exemplar of righteous living, following in his footsteps, and imitating his example as far as is humanly possible. And there is no limit to the possibilities that derive from true discipleship, when once we set our feet in the true path.

The illustrious characters of history have attained greatness because they have exhibited in exemplary degree the qualities manifested by this humble Galilean. And no person is truly great without this exemplification of the divine attributes that Jesus manifested in major degree. Think for a moment what these sublime qualities were that so impressed men of his own times and have become the ideal for untold millions in the intervening centuries. What were and are these qualities, divine in origin but forever belonging to universal man? First of all was Jesus' understanding of the God whom he so frequently addressed as Father. None other has ever possessed and exhibited so accurate, so complete knowledge of the infinite One, the only Cause, and the only Creator of all that really exists. Jesus possessed acquaintance with this Father in unprecedented and unparalleled degree.

This understanding gave birth to a faith that was unshakeable, unlimited, and constant. It took him through those terrible days from Gethsemane to Calvary; it did more: it took him

The Christ as Universal Truth

from the tomb and at last lifted him above the realm of physical sense, to sit on the right hand of God, that is, to come into full consciousness of his perfect selfhood as the Son of God, to remain forever in the Kingdom from which his Christ-self had never departed. Faith based upon understanding can move mountains, can destroy, can eliminate, the most threatening, the most potent types of error, because it is based upon Truth and its operation, upon its omnipotence and omnipresence.

Forgiveness. None other has so completely exhibited this quality as did this Man of Nazareth. Even on the Cross, tortured as few have ever been tortured, in the midst of his agony he asked his Father to forgive his tormentors because they were ignorant of what they were doing to the son of Mary. "Father forgive them" [3] are words that have come ringing down the corridors of time to arouse all who are listening to give up every form of resentment; no matter what the cause may have been, to rise above the temptation that leads to hatred and revenge and the getting even with another; to forgive to "seventy times seven," [4] if it be necessary; to heal the other of the misdeeds that stirred resentment in the heart of the injured one; this is the Christ-way. This is a "must" step in gaining the Kingdom. Forgive, as we would be forgiven!

Every mortal needs the divine forgiveness that inevitably follows upon the acceptance of the universal Truth, the Christ, which as the expression of infinite Love has never been conscious of a misdeed that requires forgiveness. Forgiveness is a mental state attained only as Truth supplants falsity in the human consciousness, as error is relinquished and the Christ-Comforter enters.

A true instance that came to my attention perfectly illustrates the quality of forgiveness, both in method and in result. A lad coming home from school was not greeted by his fox

---
[3] Luke 23:34.
[4] Matt. 18:12.

terrier, Jack. Anxious inquiry of his mother led her to the disclosure that something very serious had happened to his pet. Apparently the dog had been poisoned, and had returned to the house suffering so intensely that the mother did not want the lad to see his pet in such misery.

"But, mother," protested the lad, "when I am sick, Jack always comes to me. Now he needs me and I must go to him." Impressed by the boy's reasoning, the mother took him to the room where she had hidden the poor creature so that no one would see him. The boy shut himself in the room, and nothing was heard for some time. After an hour or more, the door opened and the lad came out whistling merrily with his pet leaping about with every appearance of perfect recovery.

When the mother asked the lad what he had done for Jack, he replied, "Why, mother, I prayed for him." "But how did you pray?" queried the mother. "I prayed for him," she continued, "but apparently to no effect." "Why, mother," insisted the lad, "I didn't pray for Jack. God was caring for him, but I asked God to forgive the one who had poisoned him. And God forgave him, for Jack is all right."

Such prayer can scarcely fail of success. It stems from faith, from the assurance that the all-knowing Father is also all-loving. And this prayer for forgiveness could scarcely fail to reach the malicious thought that would poison a boy's pet and friend. Can one doubt the beneficial effect upon the one in error when such prayer goes out to the great heart of infinite Love!

Love. Whoever loved humanity as did this man of Galilee? Whoever has proved his love by passing through such terrible experiences as did Jesus in Gethsemane, before Pilate and the High Priest, and finally on the Cross? And let us not forget that this could have been avoided; that is, Jesus, always conscious of the divine presence, could have at any stage completely thwarted the nefarious plans of his enemies. Pilate, conscious of the power of Rome behind him, inquired of the Master,

The Christ as Universal Truth

"Knowest though not that I have power to crucify thee, and have power to release thee?"⁵ To this Jesus answered in terms of deepest significance, "Thou couldest have no power at all against me, except it were given thee from above."⁶

With what assurance, with what calmness born of knowledge of the divine presence, of the infinite power of God, the only true power, did Jesus utter these words! No manner of earthly power, even the mighty power acclaimed of Rome, was aught in the view of him who really knew the omnipotence of God, of good.

Again, when as he was about to be taken in the Garden one of his companions resisted with his sword, Jesus admonished him to put up his weapon. "Thinkest thou that I cannot now pray to my Father, and he shall presently give me more than twelve legions of angels?"⁷ But if he were to do this, that is, successfully resist his captors as he had the power to do, the Master knew that the Scriptures which had foretold the tragic events ahead would not be fulfilled.

Could there be exhibited greater love than that which prompted this mightiest of all men, mightiest because of his knowledge of God, to lay aside all desire to escape terrible torment in order to fulfill his mission to humanity, to show them the way, the only way, to the Kingdom! How tragic, how terrible, that in the light of such love mortals have so generally refused to become its beneficiaries, to receive the limitless blessings to the reception of which Christ Jesus so plainly pointed the way!

A fundamental quality of this love was its unselfishness, its selflessness. It was wholly above and apart from egotism or the glorification of human personality. It was a spiritual quality, expressive of the perfect, infinite Love that is God,

---

⁵ John 19:10.
⁶ John 19:11.
⁷ Matt. 26:53.

The Christ as Universal Truth

of the Love that casteth out all fear. It was the type of love that impels one to give his life for another; that is, to lay down a false sense of life, a material sense, for the true sense of life, the spiritual understanding of God, who is eternal Life.

Jesus was precise in his utterance on this subject. "He that findeth his life shall lose it; and he that loseth his life for my sake shall find it." [8] He who accepts the material sense of life, life expressed in matter and supported by it, has the wrong sense of life. In order to gain the true sense of life, one must abandon this falsity. He who accepts the Christ as the Son of God, as the apostle and representative of eternal Life, has found the true sense of Life, the Life that is Love, that is divine Truth, is Mind, is Spirit. No greater benefit did Jesus bring to humanity than the true sense of Love that is also Life.

Wisdom. A quality that Jesus possessed and uniformly manifested was wisdom. He was by far the wisest man who has ever appeared on earth. And this wisdom fulfilled the many mandates of the Old Testament. To get wisdom, to get understanding, was the wise man's way of gaining spiritual progress. Jesus displayed wisdom in his every utterance, his every act. To understand this, it becomes necessary to approach his sayings from his own standpoint, the understanding of God as Spirit, omnipotent and everpresent.

How wisely did Jesus deal with the carnal mind! How completely he refuted the logic of the intellectual scribes and Pharisees whenever they tried to trap him, to propound questions that, answered as they wished, would render him answerable to the law. An example is found in the twenty-first chapter of Matthew. It appears that the chief priests and elders, becoming increasingly disturbed over the growing popularity of the Master, one day followed him into the Temple at

---

[8] Matt. 10:39.

Jerusalem where he was teaching. With the purpose of embarrassing him, they demanded to know his authority, and who gave it to him. Not to be trapped by telling the truth, that he came from God and hence his authority was divine, Jesus countered by asking them a question, saying that, if they answered it, he would tell them his authority and its Source: "The baptism of John, whence was it? from heaven, or of men?" [9] They were deeply puzzled. If they said, "From heaven," then Jesus would demand to know why they had not believed. And that they did not accept John and his fiery denunciations was notorious.

On the other hand, if they should say that John's baptism was of men, they would at once be brought into conflict with the people, for the masses had accepted John as a true prophet. Here was indeed a dilemma, neither horn of which offered them the slightest comfort. Jesus' way out was wide open. They had not answered his question. He was under no obligation to answer theirs.

Another example of his wisdom, and the Gospels are replete with similar instances, is found in the reply he made to the messengers whom John sent to inquire if he were the long-looked-for Messiah. Should John accept him or must they look for another? It seems that on the occasion when John had performed for Jesus, his cousin, the rite of baptism, the words spoken by the Baptist carried a firm conviction as to Jesus' character and mission. But it appears that later, perhaps bemused by the Master's astounding demonstrations, doubt crept into John's thinking to the purpose that he must be reassured as to the position of this most unusual man who was saying such unfamiliar things and performing works without parallel in John's experience. Hence he sent his emissaries to

---

[9] Matt. 21:25.

The Christ as Universal Truth

inquire of the Master himself as to his real character and mission.

Jesus' response was inspired by wisdom itself. He did not declare himself. He made no effort to reaffirm John's credulity by a spoken message. He did the most impressive things he could possibly have done. He did, right before the eyes of these messengers, the very things that would establish his identity beyond possibility of refutation. In their very presence the blind were made to see, the lame to walk, the lepers were cleansed, the deaf made to hear, and even the dead were raised to life again. And, furthermore, he was preaching the Gospel constantly to the poor, to all receptive to his messages. "And those who are not repelled by me are blessed. Go and tell John these things that you have witnessed." [10] Surely no more convincing message has ever been borne to an honest inquirer, eager to make sure that neither had his confidence been misplaced nor had his judgment been wrong.

The strongest proof of the truthfulness of Jesus' words lay in his works, invariably performed in demonstration of his knowledge of God and of the practicability of that knowledge in overcoming error in its every phase. Surely the wisdom displayed by this Nazarene was the reflection of the one Mind, the Mind that Paul urged his friends to receive. Paul knew as divine the Source both of the wisdom and of the intelligence invariably manifested by the Master. No other explanation is adequate. So superior to human intelligence or the wisdom of men was his state of consciousness that it must be attributed to some higher power.

It is not unwarranted to assert that Jesus was the most intelligent man that has ever trod the earth. That he expressed in greater measure the infinite Mind with its unlimited intelli-

---

[10] Luke 7:22.

gence is the conviction of many Christians. It should be the conviction of all, for upon true intelligence, which knows and understands, and upon its expression, must the permanent structure of Christianity be erected. That the unseen power, the creative influence that has set the stars in their courses and brought the vast, limitless universe into being must be an infinite Mind, an unlimited intelligence, is becoming more commonly accepted by thoughtful religionists.

Tolstoy translated the opening sentences of the Gospel of John thus: "In the beginning was divine Intelligence, and divine Intelligence was with God, and divine Intelligence was God," a very appealing rendition of a familiar passage, a passage, however, that has caused unlimited discussion and almost an equal volume of disagreement. The Greek "Logos" has had a great variety of meanings assigned to it, but it seems that the words "Mind," "Intelligence," or spiritual consciousness best represent the creative power of the omnipotent One whose Word had created the universe, that is, the universe of reality.

How logical, then, to agree that this Son of God, Jesus the Christ, who understood God, the divine Source of all intelligence, should have been the best educated, that is, the most intelligent, man who has lived on earth. And the degree of his intelligence was precisely in proportion to his recognition and understanding of God as Mind.

Love, intelligence, wisdom, and mercy are qualities that the Nazarene expressed with utmost humility. He invariably recognized the divine Source of the ability that he exercised so impressively throughout his entire ministry. Fearless beyond the point of doubt, courageous to an unparalleled degree, yet always the very symbol of humility and modesty.

How rare is the quality of true humility among mortals. The egotism, the intellectual arrogance, the superior attitude so often assumed by the rich and prominent, the intellectually proud, how far are these qualities from those that stem from

The Christ as Universal Truth

God! Yet it is probably true that there are few who would not sell all they have for the attainments gained by this humble man who had "not where to lay his head,"[11] who apparently had not accumulated material possessions whatsoever except the clothing that he wore. Far above all worldly riches, all material possessions, did he value the gifts that a gracious Father was constantly bestowing upon him. He knew the relative value of spiritual things as compared with material. He gladly withheld any desire for common possessions in order to maintain his freedom to worship the Father who had sent him. And this worship was in proving to humanity what the blessings of God may be to those who are willing to pay the price for them.

It seems that many who seek the Christian ministry as their opportunity to serve the Master and thereby to glorify God go only part way in their preparation, else they would assume the entire ministry which Jesus set forth: to kindle in the hearts of men the spark resident there until the whole purpose of life is aflame with a passionate desire to follow step by step the great Exemplar. No halfway loyalty, no wearing of only a portion of the mantle, but wholehearted acceptance and promotion of the spiritual idea in the completeness of its demands is the way to the Kingdom for each and for all. Great is the demand for purification of thought and deed! Great is the reward to those who have the consecration, the courage, and the fortitude to pay the price!

---

[11] Matt. 8:20.

X

Christianity and Natural Science

IN THE realm of physical science in recent decades the expansion has been nothing short of marvelous. In chemistry, in astrophysics, in pure physics, in electrical development, the unfoldment has brought many wonders—discoveries and inventions sufficient in their magnitude and diversity to startle the intelligence of humanity. For the most part these inventions have benefited mankind, have somewhat lessened the heavy burdens of men, have in some measure alleviated the weariness of mortals, inherent in the task of earning their bread by the sweat of the brow.

The evils that have resulted are also very great and pose serious problems. Has the development of motion pictures to their present high state of perfection really benefited the race? Do they in any measure urge one forward on the journey that has the Kingdom for its goal? The answer must be based upon the balance between the good and evil that they so vividly present to the expectant throngs that crowd the cinema houses of the world. Are they enlightening the masses upon subjects that truly benefit them; or do they furnish a type of entertainment that adds substantially to the burden of materiality of which mortals are to be divested in order to gain that spiritual understanding that constitutes the forever existence? In other words, does entertainment that merely gratifies the physical senses truly benefit humanity? The answer must be in the negative.

This, however, is but a general characterization. Many motion pictures are both entertaining and instructive, even uplifting in the sentiment expressed. It is not the vehicle that is bad. It is the use made of it that leads to its prostitution. Again the balance must be struck between the good and evil. It is indisputable that alert parents and many educators see in the sordid features of the "movies" presented, as in the "funny" section of the daily press, that which distorts the vision of youth, which often portrays evil in an attractive garb, thus demoralizing and degrading with false standards.

The remedy is, of course, to make better types of pictures, to portray good instead of evil, to exalt and purify the best instead of the worst in human nature. This end will be obtained only as the producers and the entire industry learn that only that which serves God—which serves good—can be to their lasting benefit. If promotion of the low and mean, of evil in its various forms, is the highway to success and true happiness, then the whole structure of the Christ-teaching is nullified, is rendered wholly destructive to spiritual progress.

If the true answer to the query, What would Jesus do? could be the criterion to guide mortals in their affairs of life, the road to the Kingdom would be thronged, where now the travelers seem few and too often uncertain of their course. Consciousness awakened to the needs of the hour, a thirsting for righteousness, and willingness to obey the divine mandate; these will hasten the advent of the Kingdom as nothing else can.

The destructive uses of modern inventions are perfectly illustrated by the airplane and the undersea boat. The former, especially, has already reached a state of great usefulness in legitimate transportation of passengers and goods. It ties the nations together with a bond the value of which could be immeasurable. That, following the close of the present conflict, air travel and transport will receive tremendous impetus, is now a certainty. But meantime, the use of the airplane as perhaps the most potent instrument of war has reached a stage that is nothing short of appalling in the extent of its destructiveness.

Unless the war psychosis is to be extirpated, the threat to human safety offered by the expanding possibility of the airplane as an engine of destruction is unlimited. Justifiably the query arises, can civilization withstand the use by an aggressor nation bent upon world conquest, if this engine of destruction be carried to the limit?

The airplane is but one of the many inventions that bless or curse humanity exactly in accord with the mental state behind it. Hate, false ambition, and desire for dominion over others are mental states that make use of the instruments at hand to serve the purposes of evil. Likewise, the development in chemistry has been especially the servant of good and evil. None will gainsay the benefits that have followed upon chemical discovery and its application to the meeting of human needs. Yet it also has developed lethal gases so deadly that only the most depraved mentality would use them in warfare.

Here, again, the balance between the good and evil rendered is wholly determined by the mental status of the individual or group responsible for its use. If the purpose is to serve God through serving humanity in some constructive manner, chemistry can be of incalculable service. If the opposite purpose, to satisfy personal or national ambition, be the promotive influence, its destructive possibilities with respect to both property and human life are also incalculable.

Many more modern inventions and discoveries may be similarly analyzed with like results. The whole problem reverts to the state of thought, the type of mentality, behind the use of the instruments portentous of good and evil. Plainly, then, the need is to transform the evil thinker into a servant of good. An evil course never exalts humanhood. Therefore, it becomes plain that success in evil never progresses one toward the Kingdom. The evildoer pursuing his evil ways never promotes his own welfare or that of others. His course is down-

Christianity and Natural Science

ward, with a speed exactly in proportion to the degree of his wickedness.

The stories of cruelty and barbarism coming out of the countries occupied by the Germans are enough to appall the stoutest-hearted. Can one doubt what the end of such a regime must be? If such a course can succeed, then is the situation of the world hopeless. Chaos and old night will settle upon this earth a pall so dense and so dark that only the rays of the Christ could ever penetrate it. Such is the fact. Good has behind it divine omnipotence; while behind the terrible forces of evil stalking about the world just now is no permanent power, no eternal mandate.

God has no part in support of this miserable situation; and only as His representative, this redeeming and saving Christ, comes into human consciousness, only as the transformation takes place, will there be experienced upon earth the peace that Jesus came to proclaim. He well knew the struggle that would follow promotion of the acceptance of the Christ-Comforter. None ever was so keenly aware of the conflict that would usher in the Prince of Peace, and none other was ever so aware of the ineffable blessings to follow when the Comforter is accepted as the true way of life.

XI

Summary

IT IS traditionally true that individual observers of an incident or a series of incidents will inevitably report what they have witnessed, each in his own way. No two observers see events in precisely the same pattern, hence their reports will vary. This variation will depend in large measure upon the mental status of the observer. Each has his own mental makeup, his individual interests, his own standard of judgments. And as each has his own purpose, consequently there arises the difficulty of presenting wholly objective accounts of events, even from eye witnesses.

Perfect objectivity is beyond reach. This is a condition of understanding important to the most practical approach to the Four Gospels. Here are four narratives, largely biographical, relating the conclusions of four individuals who companioned with the most important man ever to appear on earth, or with those who had been thus blessed. Each saw events through his own mental lens; each recorded in his own way what he had witnessed and what he had heard. And the wonder is that the four witnesses are so much in agreement that the fundamentals are surpassingly alike. The differences and disagreements for the most part relate to the events of lesser importance.

In that marvelously inspiring presentation of the King James Version of the Bible, *The Bible for Today*,[1] the editor, John Sterling, makes very impressive observations regarding the point

---
[1] The Oxford University Press. Quoted by permission.

Summary

of view of each of the four biographers. Luke is interested in locality. His Gospel is replete with geographical reference. He defines the journeys of the Master, the direction in which he traveled, where he stopped, as on and on he went in his tireless marches, invariably undertaken in the fulfillment of his mission. He was as tireless as he was faithful. Luke is geographically minded.

John's penchant relates to time. He especially injects the time element into his spiritual interpretation of the sayings and works of his Teacher. While it is apparent that John's vision more accurately than the others evaluated the spiritual import of the Master's mission, yet he peculiarly and definitely introduces the time element. The day and the hour of events are specifically indicated.

Beyond doubt John saw the true relation of what he witnessed and heard to the timeless and spaceless universe, the Kingdom to which the Master so constantly referred. But it is equally certain that he was deeply interested in the precise order in which the events he was recording took place. He even opens his Gospel with reference to time. "In the beginning" was to him a definite designation of the occurrence of the most important of all events, the creation. Sterling says that where the keyword with Luke was "where," with John it was "when."

Careful study of Mark's Gospel reveals that he was less interested in place and time, as his references to these are vague. It is the people that command his keen interest. Who were the important characters in the great drama which was being worked out around its central figure, Christ Jesus? Mark goes to some length in defining these personages, both the individuals as they appear on the stage and the masses as they throng about the man who was telling them truths entirely new and performing works the like of which they had never heard, much less seen.

Surely the *dramatis personae* of this greatest, most significant of all life's dramas could not fail to attract the interest and the eyes of so intense an observer as Mark. He saw the multitudes

Summary

attracted by the words and works of the Messiah as a feature of the Master's experience worthy to be recorded by him.

The completeness of the narrative is the central fact in the Gospel of Matthew. This Gospel sets forth the background against which the life of the Nazarene was projected; it sees in him the fulfillment of Scriptures. It presents in the most sequential form the essence of his teachings. It was manifestly written for the Jews themselves; and although not the first Gospel written, yet it is placed first probably because of the completeness with which it presents the advent, the mission, and the historical incidents of Jesus' career.

These four stories constitute a symposium in which each presents a factor that could not be omitted without serious loss of the meaning and importance of the most precious of all human experiences. Each is individual, in a goodly degree complete in itself, yet the four are necessary to the whole story. The loss of any one would seriously impair the Gospel story. Together they constitute the most priceless message ever sent to mortals by an all-loving Father. Combined, these Gospels present the best news ever sent to bless humanity, for they disclose the way of life, the assurance of individual persistence and unchanging blessedness. It is this good news that makes them priceless.

The tragedy of our times is that, having all this presented in glowing terms, alight with the "Spirit of truth," it has not been generally accepted in the fullness of its significance, and at most has been only partially believed. It is little wonder, then, that one horrible catastrophe after another has characterized human history. And now, after nineteen centuries of opportunity for gaining the Kingdom, through accepting the way of life opened by the Nazarene for establishing on earth the reign of righteousness, humanity is assaulted by barbarity of a degree of cruelty and destructiveness never approached in the entire era of recorded history.

Reflective people throughout the earth are analyzing the

Summary

causes that have led to this terrible calamity, are striving to find a formula that, if agreed upon and adopted, will make impossible a recurrence of this devastating evil, which, if continued, would utterly destroy what is known as Christian civilization. And yet the way has been charted and the beacons lighted, a way that, if trod faithfully and in strict accord with the recorded instructions, would bring to earth, here and now, the Kingdom of God, the brotherhood of man, never again to be disrupted by the horrible conditions of war.

The blueprint was drawn by the Man of Nazareth. The need is to recognize this fact, to accept it, and to build the foundation of our spiritual structure in accord with its definite provisions. Nothing is lacking, no least detail omitted, and, combined, it constitutes a perfect chart to the status of peace and blessedness.

The Gospel of Matthew, as we have seen, is more nearly a summary of the Master's teaching in sequential form than any other gospel. The Sermon on the Mount, as this summary is usually termed, is the most complete compendium to righteous living ever set forth. It is practical and comprehensive in that it charts the way out of the darkness of human experience into the light of true being. It portrays the remedy for every form of evil, of disaster, and for any manifestation of lack with which a mortal may be confronted.

This completeness of the sermon is unprecedented and unparalleled in incisiveness and practicality. And not only does this completeness characterize it, but, when its truths are learned, accepted, and applied, this sermon furnishes the universal salvation to every adverse condition in human experience. Its importance, then, demands a careful analysis even in its slightest detail. The author regrets that the space and purpose of this volume make possible the consideration of but a portion of the major tenets of this great sermon, particularly those now relevant to the chapters appearing in Part Two.

The wisdom of the Nazarene, so frequently manifested

Summary

throughout his ministry, is especially apparent in his delay in announcing himself as the Messiah. Had he at the beginning of his career proclaimed himself as sent of God, as the long-looked-for One who would restore all the glories and prestige of Israel, all might have regarded him as an imposter. It is doubtful if, without his works, his teachings would have made more than a slight impression upon the people. A gradual process, developing little by little, of words illustrated by works, declarations proved by demonstration, was the method adopted by this wise and practical man.

Proof of the wisdom of this course is found in the numbers of his adherents and followers, the depth of their convictions, and the ardor with which the immediately succeeding generations of Christians took up his Cross, to bear it bravely forward. Another course, it seems likely, would have been less productive of the fruitage of the vine he so successfully planted.

Whether or not the Sermon on the Mount was delivered as a single message and on one occasion is of little importance. Its value consists of the golden nuggets that it contains. Its truth is universal, is timeless and limitless in its sweep and application. It may be asserted without fear of contradiction that down the centuries since its utterance, no individual man or woman is entitled to the characterization as "great," except as their lives have expressed the gist of the pronouncements contained in this sermon.

No mere human ideas, no products of the carnal mind, ever produced great deeds, ever inspired to the heights of possible attainment set forth in the Master's teachings. Above all mere human ambition, attainment, or capability they alone lift to the heights bathed in the light of true Being, of the Life that is eternal, that is above all material conditions, limitations, and restrictions, the Life that is God. It is this Life that Jesus declared to be eternal, to be gained by mortals only through knowledge of God and of Christ Jesus, sent of the Father to light

Summary

the way for all humanity out of the darkness of despair into the glow of forever being.

It is fitting that this superlative sermon should have been introduced by statements of assurance. The Beatitudes set forth in simplest phraseology the mental conditions most conducive to the reception of the great message itself. They create an atmosphere in which the truth most vividly appears. They are the perfect prologue to what is to follow.

How simple, how appealing the language! "Blessed are the poor in spirit,"[2] they who recognize their spiritual need; they who need comforting; the meek: they who are hungering and thirsting for spiritual food and drink; the merciful: they who respond to another's needs with succor and words of kindness; the pure in heart: for it is they who, lifted above the plane of material sense, envisage God, the infinite good, unchanging Love; the peacemakers: who are blessed because, knowing both the value of peace and the method of attaining it, they are eager to share their blessings with others.

It is these spiritually minded ones who recognize their true selfhood, made in God's likeness as truly the children of God; they who, having risen above the limitations of materiality, who, having divested themselves of every trace of carnality, are conscious of their sonship with the Father, infinite Spirit. And surely no phase of materiality could possess the slightest semblance to Him who is infinite Spirit.

Those who, through standing firm for Truth, for God and His Christ, are persecuted, these are they who will receive great reward. Why? Because it is these consecrated ones who have gained a knowledge of God the Father, which reveals man's true selfhood, made in the perfect likeness of the divine nature. And how impossible for this spiritual attitude, once gained, to depart from the holiness that it embodies!

---

[2] Matt. 5:3.

Summary

The holy ones of old were thus persecuted. From time immemorial have those who have climbed the heights of spiritual understanding been assaulted by the carnally minded, who see in the Christ their sure nemesis. What a perfect preparation for the message that follows do these Beatitudes constitute!

At the very beginning of his discourse Jesus makes clear that those who accept him and his mission, who see his teachings as truth, are the very salt of the earth. But to be of use in seasoning the carnal mind, they must maintain the spiritual ethos with which they are being anointed. If they gain and retain this spiritual truth, they will light the whole world, illumine human consciousness with light ineffable because it is from "the Father of lights." [3] They, illumined, will reflect their sacred illumination by letting it shine. Not in the cloister, not in a hermit's cave, does this spiritual illumination shed its rays, but in the world of men and affairs, where its healing radiance will illumine those receptive to its influence.

It was not to break the Law to which the Hebrew nation had so strenuously adhered that Jesus came; rather was it to bring grace and peace, to interpret its provisions more nearly in accord with human need, to apply it more understandingly and more mercifully; to bring joy and peace through revealing the Law of Love, thereby softening the stern mandates of the thunderous Law of Sinai. It was grace and truth humanity so much needs that the Nazarene came to bring. The Commandments are to be kept, but they must be accompanied by the spirit of love and kindness, of mercy and forgiveness, if the Kingdom is to be established in earth.

Mortals are to forgive their debtors, those who maltreat them; those whom the carnal mind calls enemies are to be loved, for in the heavenly Kingdom there are no enemies. Enemies arise

---

[3] James 1:17.

Summary

from belief in a mortal, the unlikeness of God, as man, from lack of knowledge that the so-called mortal is but the counterfeit of a son of God, who is truly made in His likeness. How quickly does love of the real man supplant the concept of an enemy to be hated when once the truth about man is understood!

The question is often asked, How can I love my neighbor who is not lovable, manifesting traits of character altogether unlovely? That type of mortal is not man, but a false representation, often a horrid counterfeit of God's likeness who is rather to be pitied for his ignorance of himself, of his true nature.

It is no impossible thing that the Nazarene enjoins upon us. His admonitions are perfectly practical of application when once the facts about the real man are learned. Mortals are to come under a selfimposed discipline that seems saner when viewed from their own position, that is, the belief that a mortal is the real man.

In order to put off these false beliefs, to promote spiritual growth and the blessedness that is its reward, some cherished beliefs must be put off; some things that are as dear and as necessary as one's right hand are to be extirpated, put out of consciousness. Even the right eye, the most cherished habit, is to be plucked out of consciousness, abandoned for the corrective truth, the redeeming Christ.

Severe, it seems, are these demands, but absolutely necessary in order to gain the freedom that belongs to the man of God's creating. Moreover, the seeming loss attached to the abandonment of these dearly cherished beliefs is compensated for a hundredfold by the possession of the pearl of Truth for which the exchange is made.

Adultery is primarily a mental state that is to be eliminated by the abandonment of belief in a physical mortal as man. In

Summary

the Kingdom, God's children neither marry nor are given in marriage, for each child of God is complete in his own selfhood as the likeness of all the deific qualities.

Nothing is to be gained through taking God's name in vain. It adds nothing to the strength of an assertion to add on oath. Rather does it detract from its impressiveness, for the user of oaths lacks faith in the truth and power of his own words. When our communications are restricted to "Yea, yea; Nay, nay," [4] they not only avoid the temptation to misrepresentation but they gain in forcefulness by their very simplicity. Since truth is unalterable, is wholly above the ability of mortal man to change it, nothing is gained, no profit arises, from inveighing against it. Profit of inestimable value derives from gaining the spiritual truth, submitting to its control, for this is the road direct to the Kingdom, wherein all blessedness awaits.

The Master's words regarding resistance to evil have been a stumbling block to many of his faithful followers. It has long been the cherished concept that to get even with our enemy who has wronged us, revenge must be taken; that injustice and evil done one should be avenged; that one sinned against is justified in administering adequate punishment: these mental states are not found on the way to the Kingdom. Rather do they point in the opposite direction, to that state of mental torture and unhappiness that has been accurately characterized as "hell." And since these are mental states of the carnal mind, they have no actuality. Moreover, since the constituent elements of hell as commonly viewed are unreal, have no actuality, their aggregate seeming is but a myth. Hell has no relation to the Kingdom. It is a state of carnal consciousness that disappears under the influence of spiritual illumination.

Nowhere does Jesus set forth more emphatically the need to maintain the true sense of forgiveness than in these verses

---

[4] Matt. 5:37.

Summary

in the fifth chapter of Matthew's Gospel. To be sure, the demand is for a high degree of spiritual attainment, but no higher than entrance to the Kingdom demands. No matter how grievous seems the offense, how great the temptation to return like for like, to use the material means at hand to wreak a just vengeance upon the aggressor who has injured us, to indulge the spirit of vengeance, is to fall away from companionship with the Master.

Remember Jesus' words on the Cross. "Father, forgive them; for they know not what they do" [5] comes ringing across the centuries with a forcefulness that may not be denied. Returning evil for evil has never brought healing to the "enemy" in need of it. Use of force against force has not stopped war, has not, in fact, lessened its occurrence or mitigated its frightful conditions. Rather has it intensified the hatred and bitterness that are prominent forerunners of the war spirit.

Jesus' admonition to turn the other cheek to the smiter, in assurance of the absence of fear of the tormentors, is based upon the possession of a degree of spiritual understanding that commands the power of the Spirit sufficiently to nullify the seeming power of evil. This is undoubtedly the goal to which humanity should mightily strive, for it is an inevitable condition of the Kingdom.

It seems, however, that until sufficient spiritual understanding is won to justify fearless facing of the enemy, belief that such forbearance might lead to disaster might lay Christian attainment open to a degree of destruction from which it would take long to recover. The teachings of the Master are the goal for all mental and spiritual attainment. But to force one's demonstration beyond one's spiritual attainment is neither scientific nor obedient. Faith in God based upon clear understanding of the divine nature makes both possible and practical

---

[5] Luke 23:34.

Summary

the accomplishment of what to the carnal mind seems radical and impractical.

On the other hand, when the understanding that all true power is derived from the divine Source, and that this divine power is omnipotent, everpresent, and available through spiritual understanding, then the other cheek may be safely turned, the enemy faced with perfect assurance that no harm can befall. When one truly dwells "in the secret place of the most High," [6] that is, in the consciousness of the divine presence and power, then it is that no harm can befall, no plague annoy or harm.

It does not seem practical for one to expose himself to the machinations of evil, to permit himself to be robbed by the dishonest and avaricious. But when one has gained the knowledge of God and His Kingdom, this understanding will enable one to give generously of his spiritual substance, feed the hungry, comfort the sorrowing, heal sickness, and bring redemption to the sinning in the ministration of true and merciful experience. Then it is that the Christian goes the second mile with one in error, even the third, so far as may seem necessary in order to guide his steps in the right way. Surely there is no limit to the mercy and loving-kindness which may be successfully poured out upon one receptive to this blessed ministry.

That the divine Father of all is no respecter of persons, that He makes His sun to shine and the rain to fall upon all alike poses an important lesson. Since all are equally blessed by the sun and the rain, we may conclude that divine Love is constantly bestowing its infinite, spiritual blessing upon all. None is forbidden to receive this, none denied the benefits of God's gifts. All are equally free to receive and enjoy the divine beneficence.

The problem that mankind faces is the need to make use of these heavenly gifts. The poverty, misery, and lack so common

---

[6] Ps. 91:1.

Summary

in human experience are due to the failure to understand the Giver of all good gifts. Knowledge of God conveys understanding of and appreciation for His constant bestowal.

While these gifts are wholly spiritual in their inception and quality, yet they find expression in terms of humanity's needs. Mortals reaching out for what is deemed necessary to support life touch this Law of Love that in its constant and continuous activity meets every requirement necessary to material well-being. To receive these blessings, it becomes obligatory to know God, His attributes and qualities, His Law of Love. And with this knowledge are coupled obedience and humility.

The conviction that "I can of mine own self do nothing" [7] opens the way to the recognition of the great fact that "every good gift and every perfect gift is from above, and cometh down from the Father of lights, with whom is no variableness, neither shadow of turning." [8] Once this conviction is gained, the way is opened to receive the divine bestowal that, in its quality and abundance, will meet mankind's every need.

Associated with the injunction to love one another, to love one's neighbor as oneself, even to bless them that curse you, is another statement that has given pause to many an earnest student of the Master's words: "Be ye therefore perfect, even as your Father which is in heaven is perfect." [9] If mortals are to be regarded as the children of God, then it seems quite impossible fully or even partially to obey this direct mandate. How can a mortal, a creature born of the flesh and hence material and subject to all the imperfections that accompany material selfhood, with its susceptibility to discord, sin, and disease—how, pray, can this creature, so frail and imperfect, become perfect?

It is completely impossible to accept, through either faith or reason, the supposition that mortals are made in the likeness of

---

[7] John 5:30.
[8] James 1:17.
[9] Matt. 5:48.

Summary

God. For, if the mortal is in actuality the likeness of God, then the assertion of divine perfection falls to the ground. Yet the statement closes with "even as your Father which is in heaven is perfect." Accepting the premise that God, the Creator of all, is perfect and that man is made in God's likeness, then it inevitably follows that man, the son of God, is as perfect in a degree as God Himself. This resolves the problem completely.

God's likeness is spiritual, is forever perfect. And it is the obligation of mortals to lay off the false material sense of man, of the counterfeit, which has developed through aeons of time, and seek man's true selfhood, the only selfhood that is real, perfect, and permanent. Thus do the words of the Master become a wholly practical admonition, one worthy of strict obedience.

The giving of alms was a subject of attention in this all-comprehensive sermon. Alms were not to be given in public, that is, that the giving might be known of men, and accordingly with the purpose to attract attention to one's generosity. Give for the joy of giving, out of love for those in need, and find your reward in the knowledge that such giving is after the pattern of God's bestowals and hence in conformity with the perfect Law of Love.

The size of the bestowal does not measure its highest quality. It was the mite cast into the Temple box by the widow that Jesus declared to be a greater gift than the offering of the rich. Not the magnitude of the gift, but the spirit of the giver really determines its value and its status as a genuine gift. Giving what one can readily spare, what causes no sacrifice to the giver, does not meet the implication of the Master's words. A little given in the true spirit carries a far greater sign of Christian spirit than the larger gift that may cause no inconvenience, no hardship to the giver.

The Master's injunctions regarding prayer are among the most impressive and important of all his precious sayings. All

Summary

genuine praying should be done in secret and not to be heard of men. The prayer in secret, in the innermost sanctuary of human desire and purpose, lifts thought to the plane of reality where God and His offspring forever co-exist in harmony, joy, and abundance.

This realization, reached and held to, brings the perfect assurance of the inseparable relationship of God to His children, a relationship continuous, eternal, forever inseparable. Moreover, it brings to the seeker perfect assurance that God has already bestowed upon His beloved children every good and every perfect gift, all that infinite Love, the Love that knows only man's present and eternal perfection, could bestow. For manifestly, God's likeness could know no lack, could have no unfulfilled desire, no unsatisfied longing.

Can one doubt that this realization gained and firmly held to would bring into human experience that which would meet every need? The prayer of realization would demonstrate the perfection of Being, of Life always manifested as perfect. Perfect God and perfect man is the forever status of the divine economy, the Kingdom of Heaven.

There then follows the perfect type of petition and affirmation known as the Lord's Prayer, the prayer that completely recognizes the divine presence and sovereignty, ever bestowing upon God's children the divine beneficence in a fullness that knows no lack, no imperfection. This is the prayer that heals the sick, reforms the sinful, restores the distressed to man's ever perfect state of peace and blessedness. It is this prayer, uttered in recognition of the beauty of holiness that knows no lack of forgiveness, no enmity, nothing foreign to the likeness of infinite Love.

Prayer in a definite sense connotes fasting. For the spirit of true prayer is attained only by rising above material sense into the realm of reality, into the divine consciousness, the Kingdom of Heaven. Withdrawal from the world of matter

Summary

to the universe of Spirit, God—this is true fasting. Abstinence from material food is but the symbol of true fasting. It is beneficial only so far as it aids in the gaining of the spiritual heights where are revealed the allness, goodness, and perfection of God's universe, the realm of Truth, of Life and Love.

The central thought of Jesus' teaching, its very heart and soul, is reliance upon God, reliance based upon the divine nature, purpose, power, and presence. The closing assertion of the Lord's Prayer not only implies this but emphatically affirms it. "For thine is the kingdom, and the power, and the glory, for ever," [10] beyond possibility of doubt or refutation, posits with God all power, the everpresence of that state of consciousness that is the Kingdom of Heaven. And to this almighty and all-loving Father is attributed all glory. No true glory, nothing worthy of emulation, stems from any other source. To Him be all glory who is all might, all goodness, all Love, all substance.

It is to this all-inclusive One that the Master demanded obedience, radical reliance, and true worship. Thus it was that he admonished his hearers against the seeking for and the laying up of material wealth. Knowing as he knew the transitory nature of everything material, he urged his hearers to turn away from the temptation to place reliance upon material wealth and rather to turn to God, in whom inheres all that is of permanent value.

Moreover, this reliance upon Deity, if buttressed by understanding, would insure that all material needs would be supplied. And there is implied in his words a definite distinction between needs and wants. The carnal mind is acquisitive, is forever seeking to accumulate not only that which it believes necessary to sustain its own sense of life, but that which satisfies

---

[10] Matt. 6:13.

Summary

its pride of possession. It loves to lord itself above its fellows because it has accumulated not matter alone, but whatsoever bespeaks unusual capability in administering human affairs.

It is to refute and expose this false sense of possession that the Nazarene took his radical stand. No man can love materiality, can prize it above spiritual attainment, and gain the Kingdom. Materiality can never accompany one into the Kingdom. Matter and Spirit have nothing in common. Only as love of mammon, the god of materiality, is extirpated, can the spiritual ascendancy be found that meets the need. When this attitude is gained, there will be no need of taking thought for the morrow, regarding either food or raiment or, in short, any material thing. All will be supplied through understanding of and complete reliance upon the Father of all, whose storehouse of blessings is infinite and from which all needs are supplied.

These gifts, however, are to be sought. "Ask, and it shall be given you" [11] definitely implies the necessity of asking. For mortals to gain that which is automatically bestowed upon the children of the Kingdom in fulfillment of the divine order, they must ask for it, must valiantly seek it to ensure its reception, a wholly logical situation. If one be given a large sum deposited in a bank, one must acknowledge ownership and must draw checks in order to receive the bequest, that is, in order to possess and utilize it. Likewise, effort is necessary in order to gain from the storehouse of infinite Love its spiritual treasure. And this effort requires the gaining of the spiritual vision, the understanding of God and His Kingdom, in order to bring His beneficence into the human experience. "Ask, and it shall be given you; . . . knock, and it shall be opened unto you."

No more perfect pattern for right living has ever been propounded than inheres in the Golden Rule. To be sure, it was

---

[11] Matt. 7:7.

Summary

not original with this Man of Nazareth. Yet so universal is its truth, so complete its thesis, that no ethical teacher, so aware of the divine presence as was he, could fail to present it in its most impressive form. That this truth is universal and has been glimpsed by great religions of all time is an obvious fact, as every searcher for reality finds. Hence it was that these words in which Jesus gave utterance to an age-old spiritual fact were so obviously just, so impressively righteous, that none could gainsay its importance.

No treatment of another that does not epitomize what one would wish another's attitude toward himself to be, could be the very acme of true relationship. To receive justice one must deserve justice. To win fair treatment, one engages in fair treatment toward all and sundry with whom he becomes related. And it must not be overlooked that as one's own mentality is spiritualized, his treatment of others takes on a new aspect; and this implies a reciprocal improvement in that which he receives. The Golden Rule is a perfect axiom for righteous relationship between men. If it were to be put into general use, the conditions of humanity would be markedly improved. Like all the Master's teachings, it is a truth—beautiful, to be sure—but proved effective only as it becomes utilized.

Jesus was keenly aware of the false prophets, they who assumed the appearance of true disciples of the Christ, yet were dishonest, deceitful, devilish. They would turn the most sacred words of the Master to their own advantage, thus violating the very spirit of the message. These falsifiers often strode about in the garments of righteousness, sometimes so cunning and convincing as to deceive the very elect. These were to be guarded against as one protects his household from the thief and robber. Sheep's clothing never hides the true character of the imposter from the keen perception that understanding of Truth bestows. This understanding, however, must be utilized to guard against the false prophets. When the proof of works

Summary

is a requisite to the acceptance of any presentation, the defense against imposition is well built.

No more impressive ending to a priceless document could the Master have spoken than that which appears in the last verses of this supreme sermon. The wise man appears in bold contrast to the foolish. It was the latter who built his house on the shifty and unstable sands of the mortal or carnal mind, that state of consciousness which deals with materiality in its multifarious phases; with the unreal in contrast to the realism of the Kingdom. Built upon so insecure a foundation, there was no chance that it would withstand assault from the evil forces of its own conspiring. Of course such a structure fell because it was falsely planned and jerry-built.

Not so with the wise man, instructed in things of the Spirit, conscious of their value and lasting quality, convinced that this alone furnished the sure foundation for all permanent building. Convinced of these, he could do no less than to follow what he had determined was the way, the entrance gate to that "house not made with hands, eternal in the heavens." [12] Convinced that unless the Lord builds the house, all building is vain, the wise man proceeds to surrender all human plans to the All-Wise, rendering willing obedience to the true pattern of life as it unfolds.

The house thus built stands against the vicissitudes of human experience, however powerful, however threatening they may appear. With its foundation stones laid upon the rock, Christ, and joined with the cement of spiritual understanding, the house thus founded stands forever. All structures, mortal and material, go forward to decay. They are inevitably destined to disappear because their foundations, their very premises, are false. How important, then, that we build our houses, our state of consciousness, upon the stones of spiritual truth which this

---

[12] II Cor. 5:1.

Summary

Master Workman has wrought from the quarry of Life everlasting. He has shown the way. The need is to follow it precisely as he charted it for needy humanity.

If search were made for a single statement that summarizes the teachings of this Nazarene, it might be found in these simple words, "But seek ye first the Kingdom of God, and his righteousness; and all these things shall be added unto you." [13] As we have seen, so important is this statement that it deserves close analysis. The "Kingdom of God" is to be sought: the state of consciousness from which all materiality has been banished; the mental state that perfectly reflects the divine—this is the first requirement. Mortals may not be able, in fact, never are able, to gain this degree of spiritual altitude in a moment, hurriedly, or in a brief space of time. Earnest desire, however, coupled with persistent prayer, leads onward and upward to this goal of complete triumph. Self-surrender to the divine afflatus, banishment of egotism, greater humility—rising from the understanding that all true capability springs from the divine Source—all of these are requisites in this seeking and finding of the Kingdom.

The word "first" in this passage is of signal importance. The rewards, the blessings that accrue upon entrance to the Kingdom are not to be obtained until all these preliminary steps are taken. None can be omitted, none overlooked: all are necessary to be taken *first*. Moreover, seeking the Kingdom is to be accompanied by the gaining of "his (God's) righteousness." And surely this can mean nothing less than the state of right living, the true sense of Life, the understanding of the nature, attributes, and qualities of Deity, of Truth, of Love, of Mind, of Spirit.

When this understanding is once attained, it becomes the

---
[13] Matt. 6:33.

Summary

way of life. Thus the seeking is rewarded in the fruits of the Spirit, in the blessedness that forever characterizes the children of God. Upon the attainment of this exalted state, the results are assured—"all these things shall be added unto you." And there is complete justification in the conviction that "these things" will include whatever is necessary to the demonstration of a harmonious and successful experience. These things do not satisfy false desire; they do make for the type of experience most conducive to spiritual growth. In other words, these things include whatever is needed to aid us in the journey from material belief to spiritual understanding, from the uncertainty of experiences based upon materiality to the perfect assurance of spiritual well-being in the Father's house. These are the "added things."

It is little wonder that when the Master had concluded this masterly pronouncement, the most important message ever delivered, the multitude should have followed him from the mountainside. To a complete summation of the teachings of the Old Testament, its ethical and moral code, had been added the grace and truth of the Spirit, the very essence of spiritual truth. The demands were high, the mental discipline required drastic, the sacrifice of material things great, but the rewards were of infinite blessing, an eternal state of joy and peace far above all human conception.

This was the very acme of the teachings of the matchless Master wherein he ascended to the sublime heights of spiritual grandeur, the heights that he had attained through speechless prayer and great travail of spirit. This he poured out without stint and with convincing earnestness.

No one can read this sermon without gaining something of "the Spirit of truth" that breathes through its every line. If and when humanity accepts it and orders the affairs of life in accord with its lofty but true idealism, not only will the indi-

Summary

vidual experience complete salvation, but society itself will compose its manifold problems.

The present terrible chaos of the world is proof that these teachings have been ignored: that the effort to make them effective has been abortive because of the distortion and misdirection of that which is simple in its essence and wholly practical in application. None can justifiably assert that the Christianity which Jesus set forth in minutest detail has been generally accepted and adopted by Christendom, either individually or collectively; that the Church founded upon the rock, Christ, has followed the directions he so plainly charted. In consequence, after nineteen centuries the world still wallows in the mire of materialism and selfishness. The conditions are unmistakable; the situation grave, even desperate.

There is serious doubt whether the so-called Christian civilization can endure if the catastrophic strife with which the world is now encircled should be repeated. Jesus has given the perfect remedy. Nothing is lacking in its detail or the practicality of its character. The one problem is to understand its method and gain the spirit of the Christ-message. The time is now, if the world is to find peace in place of the terrific cataclysm that now enshrouds it.

The Ecumenical movement that is now launched in both America and Europe is grand in its inception. Its success will depend upon the measure in which it gains the spirit and learns the letter of the Master's revelation. No longer need there be mystery as to the nature and quality of Deity. No longer is there room for doubt as to the practicabilities of the Master's teachings.

That the nature of God was revealed to Jesus is now an admitted fact. The letter is revealed in the "Spirit of truth"; the remedy is complete. The Christ-Comforter, the Holy Ghost or spiritual truth, is at hand and available to meet every type of need in correcting the evils of the times. God is omnipotent

Summary

and omnipresent. He is everywhere available to solve every problem. Neither pride, prejudice, nor passion should prevent the use of this divine Almightiness, adequate to lift humanity above itself into the realm of reality, where alone are peace and prosperity established forever for all of God's children. Permanent peace will be attained when the Christ dominates the Peace Table.

PART II

XII

A Broad View

ALL Christendom is convinced that there is an overruling power, almighty and everpresent, termed God. There is also general agreement that God was revealed through Christ Jesus, His Son. The following chapters are based upon the conviction that the Comforter (Helper)[1] which Jesus promised should come, was and is the Christ, the "Spirit of truth," the truth about all things; that this Christ-Comforter is co-existent and co-eternal with God, is present here and now, available to heal the evils that so grievously beset mankind; to set in accord with righteousness the affairs of humanity; to compose the difficulties of men and nations; to establish a sense of brotherhood that will in fact constitute peace, lasting, just, durable—the peace that passeth all human understanding.

It is becoming increasingly manifest that the present world chaos is due to influences reaching far back in the human economy, to wrongs and evils arising from the sins of the people, of individuals, groups, and governments—sins that manifestly the Church has not healed. With this conclusion there has also arisen the firm conviction widespread throughout Christendom that inescapable responsibility rests upon the Church to introduce the reforms necessary to correct the evils that have resulted in world-wide calamity. The certainty is that humanity of itself apart from divine aid can never accomplish the task. It has tried and failed. And the Church, divided and weakened, with the spiritual animus of Jesus' teachings watered down to a

---
[1] Moffatt's translation.

A Broad View

feeble content, has so far departed from the primitive Christianity, in a measure established by the early Christians, that it has become ineffective in giving direction to the affairs of government and to the development of international amity.

The task that lies ahead of rebuilding society upon a basis of lasting peace is a task calling for the leadership of God, of the divine Author, which is available through the everpresent Christ to guide, direct, and improve the affairs of men when once approach is made with humility and willing obedience to the divine Will. The unity that alone makes peace possible derives only from the basis of the Fatherhood of God and the inevitable corollary, the brotherhood of man. Since this Father of all is Spirit, the brotherhood comprises His spiritual offspring, bound together in the one Christ, the infinite manifestation of this infinite God. Upon this foundation alone will the brotherhood be established; the brotherhood that recognizes that all men in reality are created equal, that all have the same status in the divine economy, that all are equally loved of the Father, who is infinite Love.

This healing Christ, this Holy Spirit, is everpresent to solve the problems of humanity of whatever form, of whatever seeming difficulty of character. But the Christ-Comforter must be recognized, known, accepted, and applied in order to introduce its healing and corrective power into the affairs of the world. That the multiplification table is true, reliable, and ever at hand, always available to solve our problems in arithmetic all agree. But it had to be learned and accepted and the method of its application acquired before it became an effective agency in this solution. Precisely the same reasoning applies to this divine agency, the Christ. It must be known, accepted without doubt, its presence realized, and its potency acknowledged in order for it to perform that which it will perform in meeting the human need. There is no mystery attached to this power, but it must be understood in order to become effective.

A Broad View

Nothing is impossible to the Almighty, whose power and influence are ever to be invoked through the righteous prayer, which the faithful James assures us "availeth much."[2] Likewise nothing is impossible to this Christ-messenger, His beloved Son. Upon this basis are the following chapters written, with the purpose of examining the present problems of humanity, of determining in some measure their cause, and of illustrating the application of the Christ-Comforter, the agent of divine will, to their solution. The task has been undertaken with a deep conviction that not humanly but divinely must the approach be made. With this approach, the Christ becomes the perfect agency for the composing of all difficulties, for the removal of all error in the social economy.

Even casual examination of the governments of the world as constituted before the opening of the present conflict reveals that contained within them were the seeds of disunity and distrust, qualities that, if allowed to grow, would ultimately lead to open warfare.

The portent was not inaccurate. The inevitable happened. The blow fell with a severity that is shaking the whole world. So severe is the blow that nations are trembling to their very foundations; and already, rising from this furnace of hell, are conclusions that demand a new order, if Christian society is to endure.

Among the Allied Nations the belief is general that the conflict is a titanic struggle between good and evil, between the right and wrong way of life; between righteous and unrighteous ideologies concerning government. This conviction is erroneous if it stems from the belief that the Axis Nations had no basis for their conclusions that they were not being fairly dealt with by the great Democracies. Their conclusions were justified, at least in part. That their deep-seated dissatisfaction was

---

[2] James 5:16.

A Broad View

bound to lead to war was overlooked, or at most but half realized. It was and is not only unjust but impossible to hold great and virile peoples in bondage either through lack of territory necessary to support increasing populations, or through want of the raw materials that underlie manufactures.

There is no mistaking the fact that the economy adopted by the victorious nations in the first World War was of a kind to bring disaster to those against whom it was directed, while at the same time it was bringing unprecedented prosperity to the victorious nations. Not the Versailles Treaty alone, but the course afterward pursued toward Germany could but result in a desperate effort on her part to regain the power and prestige that she regarded as her inherent right as a great and powerful nation. This is no justification for the biological theory of a superior race or of a people determined by Providence to rule the world. No more is there justification for the development in a civilized world of a National Socialist philosophy, godless and hence ruthless and cruel beyond comprehension. The philosophy that posits right as the possession and use of material might to gain what is coveted is nothing short of paganism.

In his little volume *Christocracy*,[3] J. Middleton Murray goes so far as to say that the Germans had no course open to them, no way of overcoming the appalling unemployment situation following Germany's economic collapse, other than to turn to the production of armaments for a future war. Two purposes, he avers, were served by this policy. Germany was preparing for her future adventure in gaining world dominion, and at the same time providing labor for all. This, it seems, met their common need. On the other hand, the author points out that England accepted a policy, however reluctantly, of undernourishment for her children because of unemployment. England failed in her economy where Germany succeeded in hers at the expense of the world. Meantime the United States

---
[3] Andrew Dokers, Ltd., London.

A Broad View

drifted along, somnolent and at ease, while the god of war was building a war machine unprecedented in its extent and power.

These conclusions are not wholly warranted. Yet unprejudiced analysts, those who are able to survey the situation objectively, are convinced that no nation concerned was blameless, since no one nation was wholly actuated by a Christianly desire to serve humanity in a manner to promote true brotherhood. The high Christian character attained by numberless individual Christians throughout the earth had not made its way into the national capitals, there to enforce a policy looking to the service of all. National lines still constituted a barrier within which self-interest was uppermost. The spirit of nationalism was paramount. Tariffs were raised by the one creditor nation, thus preventing the flow of commerce that not only would have enabled the debtor nations to meet their obligations but also would have tended to break disunity and distrust. The great American Republic became in the eyes of the debtor nations the veritable Uncle Shylock of the international economy. The promoters of the Smoot-Hawley tariff bill became aware of their serious error, but too late to advance international amity.

So thoroughly have the causes of the war been exposed, analyzed, and discussed pro and con that there is little occasion to recount them further. Accordingly, they will be referred to only in connection with their remedy. An avowed purpose of the Allied Nations is to preserve Democracy and to prove through exemplification that it is the best form of government yet devised.

It is becoming painfully apparent that the one-time popular slogan, "The world must be made safe for Democracy," sprang from a misconception of the problems facing the world. When Democracy is proved the ideal mode of government, the world will be the benefactor. The demand is that Democracy be made so practical, that its idealism be brought so perfectly into

A Broad View

realization, that all the world desiring true freedom will seek its adoption. This, then, is the paramount issue—to bring into realization the idealism inherent in Democracy. Democracy must be made safe for the world.

The contention that because Democracy represents the will of the majority of an electorate it is in consequence the divine method of Government, is far from accurate. The old cry, "vox populi, vox Dei," has been found far from realism. Many a time has the majority adopted a course that led directly away and far from the status of righteousness. The voice of the people is expressive of divine Will only in so far as it conforms to the tenets of Christian teaching—Fatherhood of God, the correlative, brotherhood of man, and the divine Father incorporated in the Golden Rule.

These are the foundation stones of all true building, both in individual life and as the national policy. The brotherhood of man, the unity of God's children, is an eternal fact in the divine economy. This brotherhood, this forever unity, is government by divine Will, the Will that is beneficent and good beyond the power of words to express. This government is changeless, since it expresses omnipotence, fixed and inexorable divine Will. But this divine Will is Love, the irresistible, irrepressible desire to bless. Hence its rule is wholly beneficent. How could the rule of infinite Love be less than blessed for all under its ineffable dominion?

Now Democracy, as humanly devised and operated, rule by the people, is at most simply the approximation in terms of human capacity of the pattern of the divine. And it will succeed only in proportion to that approximation. And in the degree in which it becomes the counterpart of the divine government will the voice of the people become the expression of divine Will.

Too long has the welfare of the nation been uppermost in the purpose of the government. Save our skins, regardless of

A Broad View

the welfare of other peoples and nations, has too long been the guiding purpose of governments. To care for one's own is commendable; but it may fall far short of the ideal in promotion of the grand brotherhood of all humanity, which, under God, is the only worthy perspective. Exploitation by an imperialistic nation, organized under the aegis of Christianity, is an anomaly. The Editor of the *Christian Advocate* recently put it admirably: "We are discovering, for instance, that ours is all one world. Races and nations are interdependent. It is not only that the democracies need the oil and the rubber of the East Indies, but they also need the East Indians. The tin and bauxite as well as the petroleum of Burma constituted a serious loss to the United Nations, but before we lost those precious minerals we had lost the Burmese." Not material gain but the welfare of the people must be the purpose of the New World Order, the establishment of true Democracy.

Greed, inherent in mortals and hence expressed in national policy, has long exploited the humble peoples of earth in order for the citizens of dominant nations to dwell in comfort and affluence, in ease and luxury. Now the error is uncovered. The remedy is at hand. So universal has been this condition of master and subjugated peoples that it not only constitutes a black spot on the escutcheon of the master nations, but it has morally degraded those who have seemed to be its beneficiaries. It matters not whether we look at the Dutch East Indies, the Belgian Congo, the French Equatorial possessions, or the English possessions widely scattered over the earth, the purpose primarily has been to profit from the labor of the native populations, often with little regard for the well-being of the exploited. Profit has commonly been the impelling purpose, profit both for the government and for those having vested interests in these primitive localities. Conditions in certain instances have improved, and a more just attitude toward the exploited peoples has been adopted. This is especially true

A Broad View

in the East Indies, where the Dutch rule has adopted some measure of benevolence.

It may not be contended that all efforts to gain and control territory and peoples have had an unholy purpose. When England reluctantly took over the mandate for Palestine, the United States having refused to accept the responsibility, the task immediately assumed the aspect of helping the population, both Arab and Jew, to a better way of life. It was the avowed purpose expressed to me in 1927 by the Governor of Jerusalem to develop more healthful conditions, to remove squalor and poverty by establishing modern sanitary methods, to promote facilities for education, and to stimulate the processes of agriculture and industry. For example, when it was found that the Dead Sea, long the symbol of death and desolation, was a veritable mine of valuable minerals, the terms made by the British companies that undertook their recovery were very favorable to the people of Palestine. In 1927 there was no, or almost no, display of military authority. The declared purpose was to help the people to a better way of life. By contrast, in Syria the French tricolor was everywhere displayed and "the glory of France" was the watchword of the day.

This but illustrates the trend of an improved purpose and method evolved by Great Britain through several centuries of experience in colonization. Far from inspired by Christian motives were her methods in China and India when first entrance was forced among these peoples. Imperialism was the modus. Profit was the purpose, with little regard for the welfare of the people that were exploited. Gradually, however, enlightenment has come in her national policy, and the conditions imposed upon subject peoples have been greatly improved. This is not to say that much more does not await the doing before the spirit of true Christian brotherhood motivates the powers. But an assessment of England's attitude in the Indian situation would be far from just did it not give full consideration to the difficulties arising from racial and religious traditions in their intensity beyond anything known to the Western world.

No nation has a clear record. Even in the Philippine Islands, toward which the United States adopted a policy providing for citizenship and ultimate self-government, private interests entered under the flag and exploited the native population to their own purpose. However, that President McKinley had the high purpose of elevating the native population to a degree of intelligence that would first prepare them for citizenship in the great republic and later for self-government is a historical fact. There is, however, an improvement manifest in various ways, but much of self-interest is yet to be overcome before the establishment of true Christian government in the rule and purpose of the nations. Divine direction is yet to be accepted and demonstrated as the one and only basis for the establishment and maintenance of true Democracy.

A Democracy as administered is expressive of the will of its citizens. It is the measure of the morale of its constituents. It exemplifies, illustrates, the mental status, purpose, and direction of the electorate. It is good or bad as the desire is for righteous or unrighteous government. It is improved as the understanding of true government is gained by its constituents and the purpose rises to bring it to conform with high purpose, with service of the people. When the people have gained the right concept of government as the means whereby the greatest opportunity is brought to the individual for mental, moral, and spiritual growth, for the fullest expression of life, compatible with the general welfare, Democracy will attain new heights. It will become more effective and its spiritual animus will draw support of the electorate in proportion to its adherence to the idealism upon which it is founded.

The oft-repeated axiom, "Charity begins at home," as applied is less than a half-truth. It may be that charity is first and

A Broad View

best exemplified at home, but only as it spreads its influence to include each and all will it be worthy of the name of true charity, the motive of true Christian government.

In every country the need is imperative to conform its government to the Christ demands, if a truly Christian civilization is to emerge from the dense shadows of the present. Education of the citizen primarily in knowledge of God and His Christ is the starting point, the very first step in the holy purpose to establish the brotherhood of man as an actuality. The constituent members of a Democracy strong in the faith, the faith based upon understanding, will choose its government of like-minded individuals. These representatives of the will of the people will ordain policies in accord with Christian purposes.

Governments thus motivated reach across the national boundaries with one desire, to bless their neighboring peoples. Each will visualize the other's need and, seeing, will seek to supply it, thus filling the measures of the Golden Rule. A unity of peoples and nations will emerge, a symbol in terms of a unity of peoples that approximates the true brotherhood of all God's children, the spiritual brotherhood that forever persists in the Kingdom of Reality. It will be and is contended that this attainment is impractical, that such a goal is impossible of attainment, in a world ordered as society now is. To be sure, the true brotherhood is not attainable except through spiritualization of thought, through the gaining of that understanding of God and Christ Jesus that constitutes eternal life. But the beginning may be undertaken now, at once. Time is running out and the emergency is great.

The rewards will accrue progressively as the governmental acts are brought into accord with the divine Will. Innumerable ways will open for uniting the peoples and nations of earth with the cement of good will, of brotherly kindness, and the love that the saintly John enjoined upon his friends in the Faith. This is no impossible program. All things are possible

A Broad View

to those who humbly seek to serve God "in spirit and in truth." [4] The time is now and the need is imperative.

The national consciousness but reflects the mental status of the people. It improves, rises, as the individual, hungering and thirsting after righteousness, spiritualizes his purpose and determines to serve God first. When this is done, and His righteousness is ardently sought, the "things" will be added; and those things will include righteous government, based upon selfless service to all humanity. Whatever is possible and practical for demonstration by the individual is equally possible and practical of attainment for the combined will of the people expressed in terms of government.

No nation has arrived at the goal of true Christian service. No nation has risen above the primary desire to serve, care for, and protect its own. What reputation does the citizen gain whose purpose, primary and exclusive, is to care for himself and his family? He is known as a self-centered and selfish mortal, failing in the ministry of the good neighbor. No more can a nation, great or small, that is concerned alone with its well-being attain to heights of spiritual blessedness. Jesus' words, "And I, if I be lifted up from the earth, will draw all men unto me," [5] have a direct pertinency to the national situation. The nation first illumined with the holy light of spiritual understanding and attaining to the mountain peak of demonstration will become the leader in the procession headed for the Kingdom, the Realm of perfect peace.

---

[4] John 4:24.
[5] John 12:32.

XIII

Total War, Total Peace

EACH stage of human experience produces new terms, new uses of words that have perhaps long been a part of the people's vocabulary. War is especially prolific in this respect, since it is extremely fecund in the variety of its attendant conditions, many of them novel and without precedent. An example of such terms is the use of the expression "total war" introduced early in the present conflict. As applied by the aggressor nations, there soon developed for this term a double meaning. At first it signified a whole, complete, utter state of war, as used by the Axis powers, an all-out effort to accomplish their nefarious purposes; an effort in the prosecution of which were involved all their resources, industrial and manpower as well—not only all the resources to be obtained within their own borders, but all that could be wrested from the nations they were able to crush and conquer. It was an out-and-out act of piracy, projected by a people raised to the highest state of enthusiasm, a resourceful people who had occupied the years following the last great conflict in preparing to carry out an unholy purpose. It was an effort, soulless and ruthless, prepared and launched on a scale never paralleled in history. This type of enterprise was characterized as "total war."

As the war progressed, another meaning was attached to the term. It came to imply total subjugation of peoples on whom their heinous purpose fell, total destruction of all semblance of national sovereignty, total domination of the lives of the conquered peoples—a state but little short of abject slavery. In

Total War, Total Peace

fact, so far has the heavy hand of the Nazi authority gone that enslaved peoples in France, Belgium, and other countries are forced to labor at home or in Germany to keep the wheels of the war machine turning and to provide subsistence for the German people. The program as planned and initiated implied the employment of all the enginery of modern warfare produced in two decades by a people noted for ingenuity in devising new inventions and for the technical ability to render them practical.

The whole world was to be brought into the orbit of the New Order, but so subdued and organized that all profit would accrue to the victorious nation of supermen. Under this regime, total war took on the added significance of the complete subjugation of every people or nation that had the temerity and the stamina to dispute the progress of this gigantic monster, a modern horrendous one, indeed. Those offering no resistance would be admitted to the New Order, but only on the periphery. Thus "total war" took on a double significance, to include both the efforts of the aggressor nations and the complete subjugation of all the nations brought under its heel.

When the affair at Pearl Harbor suddenly catapulted the United States into the conflict, the term "total war" took on a third significance, one that differed completely from the meaning of the term as used by the aggressor nations. The United States, like Great Britain, China, and the Dutch East Indies, suddenly had thrust upon it a wholly unwelcome situation, one that the several governments involved had striven earnestly to avoid through prolonged and patient efforts to arrive at a peaceful settlement of the international problems involved, utilizing the generally accepted channels of diplomacy and exercising commendable restraint; even the mistaken policy of appeasement was employed.

All these efforts were in vain. The aggressors turned deaf ears to every effort toward peace unless it recognized the justice of their infamous claims. All efforts to compose the questions

[121]

Total War, Total Peace

at issue failed. England in dealing with Germany had gone almost to the point of subservience in her desire to avoid so terrible a calamity. The United States, instantly as it were, was plunged into a state of war, a situation from which there was no escape with the preservation of national honor. Pearl Harbor left no other choice except to surrender to a pagan nation actuated by the same purposes as her partners, namely, to take whatever she desired and believed to be of advantage to herself to possess.

Instantly opinion, which had been at notable variance in the Congress and between the Congress and the Administration, became fused into a unified national purpose. As by a miracle there was displayed the readiness and stern determination to embark upon total war with no slightest purpose of national aggrandizement, no desire to enlarge its borders, no wish to extend or create an empire, but for the one purpose of laying once and forever the evil known as a war psychosis, which, if victorious, would enslave all mankind.

This attitude on the part of the United States gave a new meaning to the term "total war." To make possible the peace for which the Allied Nations long, they are indissolubly united in a grim resolution to wage total war, total in a complete unity of purpose to employ every ounce of their unlimited resources to destroy the gigantic evil manifested as unprecedented cruelty abroad in the world today. Total war to the thirty-one Allied Nations means the use of so much of their wealth, energy, and combined force as may be necessary to accomplish the enterprise so reluctantly embarked upon: complete victory over the aggressor nations.

This brief review of events is necessary to understand the task of winning the peace after the military victory shall have been won. The problem of winning the war not only entails the necessity of discussing a plan to operate immediately after the cessation of hostilities, but it involves the planning for a total peace, just, permanent, so incontestably righteous in its

Total War, Total Peace

fundamentals and details as to preclude for all time the recurrence of the terrible tragedies of the last three decades. Something more is needed, something vastly more potent, more effective than has yet been devised to ensure all peoples safety from the plaguing evil that is now shaking the very foundations of civilization.

Already hosts of thoughtful persons, peering through the mists that seem so darkly to enshroud the future, are undertaking to formulate peace plans that will make future international strife an impossibility. Earnest men and women are employing their highest capabilities, their most earnest prayers, to discover the way out of the darkness of devastating war.

Naturally, it seems, under the circumstances, the query arises, Should not the peace-loving nations that are able to enlist an all-out effort in prosecuting total war be as able to undertake equally strenuous efforts for the holy purpose of establishing just peace? Is not "total peace" as worthy of the combined, the all-out efforts of the nations as the prosecution of "total war"? The purpose of this unprecedented war effort is to make way for the peace to follow.

War does not by any means make peace. It simply establishes conditions whereby the Peace Table may become the successor to the strategy board, where planning peace may supersede the planning of campaigns. Peace does not come by decree. It is not a self-existent entity: it is a mental state wherein, in some measure, the harmony of Heaven prevails in place of strife and the promotion of self-interest.

In consideration of this all-important question, it may be queried: Have the nations now struggling for opportunity to establish peace ever, even individually, or in unity, approximated the winning of peace with an effort entitled to be characterized as total? The only answer is negative. No nation has ever shown the same determined purpose to win peace that it has employed in the prosecution of war. No nation has ever advanced to the state of Christian consciousness that would enable it to command all its resources for the promotion of total peace, just and lasting, the peace that can only follow the extirpation of basic national evils—the self-interest, pride, and lust for power and prestige that in some degree have characterized the national life of every people.

If total peace is a just and worthy cause, then there should be explored thoroughly and in every aspect the ways and means of accomplishing the kind of peace that will be permanent because it is just, because there have been removed the old sprouting seeds of self-interest that, unless uprooted, would lead to future strife. In the modern types of government adopted by the nations of the world, there has been a certain common pattern. Whatever the specific form of government—Democracy, limited Monarchy, Totalitarian—there are commonly devised departments of war, navy, state, finance, labor, commerce, education, et cetera.

In no government has there ever been a department wholly devoted to the cause of permanent peace. Never has any nation been so determined upon seeking the blessings of peace, peace total and impregnable, as to undertake its promotion through a government agency, bureau, or department having no purpose other than the promotion of peace, a department equal in standing with all other departments.

The tentative answer to this proposal, sometimes offered, namely, that various departments of governments are devoted to the activities that promote peace, does not adequately meet the situation. Rather is it an evasion. The evidence that these departments have not established a state of peace is the perfect answer to the proposition. They have failed to bring to many peoples of the earth a mental state that finds both prosperity and happiness in the prosecution of the arts of peace rather than in armed strife prosecuted for the satisfaction of false desires for mistaken ideals somewhat common to mankind.

It cannot be denied that the efforts of governments toward

peace have been desultory and ineffective in comparison with the energy and determination displayed in the preparation for and prosecution of war. This is not to deny the need for departments of education, commerce, labor, finance, foreign affairs—all are necessary to orderly and effective government. But it must be admitted that they are only indirectly engaged in peace-making.

If it be asserted that the preparation for peace is primarily a function of the Church, then it must be recognized that the Church has a direct influence in the affairs of government. Otherwise, its most earnest efforts founded in its understanding of divine government could easily be nullified by act of a political government. Moreover, in the United States, Church and State are so completely separated by constitutional provision that such relationship would be impossible. There remains, however, the possibility of electing to office those who are so thoroughly impregnated with the Christian attitude that the moral and spiritual law would become the directing power in all acts of government. This is the direct and only practical manner of inspiring the righteous ethics that make for lasting peace.

It is commonly agreed that victory in the present conflict must be followed by such unity of effort and purpose on the part of the Allied Nations as will render impossible the recurrence of such another devastating calamity as global warfare. Surely all Christian peoples and, almost equally surely, all civilized nations, earnestly desire to escape the consequences of armed conflict, which inevitably set civilization backward immeasurably. The exceptions are those which, like the Axis Nations, glorify war.

The cost of war in lives and treasure is increasingly appalling. Innocent peoples, noncombatants, suffer even more than those actually engaged in the strife. The decline in moral status of the peoples engaged in total warfare, while imponderable, is none the less a serious calamity; war engenders a degree of hatred and resentment obliterated only after long periods. Such results are commonly recognized as the unavoidable by-products of warfare. So tremendous are its repercussions that if civilization is to endure, all possible means should be taken to remove this scourge from human experience.

In the examination of this vital problem of total peace, the past must be explored for its possible lessons. What may be taken from previous experience to guide in the determination of the way to this desired goal of lasting peace? What mistakes should be avoided? No unprejudiced person will deny that the League of Nations was conceived in a high purpose—the unity of peoples and nations in a brotherhood in which the good of all, the commonweal, would be paramount to the desire of any individual member; in a unity that would pave the way to permanent peace. Hopes ran high in many hearts.

The people of the embattled Allied Nations looked upon President Wilson as the veritable Apostle of Freedom for the whole world. The victorious nations, fresh from the terrible sacrifices of four years of carnage, had become hopeful, and at least partially sure, that they at long last were nearing the goal of their desires. They were becoming convinced that only through a federation of the nations of the world could peace, just and lasting, be assured.

The purpose was noble; the results ignoble. The nations were still nationalistic—selfish to the point of refusing to surrender the degree of national sovereignty necessary to ensure unity with authority and power to carry out its mandates. Self-interest was too deep-seated to yield to the common welfare. The United States failed to support its own child. It laid its offspring on the steps of the temple it had conceived and ran away, withdrew into that state termed "splendid isolation." The total peace so poignantly sought became a shadow to be materialized only in the far future. A lesson learned in the intervening years between World War I and World War II, one that even the most hardened nationalist must acknowledge, is that no nation can longer live to itself, isolated and apart from its fellow nations. Global war has taught the lesson of national interdependence. There can be no isolation when frontiers no longer exist, when oceans no longer serve as barriers to separate. The nations of the world are geographically neighbors. The problem is to unite in a material and spiritual unity that constitutes the best attainable counterpart of the true brotherhood, the infinite family of God's children.

Education, as we have seen, does not meet the need. As commonly conceived and provided, it goes but part way to the ultimate goal. Commonly based upon purely academic courses, it misses the fundamental instruction in the nature of true brotherhood and the means of attaining it. It lacks the magnet of knowledge of spiritual values that alone draws mortals together.

Jesus' words, "And I, if I be lifted up from the earth, will draw all men unto me,"[1] have a profound and all-important meaning in gaining the true sense of brotherhood. The spiritual exaltation gained through understanding God and the divine economy has drawn uncounted millions to that masterful character, the Founder of Christianity, the Way-shower to the Kingdom, Lord and Saviour to all Christendom. The human need is to accept his pregnant words, to motivate them, for the Nazarene alone has shown the way to the goal so yearningly sought by all Christians; he has pointed the way to a peace that will stand, to the mental state that makes for the highest degree of well-being for the human race.

Material means have failed. Educators have increasingly omitted the vital element in education—spiritual values. Despite all the progress in education along physical lines, the

---

[1] John 12:32.

present crisis has not been avoided. Pursuit of the natural sciences has gone far in the development of their respective field. Great benefits to humanity have resulted. Great prosperity has followed. But at what a price! What avails it if by winning material possessions, spiritual values are ignored, lost sight of? Not long ago in a convention of chemists where many of the recent discoveries in that science were made known, an enthusiastic chemist asserted that chemistry will meet all our wants. We no longer need God!

Much has been accomplished to make material experience easier, more pleasurable. Many of the burdens borne so heavily in the past have been lifted. Much, however, remains to be done. The picture of human beings drawing the plow and the harrow in the evening twilight as I left the old walled City of Peking made an impression I shall not soon forget. The sight of men sawing planks from hardwood logs was a type of labor I had thought was known only in the distant past. That laborers in public service in India had but one meal a day of rice, and that at night, as told me by the Anglo-Indian foreman whose acquaintance I made, convinced me that much is yet to be done to relieve humanity of its self-imposed burdens, to bring a living wage to the underprivileged working class. These are but a few of the conditions to be adjusted in the final determination of the ways to peace.

Practical application of modern inventions has done much in lifting the burdens that so long have weighed heavily on the shoulders of mankind. Much more remains to be done through improved distribution to ensure the abundant life that belongs to all. It must be recognized, however, that no measure of relief from these physical burdens and inhibitions can substitute for the knowledge of spiritual things, for this understanding alone opens the way to the Kingdom.

Moreover, this knowledge of God is not, as commonly believed, a preparation for future existence alone, that is, for an other-

[128]

world state; but it is an eminently practical remedy for every type of evil, every phase of material limitation to which mortals seem here and now to be subjected. It is, in fact, the only true and effective remedy for all humanity's needs.

Is there a single phase of human need that Jesus left unsolved in his brief ministry? The Comforter, which he assured his followers would come, was declared to be the Helper to humanity in the meeting of every condition that might befall. And since no need is greater than the need for a condition of peace, the attainment of the atmosphere of brotherly love—the handmaiden of peace—is the problem that humanity has to solve. In the hatred and malevolence of warfare, the seeds of love fall upon barren ground. The training for combat even in the so-called Christian nations implies a mental state where love for one's fellows, the enemy, has no part. A warrior is trained to kill. And while this awful necessity confronts the warrior enlisted to save the Democratic and Christian way of life, yet it leaves a mental impression difficult to erase.

I recall the case of a young soldier in the last war, who told of the frightful revolt against war that came to him during his training in bayonet fighting, even though the object of attack was but an effigy. To retain one's mental poise when that which has been done in training becomes the necessity in actual combat is only another revolting picture of what are described as war's necessities.

It is just these debasing experiences that, multiplied to the nth degree, should stir the nations to the adoption of the most efficient means to make impossible the recurrence of warfare. No national interest as such, no mere pride of empire or prestige in power, should stand in the way of laying once and for all time this frightful ogre of modern warfare. There is no need for further experience to prove its frightfulness. Its character in all its debasing viciousness lies fully exposed. The crying need is for a permanent remedy.

Total War, Total Peace

The gravity of the situation should by no means be regarded as a night of Stygian darkness. That better conditions for human experience have not been developed should by no means lead to the conclusion that there is no remedy. To accept such a belief would be to join in a counsel of despair. If it be contended that nothing in the past material experience of the race promises a better way, a way to prevent the recurrence of sanguine and devastating strife, then in the experience of the servant of Elisha may be found an encouraging example of faith based upon understanding of the spiritual nature of man.

However, on that fateful night in the Garden when Jesus assured his companions that did he so desire he could call twelve legions of angels to his defense, he recognized the presence of a spiritual power operating through spiritual law to meet his immediate need. Whether it be the Syrian host or emissaries of the Jewish Hierarchy sent to arrest and crucify the noblest, most humble, yet most potent man who has ever appeared on earth, that is to be overcome, the same power is everpresent to protect mortals from any threatening enemy. There is no reason for alarm; no cause for despair. Attainment of the most favorable conditions for humanity is a present possibility.

To be sure, mistakes due to accepting the ways and methods of evil must be seen and their future occurrence eliminated. How eliminated? By the simple but wholly effective way perfectly charted by the Nazarene. Even the blueprint that it is alleged Hitler so fearlessly set forth in *Mein Kampf* is not more definite than is the way to the free and abundant life promised and charted by Christ Jesus. He left nothing to the imagination, nothing to be supplied. But it must be accepted and applied.

The next armistice group providing for a peace conference to determine the procedure whereby to eliminate the possibility for future warfare will be effective just in proportion to its

Total War, Total Peace

recognition of the spiritual necessity; and this is no distant, unattainable demand. Justice that patterns the divine, and righteousness that motivates the Golden Rule are the foundation stones. Of course, these preclude the idea of vengeance, of hatred, and of punishment beyond the restrictions necessary to make impossible a future outbreak.

The modern penal code looks to reformation, not to revenge. The old law that said an "eye for eye, tooth for tooth" [2] was superseded and outmoded by the grace and truth introduced by the Nazarene. The temptation to avenge the frightful wrongs that are being perpetrated will be very strong. But along that road lies precisely what the Christian world is striving to avoid: the nursing of hate, the spirit of revenge, and other mental qualities of the same import, which lead not to the desired goal, but directly back to the incubators where the seeds of war are sprouted and brought into activity.

The temptations will be very great to take summary means to avenge the wrongs. President Roosevelt's repeated assurances that the guilty shall be duly punished may have a restraining effect. Let us hope that it will; for if the evil passions that have been stirred to the utmost were to be motivated, a situation would follow that would darken the pages of history. Mortals are inclined to adjust the punishment to fit the crime. If this criterion were followed at the close of this war, another holocaust would ensue that would further lessen the chances for an early and permanent peace. That justice, sound and made effective by practical means, must be a prominent stone in the peace foundations, is too obvious to require argument. Any effort at peace-making that did not recognize this necessity would in itself be futile. Justice is one of the undergirders of the peace effort to be marked a *must*. No human society prospers without justice. By its provisions the rights of the hum-

---
[2] Exodus 21:24.

blest citizen are protected no less than those of the wealthy, prominent, and powerful. Justice is for all; and when it is not so regarded and administered, a chief plank in the platform of Democracy has fallen into decay.

Citizens of a Democracy claim their rights as citizens, and these rights are guaranteed by laws justly executed. One's property may be taken away or his freedom infringed; but more disastrous than these is the loss of justice. To be deprived of recourse to the law, based upon justice and justly administered, signals the death knell of democratic rights.

Laws are not static, fixed; they are changed and developed to meet the changing needs of society. Laws that seemed adequate to the Pilgrims at Plymouth or the Quakers in Pennsylvania would be found quite inadequate now in these rich and populous commonwealths with their complex social patterns. The growth of law is commensurate with the growth of the nations, but the need for the underlying justice never changes, never lessens. As the social order becomes more complex, as public and private interests multiply, greater becomes the obligation to guard the gem of justice, a prominent jewel in the crown of Democracy.

Moreover, law humanly conceived and administered, if recognized as representative of divine Law, as an expression of the divine Will, takes on an added significance. And no law that may not be so regarded is worthy or just. Law as expression of the will of a people is righteous and just in proportion as it patterns the divine. So regarded, it becomes the guardian of the inherent rights of man, the most precious item of man's inheritance.

When the writer of the Declaration of Independence declared that all men are born free and equal, he was obviously lifting his vision above the mere material concept of mortals into the realm of the spiritual, where all God's children, His creatures and offspring, are indeed created free and equal. None are privileged above others in either capabilities, possessions, or prestige. All enjoy the sacred rights which inevitably attach to the sons of the only Father, to the children of the Great King, to the Royal Household of God.

With this concept of man, spiritual and perfect because made in God's likeness, there develops a true, a higher concept of justice. It takes on a divine hue. And in the experience of mortals, it becomes a pattern of the divine economy, something to be gained and guarded in order to protect the right to justice that inheres in every individual.

This concept of law and of justice, which go hand in hand, even lifts them above the will of the state. It stems from a divine Source. Hence the state under the authoritarian claim to power is infringing the rights of man when it assumes to control his way of life—his education, his mental outlook, and his purpose. When this type of authority comes in, freedom goes out. No longer is there liberty to work out one's own salvation. It is for this reason that, in the final determination of the nations to establish peace and ensure its continuance, the rights of individuals must be safeguarded.

In the consideration of a global, lasting, and just peace, attention must of necessity be given to power to enforce the plans determined upon as necessary to the attainment of the objective. What kind of power shall it be, how extensive, how organized, and how maintained? To solve this problem practically in accord with Christian certainty, this power must be based upon the unswerving, the irresistible faith in God; that He is Almighty, everpresent and available through righteous prayer to meet the human need.

This concept of the divine plan, that God governs His universe in permanent peace; that in this divine economy man is justly governed; that his freedom is forever maintained, for he is ever doing that for which he was created—normally expressing the divine Will; when this concept of God's government is gained and understood, humanity has a perfect pattern, a practical blueprint, as it were, of the means of establishing permanent peace.

This accomplishment can be successful, however, only if the facts be clearly grasped, and the paramount purpose be to do God's will on earth as it is done in Heaven. This conclusion posits all power in the divine Will; and in proportion as this Will is invoked and motivated in the peace-making, in that proportion does the daily prayer "Thy will be done" become expressive of an honest desire and willingness to lay aside all personal purpose not in accord with the deeper meaning of prayer.

The power necessary to inspire and produce a true plan stems from divine intelligence. It can never be safely left to mere human thought-taking. Its Source must be higher. History proves this conclusively. Unless the divine pattern is more closely followed than ever before, lasting peace will be a mere shibboleth, a meaningless term with which to allay human fears. The power invoked must find expression in practical terms.

It seems inevitable that in the long period necessary to bring the peoples into a true brotherhood, incident to the establishment of the permanent peace for which the Christian world is praying, there must be provided a power sufficient to enforce law and compel order. The possibility of aggressively-minded nations or peoples again building a huge war machine with which to embark on a career of plunder and rapine must be effectually met. And averting this possibility, it seems, must be accomplished only by an international police force equal to the task for which it is provided. This problem will be considered in a later chapter.

If this conclusion be characterized as unchristian, subversive of the very basis of peace divinely ordained, it must be recalled that where an individual or a nation is too materially minded

Total War, Total Peace

to receive the Christ-messenger, the everpresent Helper, but believes only in the power of materiality, this mental state must be challenged with the means to hold it harmless until such time as its error is seen and a willingness is manifested to accept the only way to the Kingdom.

Had the League of Nations been possessed of an adequate power of this type, and had it been prompted by a willingness to use such power the terrible calamity of a global war might have been averted. Had the Japanese been stopped from invading Manchuria, had Mussolini been told that he could not be permitted to overrun Ethiopia, had Hitler been warned not to reoccupy the Ruhr, and had these warnings been supported by an adequate international police force, how different might have been the world outlook today!

XIV

What of Democracy?

Two ideologies, two ideas of government, long in contrast have come into violent, even deadly, antagonism. So opposed are they in their basic principles that they may not exist side by side without constant and destructive conflict. These are now arrayed one against the other in a competition that can have no outcome but to carry on to victory for one or the other. What Lincoln said of the United States, "It cannot exist half slave and half free," is no less true of the world now reduced in size to the extent that all nations, all peoples, are neighbors. The interrelations of the nations of the earth are in many respects as close as were those of the States of the Union in Lincoln's day.

The insistent questions confronting the world are, then, Which idea of government should prevail? Which will win? And the ready answer is, That one should win under which the citizens may attain the greatest degree of freedom, the greatest measure of liberty for the individual in working out his own salvation. That is to say, Democracy should win in the ultimate, for it is the nearest approximation to the government by divine Will of the brotherhood of man. Every Christian believes that the infinite Father is the true Governor of the universe, and this government finds its closest expression in the type of human government termed Democracy.

Nearly a hundred years ago Theodore Parker, speaking of the American idea of government, that is, of Democracy, said: "This idea demands as the proximate organization thereof, a democracy that is a government of all the people, by all the people, for all the people; of course a government of the principles external of justice, the unchanging law of God; for shortness sake I will call it the idea of Freedom." This eminent divine saw God's Will expressed in the type of government termed Democracy.

In the divine economy God governs His universe, the brotherhood of man. In the human Democracy, this finds approximation in proportion as the affairs of men are governed by justice that is divine, by righteousness based upon eternal right. And that justice and that righteousness stem only from the Source of all that is good, eternal, and unchanging. This type of government is in direct contrast to the so-called Totalitarian idea, proponents of which have set out to conquer the world, to force its concepts upon all nations regardless of the will or wish of the peoples governed.

The promoters of the democratic ideal face the necessity of proving their contention, to convince the peoples of earth that theirs is the best, the truest government because it is nearest the divine order of government. The slogan so often heard during the first World War, "The world must be made safe for Democracy," is discarded because it does not truly represent the situation. Democracy must be proved to be the best method for securing world peace; that is, Democracy must be made safe for the world. This is the problem facing the Allied Nations.

Democracy must prove in actual experience that it is the best form of government for the world, the form that not only assures the greatest degree of personal freedom but also so cements its constituency that it can withstand any assault which may be brought against it. It must prove its ability to defend itself against all aggressors.

If specific incidents are needed to prove the thesis that the Democratic way of life engenders the deepest sense of loyalty to

What of Democracy?

its ideals, the proof is found in the tremendous upsurge in the Allied Nations of the spirit of sacrifice called out by a savage threat to its basic principles. Never has individual courage been more impressively manifested than in the struggle of the hour. Whatever type of sacrifice is deemed necessary to win over the enemy is forthcoming instantly, without hesitation, without reserve.

Some time ago we had news of the destruction of the French fleet in the harbor of Toulon to prevent its seizure by the Axis powers. Frenchmen, officers and enlisted personnel as well, went down to death in the only way left whereby to show their unquestionable loyalty to their ideal, the French Republic—*liberty, equality, fraternity*—which has long characterized the true spirit of France. Not mere loyalty to personalities, but loyalty to ideals, lofty and eternal, called forth this willingness to sacrifice their human sense of life rather than yield to the domination of an enslaving victor.

While it may be tentatively asserted that Democracy more nearly represents the divine order, yet much proving awaits the final demonstration of the accuracy of these assertions. Much has been done in this direction, much more awaits the final proof. Democracy can never rise in its efficiency to the altitude of demonstrated divine sovereignty unless its citizens be imbued with the spirit of Democracy as the expression of the divine Will. This attainment insures the welfare of the many, while at the same time the individual is free to make his own way, to develop himself in any direction not inimical to the general welfare. Thus does the welfare of the individual become the policy of the Government.

The conclusion is inescapable, then, that Democracy can succeed only when it springs from the will of an intelligent citizenry imbued with the spirit of true service, inspired with the high purpose of bringing to the people the greatest opportunity for self-expression and improvement while at the same time proving its ability to defend itself against aggression of whatsoever degree of violence. Furthermore, Democracy makes for peace, and only in peace can the individual attain to the highest type of development.

The Axis nations made a great mistake in judgment when they acclaimed that the Democracies were soft, undisciplined, and consequently unable to defend themselves. This judgment mistook material might for true power. It had no concept of the type of loyalty and willingness to sacrifice engendered by a true concept of man as God-created and God-governed. It was a godless conclusion—vicious, wicked, and foreboding evil; for in the logic of human events it is only the eternal right that wins. Its ultimate victory is inevitable, since the God who is good, is omnipotent.

No argument is required to elucidate the inescapable conclusion that the success of Democracy depends upon the mental fitness of its citizenry for free government. This demands education of its constituents in the meaning and purpose of true Democracy, with the object of a clear understanding of its fundamental law and the application of its principles to the general welfare. This aim includes recognition of the privileges and duties accruing under the form of government that insures the greatest degree of liberty to its citizens. Under this regime "rugged individuality" reaches its greatest height. Education, then, is the cornerstone in the structure of truly democratic government.

Immediately are raised the questions, What type of education best prepares for citizenship in a Democracy? Does secular education as commonly conceived meet the need? Or must there be under the very foundation stones of Democracy a substratum of religious education of a type that recognizes God as the Supreme Ruler of the universe and Christ Jesus as the revelator of God to humanity?

If it be denied that knowledge of God and of true worship is

What of Democracy?

necessary to succeed in the administration of Democratic government, the challenge is met by the simple admonition, Look about you! Never in human history have so many nations engaged in so terrific a struggle as that which now is commanding the attention of the whole world. The great Democracies, conceived in the idealism of freedom, equality, and fraternity, are struggling for their very existence. And the assertion is constantly broadcast from the totalitarian countries that Democracy has failed, has proved itself incapable of developing a type of civilization able to protect itself while at the same time protecting personal freedom and providing for individual development—in other words, that Democracy cannot make its way in the present world order. Even in the Democracies, education has been secularized to the extent of omitting the most important feature of all education.

In frankness it must be admitted that there is some ground for such strictures upon free government. Democracy as yet has not been based upon the divine Will. When the premises are carefully examined, when a searching and sympathetic survey is made, the conclusion will be arrived at that the just and righteous ideals that underlie Democracy have not been given full expression, have not been sufficiently incorporated into the governmental structure of the leading representatives of the Democratic form of government. Many inherent weaknesses exist in the Democracies, weaknesses not only in their domestic affairs, in their social order, but even greater weaknesses in their relations to other nations and other peoples not yet developed to the status of sovereign governments.

It is lamentably true that indecision, self-interest, and a measure of pusillanimity on the part of the victorious Allies in 1918 promoted in the conquered countries during the years following, a state that led directly to the rise of dictatorship. Economic conditions that became masters of the political situation were allowed to develop, and Germany passed through a

What of Democracy?

semblance of Republican government only to emerge in a Totalitarian government with the one purpose of imposing its will upon the whole world.

This situation cries for a change of policy on the part of the victorious Democracies that will make a recurrence of such events impossible. And avoidance is insured only by the free nations fully recognizing their mistakes and arriving at a full determination to reform. Democracies must clean their own houses first. Then will they be prepared to bring the blessings of Democracy to less privileged peoples.

Democracy contemplates equal opportunity to all its citizens: that all shall be privileged to enjoy its full measure of blessings, its opportunities without limit or restraint upon the possibilities of individual development. This equality of opportunity is fundamental in every Democracy; especially is it a cornerstone in the type of government developed in the United States. Its Declaration of Independence states, "It is self-evident that all men are created equal, that they are endowed by their Creator with certain inalienable rights; that among these are Life, Liberty and the pursuit of Happiness"; and it asserts that to secure these rights governments are instituted among men, deriving their just power from the consent of the governed. Here are the very foundation stones of righteous government; and Democracy thus founded and administered in accordance therewith would go far toward the fulfillment of the ideals of successful government.

It scarcely seems to accord with mortal experience that "all men are created equal," either mentally, physically, or in environment. Surely there is great disparity between the highest and the lowliest mental capability in the population of any country. To gain the fundamental truth of this statement it must be recognized that God's children, made in His image and likeness, are indeed equal, all equally endowed and all under the dominion of the Father, who is perfect Love.

What of Democracy?

Only of this concept of man can equality be truly affirmed.

But does it not follow, then, that one of the inescapable duties of Democracy is to approximate as nearly as possible the divine order; to furnish to every citizen equality of opportunity to make his way onward and upward toward the goal of plentitude, of joyous membership in the social order? This is, indeed, a pertinent query, and it implies a great change, perhaps a complete revolution, in the social order.

As it was impossible for the United States to exist half slave and half free, so is it impossible to attain and demonstrate the true ideals of Democracy in a society made up of an underprivileged number, living in poverty and squalor, while an overprivileged group possess a plethora of material things far beyond their needs. Here is, indeed, a form of social injustice that of necessity must be remedied before the United States, and for that matter Great Britain, can stand before the world as exemplars of righteous government. The ancient cry, "Am I my brother's keeper?" [1] must be answered affirmatively not only of domestic relations but internationally as well. The true brotherhood of man has no divisional boundaries.

This is not to deny the commendable progress that has characterized these two great Democracies—Great Britain and the United States—in their recent history. No more does it overlook the need for definite reforms in the present social order. The tendency to develop a social order, an autocracy of wealth and opportunity far above the masses, has prominently characterized the social order in Great Britain and is only less pronounced in the United States. Wealth has brought both social position and privilege. It has developed a group of aristocrats who have assumed a superiority that many do not possess, either in culture or in intelligence. Primogeniture

---

[1] Gen. 4:9.

What of Democracy?

has no place in true Democracy; no more does the possession of selfish accumulation of immense wealth in the midst of constricting poverty.

The necessity to develop equal opportunity among all classes is a major problem in establishing a New World Order; that is to say, if this order is to be stable because just. A situation, as in the United States, in which one-tenth of the population is regarded as below the accepted social order, is one to cause grave reflection. It is little wonder that the Japanese are holding up to the native populations they have conquered our treatment of the Negro as an example of what the Asiatics may expect if the Allied Nations win the war. It is difficult to impress others with the righteousness of our ideals if we are unrighteous ourselves. This situation was accurately characterized by the great Teacher as hypocrisy.

The question has been justifiably posed, Could the Four Freedoms be established in practice without a religious background to the purpose? An affirmative answer may be made: they could be established without recognition of divine Sovereignty in the world of affairs. But would they persist? Could they be substantially founded upon a basis of morality, of humanism, unless they were undergirded by recognition of the divine Omnipotence that rules through the operation of divine Law? Could the human sense of goodness withstand the winds and waves of the carnal mind that are so frequently beating against righteous human effort? The conviction is firmly established among Christians and is gaining ground with the nonreligious that the present chaos is in large measure due to the lack of divine guidance in the affairs of the Democratic governments.

It is indubitably true that in this lack of spiritual discernment lies the cause for the intense animosity that preceded the recent outburst. Wherever one's glance may fall, whether

What of Democracy?

upon the United States, Great Britain, or France, he is confronted by instances, numerous and far-reaching in their influence, where greed, selfishness—national and individual—imperialism, exploitation in disregard of the very fundamentals of Christian virtues, have characterized the acts of government. So obvious are the instances that there seems little need to recount them.

The present treatment of the people of Puerto Rico resulting in a condition bordering on serious undernourishment, as well as the Negro problem, are rank inconsistencies in a so-called Christian government. Exploitation by England of Malaya, Burma, and other subject peoples, of the East Indies by the Dutch, of the Congo by the Belgians, reveals situations wholly apart from and inconsistent with democratic principles. The same is true of the treatment by the French of her colonial population. Even where the purposes of government have been just, exploitation by great corporations of natural resources developed through cheap labor has resulted in tremendous profit to the exploiters, and with governmental sanction.

In the face of these facts, how can it be said that Democracy has proved its claims to be the highest and best form of government? It is true, however, that these conditions that have obtained under the aegis of Democracy are not worse, are even measurably better, than the treatment accorded similar peoples under a strict monarchial form of government. But it is nevertheless true that in the New World Order these inconsistencies must be remedied if the nations are to establish the ideals of righteous government inherent in true Democracy.

Yes, the Four Freedoms are possible of attainment without the influence of religion and worship. But such establishment would be temporary and ephemeral. Its claims would be but as sounding brass and tinkling cymbal.

Tolerance is a Christian attitude when not a sign of weakness.

What of Democracy?

Democracy is best subserved when its administration has the high purpose of promoting the general welfare. Without the strengthening influence of spiritual Law cementing its foundations, any political structure will be but a house built upon the shifting sands of the carnal mind, beat upon by the winds of greed, self-interest, and special privilege that engender hatred.

Freedom of expression may be attained. But unless that freedom be tempered by the desire to serve the general welfare, it becomes a selfish and ineffective agency. Freedom of speech and expression are concomitants of individual growth. Restricted, the government becomes the mentor of thought and action, a condition subversive of independence.

Freedom of worship is the very basis of Christian living. Without this privilege, which means freedom of conscience, the right to worship God according to one's convictions, there is little if any true spiritual inspiration in worship. It becomes a matter of formula and dogmatism, of ritual and concordat. It was the desire for this freedom that drove the Pilgrims across a wintry sea into an unknown wilderness. It is this purpose that has long driven men and women over land and over sea in search of spiritual freedom, for it reaches to the deepest desires of the human heart. It has followed, however, that even the nations proclaiming the privileges of Democracy have used stern measures to limit the right of worship to prescribed modes and canons. The true spirit of Democracy is tolerant to all righteous worship, and protects it against abuse.

Freedom from fear can scarcely be gained through legislation. No assertion of a fundamental law, no legislative act or governmental proclamation, can eliminate this most common and most potent enemy of man. Whether fear arises from the danger of insufficient food and other necessities, of suppressed liberty, of loss of inherent rights, the only sure and safe remedy flows from a source far above human sovereignty. It derives only from understanding the divine government, from knowledge of God, His universe, and man as the child of God. This is the one sure remedy for fear; and manifestly this remedy is brought into actuality only through religion and true worship.

In the New World Order to be established, if justice prevails, the lesser nations will be freed from fear of enslavement by a powerful aggressor. This assurance, it seems, can come only from an international body founded upon general agreement between the nations and a police force adequate to quell any effort at aggression by an ambitious nation.

Attainment of freedom from lack, that is, assurance of the abundant life for every citizen, is a high and worthy goal. It is nobly conceived in the Christian spirit, but has too often been ignored or ignobly carried out. The millions of underprivileged should shame the Governments, Democracies or Monarchies, which, notwithstanding all their opportunities for rescue and all their unlimited resources, have provided and supported policies that have, as we have seen, enriched the few with a plethora of material possessions while a sector of the population, sometimes great in numbers, has continued in abject poverty.

There are two forms of remedy for this condition. The one that would be quickest to motivate is the awakening of the proletariat to their inherent rights, with the demand that true brotherhood be established, that the needs of the people be met through methods of the government established by and for the people: by governmental intervention to make sure that every person has the opportunity to earn a wage equal to providing the necessities of life. The Negroes and share-croppers of the South, the impoverished workers in the mining centers of Great Britain and the United States, the primitive peoples of the colonial possessions, cry to Heaven for release from both fear and want.

The other method of relief springs from an awakening on the part of the Governments to the need for establishing some social plan to relieve want and suffering among the under-

What of Democracy?

privileged. In England the Beveridge report, now made public, promises at least partial relief. The results will depend upon the wholehearted administration by the Government. This, at most, is a parental program that tends to lessen the independence of the individual. It fails to recognize that true charity is that which removes the need for charity—that provision which renders the individual independent through providing properly compensated employment.

Two somewhat conflicting opinions have been proposed as to the best way in which to bring the ideal Democracy into full flower. Partisans of one point of view have contended that only the educated who own property should be given the right of suffrage. This in a Democracy provides for the government of all by a select upper class. This concept stems from the early attempts at self-government, government by the upper stratum of society. Upon the shoulders of the masses, for the most part enslaved, rested this governing class.

In the more modern version of this type of Democracy the masses are no longer enslaved, but they are not regarded as having attained to the degree of political consciousness that would enable them to take an intelligent part in the affairs of government. It was of this concept of Democracy that Macaulay wrote a letter that has since been frequently quoted in discussing the ways and modes of securing popular government. This letter, written to the biographer of Thomas Jefferson in 1857, predicted definite collapse of any government dependent upon universal suffrage. England would not face this difficulty because, he stated, "The supreme power is in the hands of a class, numerous indeed but select, of an educated class, of a class which is, and knows itself to be, deeply interested in the security of property and the maintenance of order."

Macaulay prophesied regarding the United States that while it might go forward successfully in times of prosperity, it would scarcely be able to ride the storm during periods of depression with their attendant unemployment. And this believer in a

What of Democracy?

sort of sublimated Democracy added, "But my reason and my wishes are at war, and I cannot help foreboding the worst. It is quite plain that your government will never be able to restrain a distressed and discontented majority, for with you the majority is the government, and has the rich, who are always a minority, absolutely at its mercy."

This eminent historian further predicted that from such a state of adversity Democracy in the United States would be unable to extricate itself. Surely, a counsel of despair! What would he say of the storms that the United States has so triumphantly weathered that twice in three decades it has gone to the rescue of the Democratic way of life in his own Europe?

This point of view, however, has not yet been wholly eradicated in some of the great Democracies. It is based upon fear of the common people, of the very masses upon whom falls the burden of battle whenever danger arises. America has trusted the people, and her triumphs have invariably strengthened faith in the love of liberty, made possible through a government established and maintained by the people themselves.

Probably the most perfect as well as the most eloquent answer to the pessimism of the English historian is found in an address delivered in 1873 by James A. Garfield of Ohio, entitled "The Future of the Republic: Its Dangers and Its Hopes." General Garfield referred to Macaulay's statement thus: "I venture the declaration that this opinion of Macaulay's is vulnerable on general grounds. It leaves out the great counter-balancing influence of universal education. But furthermore, it is based upon a belief from which few if any British writers have been able to emancipate themselves: namely, the belief that mankind are born into permanent classes, and that in the main they must live, work, and die in the fixed class or condition in which they are born. It is hardly possible for a man reared in an aristocracy like that of England to eliminate this conviction from his mind."

What of Democracy?

General Garfield's characterization of England as an aristocracy was nearer the truth seventy years ago than now. Yet there are those today who see in the Island Empire a tendency to hold what the upper stratum of her society still possesses, the greater portion of her wealth, power, and prestige, and the direction of her political affairs.

The address continues: "The English theory of national stability is, that there must be a permanent class who shall hold in their own hands so much of the wealth, the privilege and the political power of the kingdom that they may compel the admiration and obedience of all other classes." And General Garfield averred that where such permanent classes exist, the conflict projected by Macaulay is inevitable.

Turning to his own country, General Garfield continued: "We point to the fact that in this country there are no classes in the British sense of the word—no impossible barriers of caste. Now that slavery is abolished we can truly say that in our political society there run no fixed horizontal strata above which none can pass. Our society resembles rather the waves of the ocean, whose every drop may move freely among its fellows and may rise toward the light until it flashes on the crest of the highest wave."

Rarely if ever have the possibilities offered by the American way of life been more dramatically set forth. Of this truth there are many eloquent examples. From the lowliest beginnings, from the log cabin and the humblest of farmsteads, from shop and factory, from mill and mine, men have risen to positions of highest honor, of greatest usefulness, in the councils of the nations.

XV

Pattern of The New World Order

GRANTED that there is to be a New World Order that will make demands for sacrifice and service upon all, the vital question arises as to the type of structure that is possible of erection. The millennium has not arrived. There are no Utopias growing on the tree of high hopes to be plucked at will. Beyond possibility of doubt there are long and arduous tasks ahead calling for the extreme exercise of faith, of patience, and of courage.

Granted that we are citizens of the world, we are to determine the sort of super-state, if any, of which we are to be the citizens. The brotherhood of man constitutes a unity to be worked out in practical terms, in a form that will safeguard each nation, large or small, against danger to its existence and to its sovereignty from an outside aggressor. It is little wonder that the smaller nations, so ruthlessly overrun by an implacable enemy, are deeply concerned that the plan of the New Order shall ensure to them their national existence and sovereignty against all enemies. Manifestly, one of the grave needs is to remove the fears of these peoples who have suffered so grievously at the hands of the invaders. It is not amiss to examine the prospects.

Many reflective persons prevision the need of a cooling-off period following the armistice that will stop the guns. Immediately to proceed to formulate terms of peace, while the ardor of battle is still unspent, while the passions engendered by the terrific struggle are still dominant, would increase the probability that harsh terms would be forced upon the stricken

Pattern of The New World Order

enemy, terms of such a nature as to preclude the possibility of establishing the lasting peace so earnestly desired.

Taking a lesson from Versailles, it seems wise to delay final terms of peace and the formation of a super-state until these problems of the greatest import to humanity may be approached in the spirit of Christianity, of service to all. Not revenge, but provision against further rape of weaker peoples will be among the primary problems to be considered and settled.

Justice demands that Germany and Japan be placed under such surveillance and such restraint as will render them powerless again to thrust the world into the maw of global warfare. That will be imperative. But this imposed restraint must be utilized by these conquered peoples to rehabilitate themselves, not as formerly through the means of a war economy, but rather upon a peace economy that will both permit and encourage the gaining of a mental state suited to render them fit members in some sort of world unity, whether that be a Confederation, a League, or a true Union.

There will be problems of adjustment that will require the exercise of true Christian understanding and solicitude. These efforts will succeed just so far as they are based upon divine Principle and are motivated by the Golden Rule, and no farther. The presence of the Christ at the Peace Table recognized and utilized, ensures the finding and developing of the proper action to secure the results so widely hoped for.

Inevitably, the great nations that win the victory will take leading part in the peace councils. Great Britain, the United States, China, and Russia will have the most prominent roles in determining the pattern of the united effort. Certain conditions seem fundamental. First, there should be a police force adequate to keep the peace; that is, to prevent another period of preparation by aggressive nations for a further uprising against the peace of the world. This, it seems, will be a large force, comprising the three major arms of modern war service—

air, naval, and army forces. Justice demands that these should be apportioned to the Allied Nations in the degree of their ability to contribute to the common purpose.

Of necessity, the smaller nations, stripped clean of resources both in material and manpower, will be able to contribute but little. Thus the greatest portion of the burden will inevitably fall upon the major peoples with resources sufficient to meet the need—the United States and Great Britain.

China, after years of struggle against a determined enemy, will have little to contribute except of her magnificent spirit and resolute determination to establish a commonwealth that makes possible the working out of her national destiny, and her ardent desire to help all humanity to attain the same degree of freedom.

Russia, with unlimited natural resources, after a period of internal reconstruction will be able to contribute her full share to the common welfare. It is plainly manifest that Russia is destined to become one of the most powerful nations. None can doubt the character of a people who have so courageously and so effectively withstood the assault of a nation trained in the art of war and inspired by a type of leadership that is nothing short of fanaticism.

Agreement must be reached as to the portion of expense to be allotted and the size of the contribution of each country in manpower and material. These problems will demand early and definite solution. Delays will but postpone a necessity, and delays in this important direction may well be dangerous to the peace establishment.

What kind of union seems most practical? What lessons may be learned from the past? It is very plain that the League of Nations, built after the pattern of a worthy vision, had inherently several weaknesses. The greatest of these was inadequate provision for enforcing its mandates, that is, for applying its sanctions. A union without power to enforce its findings is but a hollow structure destined to defeat in the face of determined rebellion. And to be effective, when an international police force is provided, it must be utilized through the mandates of the power creating it.

Another serious weakness of the League derived from inherent reluctance on the part of the constituent members to surrender sufficient of their sovereign powers to make a World League practical and potent. Will this condition be repeated, or have the nations learned the lesson that the safety and well-being of each is dependent upon the welfare of all?

It is for the safeguarding of each that all will unite in a common super-state of some type. But each nation is faced with the stark necessity of surrendering for its own and the common good something of its national powers and prerogatives. This willingness will give it prestige and prominence in the sisterhood of nations. Nothing good can result from any united action that is not based upon this primary necessity. To unite, bonds of unity must be developed; and those bonds will be wrought from the powers surrendered by the participating nations.

Perhaps the experience that brought the United States into its present status is the best illustration of what is involved in any stable union of nations. The Thirteen Colonies developed in the early years of American history had much in common. They soon learned, however, that there existed between them many conflicting conditions that could not be adequately resolved without closer unity. There were jealousies and rivalries that needed composition. Something more than mere geographical propinquity was involved. There was a need for singleness of purpose to be demonstrated through some form of political unity. And it was early seen that, to accomplish this, there must be surrender of some of the sovereign rights that each Colony had claimed and exercised for itself. There were types of interests to be administered for the general welfare that called for united action.

Experimentally, it seems, a Confederation was first formed under a loosely drawn pact. It soon became manifest that this did not meet the need. Sufficient prerogatives had not been surrendered by the constituent Colonies to make the union effective. But the experience taught a valuable lesson. There was a need for more power inherent in the over-all government to hold the structure together. Then was framed the Constitution, under which the primitive Thirteen Colonies have developed into a great nation, a Republic maintaining the primal conditions of Democracy.

It was found that in many directions the needs of the people could be met only as they were merged into the national government, especially in regard to foreign policy, and to the relationship between the young Republic and other nations. Also, there were certain domestic needs best met by the central power; among these, for example, was the Post Office Department. Later it was found that the monetary systems held by individual states led to confusion, and were, in fact, inadequate to serve the people's needs. This discovery led to the taking over of the monetary system by the Federal Government. A common currency was established and the issuance of money became a function of the general government direct, or by institutions to whom this power should be delegated under strict rules established by that Federal Government.

This summary but faintly glimpses the situation as to the Federal powers, but it illustrates the possibility of a general government successfully administering the affairs of a growing population. To be sure, there has always existed a sort of twilight zone between the powers belonging to the central government under the Constitution and the powers to be exercised exclusively by the States. No serious situation other than the question of slavery, however, has arisen that has not been amiably resolved through the medium of debate in Congress and adjudication by the Supreme Court.

Men thoroughly informed regarding the international situation are advocating a super-government, a union of nations patterned after the Constitution of the United States, with similar departments, namely, legislative, executive, and judicial. The primary question is, Are the nations of the world, especially those that are large and that have been generally prosperous, prepared to pass to a central government powers and prerogatives that they have long possessed and exercised, to the degree that would make such an organization successful? Are they ready to surrender a measure of the nationalism they have developed through great travail, upon which they justifiably pride themselves? Are the citizens of the United States, Great Britain, China, Russia, and other established states prepared to yield something of the loyalty and patriotism toward their own nation to a super-union, of whatsoever type or form, in order to secure permanent peace?

That is the crux of the situation. Without the willingness of the citizens to become citizens of a world government and to play the part that such conditions would imply, the constituent nations would hardly be able to commit themselves to the support of an over-all government, especially since this would necessitate the surrender of certain national prerogatives.

Many reflective and well-informed persons believe that this is the only means of securing permanent peace, the condition promotive of the general welfare of the whole world. There is, however, uncertainty as to the present practicability of such a plan. So diverse are the nations in racial, cultural, and traditional makeup that such union immediately seems a remote possibility. But nothing that is right is impossible of accomplishment. Righteous prayer, a deep-seated desire to promote the brotherhood of man, coupled with the exercise of divine wisdom, will unfold the necessary steps to a desirable goal. If that goal be the Kingdom, and the people are truly desirous of establishing true unity, the way will be disclosed.

Another proposal is for groups of nations, those bound by racial or ethical bonds, or perhaps geographically associated, to unite in a sort of preparatory school for training in the self-surrender and discipline necessary for a final successful union. The Balkan States and Russia, the Moslem groups of peoples, the British Commonwealth already a promising unity, the American Republics, Eastern Asia, et cetera—all, it is proposed, might be included experimentally in a series of unions.

This plan, however, would scarcely preclude the need for the international police power necessary to render impossible an uprising by one or more aggressor nations again to endanger the peace of the whole world. This, it is generally agreed, is the first and absolutely necessary step toward a lasting peace. The invaded nations must of necessity have the opportunity to re-establish themselves, to rehabilitate their industries, to reform their governments; in short, to establish again what has been taken away by a ruthless invader. To ensure this opportunity, there must be a period of peace, the absence of fear and of strife—arch enemies of the domestic tranquillity necessary to national development. None who are giving serious thought to the present world situation can fail to be conscious of the magnitude of the problems that lie ahead. However, there is no problem that is insolvable when the divine Omnipotence is invoked.

Every nation, whatever its own concept of religion and worship, looks to an ever-ruling Oneness, unlimited in power and everywhere present. The differences among concepts of the nature of Deity furnish no insurmountable barrier. The new super-state will not, of course, undertake to determine the type of religion that these citizens of the world must adopt and practice. Far from it. Such a position would make a true union impossible. Nothing so quickly breeds dissension as interference with the rights of worship.

Christendom will doubtless, as in the past, undertake through its vast missionary activities to conform to the Christian way of life the peoples now holding to other concepts of Deity and to various forms of worship. And the most potent propaganda is to exemplify to the world the results of accepting the Nazarene as Lord and Saviour. Christianity exemplified is the most effective magnet to attract the people to the true way of life.

A question that has been asked millions of times in the last three years on both sides of the great conflict is, What are we fighting for? What are the ideals for which these great armies have been created, this vast machinery provided? The Axis answer to the question has been, "World dominion; to permit us, the superior German race, to assume our rightful place as masters of the whole world by right of inherent racial superiority." The Japanese answer is not unlike that of the Germans: "We, the Nipponese, descendants of the Sun Goddess, are the superior race of earth, and accordingly should be its masters." And the pronouncements of some of its leading statesmen and teachers have been cast in the same mold of inane and meaningless twaddle.

It seems incredible that any race with a modicum of intelligence could be so deluded as these two great peoples, great in numbers only, seem to be. They represent types of thinking and statements of purpose that seem completely out of place in this twentieth century. *Barbarous, unchristian,* and *merciless* are adjectives that readily flow from tongue and pen when the effort is made properly to characterize their present attitudes.

It is important to remember, however, that both Germany and Japan, as well as Italy, are in the grasp of war parties that are leading the people on to ultimate disaster. There are in these countries a considerable body of persons wholly, or at least largely, in opposition to the policy of the war lords, and who would never have consented, if it had been possible, to these deadly assaults upon Christian countries, and who would, if they were able, end the conflict immediately. It is upon this foundation of right thinkers that the victorious nations will aid in rebuilding a sane, moral, and dependable nation in each case.

To start this process of rebuilding and to extend the spirit of Democracy to other nations, it devolves upon the great exponents of this form of government to make it attractive; in other words, to demonstrate to the world that it is truly Christian, is inspired with the desire to assist in establishing the unity of humanity implied in the brotherhood of man and with the honest purpose of lending the hand of a Good Samaritan as an earnest of its sincerity. There is a saying, "Thou the truth must speak if thou another's heart would reach." That is to say, sincerity is a prerequisite if one's example is to become effective.

The ideals of the leading nations, especially Great Britain and the United States, will have little weight in the efforts of China, India, and other great peoples to establish true government unless they prove in their own domestic experience that Democracy does work, that it does what it claims to do—that it gives to every individual the opportunity for self-development and economic independence. If these nations were to be examined in the light of these queries, some dark spots would be discovered.

The attitude of the United States toward the Chinese, for example, is a case to examine. Excluded by Federal law, the Chinese were long looked upon as an inferior race, although their civilization was several thousand years old when America was still a wilderness. Furthermore, there was the demand for extraterritoriality, providing special privileges, among them that citizens of the United States in China should be subject to trial in their own courts rather than submit to the Chinese sense of justice.

[158]

Pattern of The New World Order

That there were reasons for this situation there is no doubt. But back of the demands of foreign nations upon China was the desire for trade, to exploit China—not for her benefit, but for gain by the industrial and commercial nations. China was no longer mistress in her own house. This foreign attitude led to intense unrest, which found expression in maltreatment of foreigners.

Now, as China is regarded and actually is an Ally of the United Nations, her position has changed. Her heroic efforts in withstanding the assaults of Japan have won for her a place in the international hall of fame that will stand forever as a memorial of a people's courage and sacrifice. Her gallant leader, the Generalissimo Chiang Kai-shek, has proved himself a truly Christian leader who envisions a world in which all shall be free, with equal opportunity to progress in the higher purposes of life.

What shall be our attitude toward China and India? And, for that matter, toward all of the non-white races? When we remember that these number two-thirds of the world's population, determination of the attitude that the Democracies are to assume toward these Asiatic and African peoples assumes the proportions of a major problem. Are we prepared to approach the problem with becoming humility? Are we willing to surrender the type of thought so characteristic of us—that we are smarter than other peoples, that we can, in short, "lick the world"?

I recall a fine young man whom I encountered in a railway dining car a few months prior to Pearl Harbor. As the situation with Japan seemed to be approaching a climax, I queried him as to his views. As nonchalantly as he would speak of his assurance of his college winning at football, he replied, "Oh, yes! We shall have to slap her down." Slap her down, indeed! Pearl Harbor taught us some lessons, lessons that sobered us and brought us to a realization that not all the smart people of the world live in the Democracies.

Pattern of The New World Order

Apparently the United States, from the very force of circumstances, will have to assume a large share of responsibility in rehabilitating the stricken nations and in helping to plan and build the New World structure. The great resources of the country, its enterprise and extraordinary capability in industrial lines, its warm heart and ready hand—all must be utilized to the full in the days ahead. What is being done in aiding the cause of the United Nations is but prophetic of what may be done in winning the peace when the guns cease firing.

Will the United Nations make it clear whether they are as willing to unite for a permanent peace as they have been to impede the progress of a determined hostile force? Are we as willing to sacrifice for freedom for all nations and peoples as we have been to make an all-out effort to preserve our own way of life? It is at least fascinating to speculate on what kind of World Order would result if the United Nations would put into the peace program the same determined efforts they have exerted in winning over the enemy.

It is one of the tragedies of human experience that the zest of battle, the need for physical effort in prosecuting war, relaxes when the battle is won; and the carnal mind settles into a condition of somnolence and apathy. This has led to disaster in more than one instance. If the Allies had remained alert after the Versailles adventure, had kept a sharp surveillance upon their erstwhile enemy, how different might have been the condition today! The same mistakes must not be repeated. It is increasingly manifest that civilization cannot withstand too frequent assaults from a formidable enemy gone berserk.

When a populous and enterprising nation throws overboard all moral sense, all desire to maintain even a semblance of national honor, this type of aggression can be met only by constant vigilance, supported by an adequate police force. If there were any doubt of the extremes to which the German leaders have gone, it is entirely dispersed by the statement of their Chief of Propaganda that it is not a question of right or wrong for which they are contending; victory is their only motive. A people has gone far along the road to primitive barbarism when they have abandoned the belief that it is a just cause for which they are fighting. Warfare under such conditions reverts to piracy. It recalls the adventures of the swarming hordes of Mohammed's followers, who in the early centuries of our era took the field for the booty that could be gathered from weaker people.

It becomes clearly manifest, as the mental attitudes exhibited by Germany, Japan, and Italy are examined, that the utmost vigilance must be observed in the settlement to follow. Education will enter largely as a means of restoring these deluded peoples to a mental state of sanity and morality. The task of re-forming the mental outlook of the youth trained in the Nazi philosophy will be a task to challenge the best methods known to the Christian world. But again success will attend these efforts precisely in proportion to the degree to which the divine power is invoked and becomes the basis of the reconstruction. "With God all things are possible." [1] No task is too difficult for solution under divine guidance.

Let us not make the mistake, however, of assuming that these problems can be solved on a basis of personal gain, individual or national. The over-all cause of freedom for all humanity is the only purpose worthy of success; and success to win must be deserved. The cause must be a righteous cause and the methods in accord with the purpose of divine Will. The vision must be clear that the values involved are universal and eternal.

Much more is in the balance than the welfare of any one nation. As the war has been proclaimed by the United Nations to be a struggle for freedom for all humanity, this aim must be kept constantly before the peacemakers. And, moreover, it

---

[1] Matt. 19:26.

must be recognized that what is best for all is best for each. The security of each one lies in the security of all.

There are heartening signs of the awakening that will bring these imponderables into actual experience. Just now a prominent official of the Netherlands announces that after the war the East Indies will be organized into an independent nation. Evidence also is appearing that the very knotty problem of a freed India is nearing a solution. Hasty judgment regarding the Indian problem ignores the tremendous perplexities with which it is involved.

It is commonly held that no more difficult political situation can be named than that of finding a satisfactory and secure solution to a situation where religious antagonism borders upon fanaticism. I recall a tour made about Calcutta a decade ago with an English engineer who had spent years in striving to improve the living quarters of the city. A street had been widened to carry the increasing traffic. But in the very center of it, at an important crossing, there had been erected a shrine, about which the traffic must flow. To remove it would be likely to precipitate a holy war.

Again, I was shown a tract that had been cleared of old, ramshackle buildings to make a small park, a breathing place for a crowded quarter of the city. No sooner was the clearing process completed than a "holy man" pitched his tent in the center of it, and the possibility of its use for the general welfare came to an end. So long as the man chose to remain, there was no legal way of removing him. These incidents but illustrate the mental situation in a country of many diverse tongues and traditions, where religion is carried to the extremes of fanaticism.

Let none conclude that England's occupation and overlordship of India has not been fraught with many and great difficulties. But again let it be recalled that there is a solution to this as to every social problem, and the way will be found through righteous prayer to a just and righteous solution. When self-interest gives way to a zeal for the general welfare, ways will open that are not visualized when the vision is double.

A beginning has been made in the Atlantic Charter, which lays down the broad policy of freedom for all peoples, freedom to develop government in accord with the will of the majority. To be sure, there are many lowly peoples who will need the assistance of the more advanced nations. This is a part of the white man's burden that may not be ignored. The more privileged nations are in duty bound to aid the less privileged as they rise to a position of economic freedom and self-government.

That I am my brother's keeper is something more than a shibboleth. It must become the watchword to lead the nations forward in the grandest purpose to which human effort was ever devoted, the establishment of that state of brotherhood which is the counterpart of the true brotherhood that stems from the Fatherhood of God. The Good Samaritan did not assume an attitude of superiority to the stricken man, did not regard him patronizingly. Rather did he see the man's need and provide for it in the ways open to him. He did all that could be done to alleviate the suffering and to provide for the immediate future.

If the great nations approach the problem of aiding the benighted peoples in this spirit, how sure will be the result! There is in the heart of every mortal a something that demands expression, that looks upward and outward to a better state, however vague may be the vision. It is upon this innate desire that the improvement will be founded; and if it be encouraged and developed, these less advanced peoples will progress to the position of freedom and affluence that belongs to the children of God. To accept a lower status, or to conclude that these are impossibilities, is but a counsel of despair, a conclusion of the carnal mind based entirely upon the outward and material, an approach wholly devoid of spiritual understanding of the divine Fatherhood.

Whether the less advanced peoples should be placed under specific mandates, as provided in the Treaty of Versailles, none can at present determine. That is not the vital question. The all-important condition is the manner of approach. Is it the old desire for exploitation of a simple people for material gains, or is it the genuine desire to lend a hand, to lift a less developed group up the ladder of self-improvement into a state of independence and self-government? Democracy will never be made safe for the world unless it is based upon divine Authority. No problem is ever solved, that is, permanently, except on a basis of right, the eternal right that connotes divine justice.

The world has permitted types of philosophy, National Socialism and Fascism, to develop, with the appalling results now manifest. These as instrumented are definitely the anti-Christ, that which would obliterate in human experience every vestige of the moral and spiritual animus of the Nazarene's teaching. Now the struggle is one to determine whether or not this ogre of unrighteousness is to prevail. We are convinced that it will not, for it is utterly devoid of the might of right.

But will there follow with the victorious nations the choice of the Christ-way of life, and that in its deepest implications? The choice is before mankind. The way of evil, the way of the anti-Christ, dominant, cruel, heartless; or the way of the Christ, tender, loving, merciful, not devoid of strength, but in fact embodying through reflection the omnipotence of the infinite One. This is the choice now confronting the nations.

XVI

Labor and Industrial Peace

PEACE in industry, both domestic and international, is one of the urgent needs in the establishment and maintenance of the just and durable general peace toward which Christendom is looking and for which it is constantly praying. That the relation between capital and labor has measurably improved in recent years is a matter of common knowledge. Recent experiences, however, posit a serious situation. Even though the United States is at war, preparing for the all-out effort believed necessary to save the Democratic way of life from the totalitarian aggressor—even under these trying circumstances—labor unions have inaugurated strikes. Personal interests are placed above general welfare, even at the risk of defeat.

The number of strikes that have been called, the number of man-hours lost in the war industries, are appalling when examined in the light of the need for the utmost effort—effort to be effective only through its consecration to the issue at stake: the protection and maintenance of freedom, of the way of life won only through centuries of struggle, through the expenditure of blood and treasure almost beyond measure. Yet in spite of what is at stake, men quit their jobs, striking sometimes for higher pay, sometimes out of sympathy for fellow workmen, and sometimes for what seem trifling causes. They leave their jobs, however urgent the need for their production, and await the outcome of events.

This situation, deplorable though it be, is the offspring of industrial injustice, which runs far back into the history of labor;

Labor and Industrial Peace

in fact, so far back that its beginnings are lost in the mists of memory. All too long the condition of labor, its rights and privileges, were overlooked, or if known, were ignored. The grind of the day's work, in mine, in shop, in mill, and in the field, too long failed to stir in the employers, the great captains of industry, a sense of justice toward those whose product was the source of their wealth. Selfishness too often engendered the fashion of dealing unfairly with those who were necessary to the success of industry, whatever its nature, whether large or small.

The teachings of the Nazarene—compassion, justice, honesty, and mercy—had made very little impression upon the management of the developing industries. Those in command of capital, and those with constructive and administrative ability, claimed for themselves the lion's share of the profit they sought to make. Out of these conditions grew the labor union. Unions sprang from the necessity for labor to improve its conditions. They sprang from the logic of events: labor had to protect itself. If employers would not improve the situation and rectify their mistakes, then the only alternative was for labor to take the situation in hand and, through united effort, demand and secure their rights: a larger share in the product of their toil, better wages, shorter hours, and improved working conditions. It is little wonder that, realizing their power, they often went too far, until, as they ignored justice between labor and capital, between employer and employed, the pendulum swung to the limit of its arc and industry suffered, ofttimes to the point of disappearing. Labor imposed conditions that made impossible the maintenance of industry with profit—and neither capital nor employer has the incentive to carry on without the prospect of material gain.

Out of these conditions has developed the present situation between capital and labor. Much progress in the demonstration of justice has been made on both sides. Employers have

[166]

Labor and Industrial Peace

learned valuable lessons. Labor has come to understand, in some degree at least, that industry must be prosperous in order to continue. Neither can prosper at the expense of the other. Co-operative endeavor is the need. Each must recognize the position of the other. At its best, each must have as the high purpose true service. Labor cannot prosper, even in a rich industry, if it is strangled by greed. No more can profit accrue from dissatisfied and rebellious labor. A righteous medium must be established, where both can meet in a common purpose: true service. This brings us to the problem of service. What is it, and what is its purpose?

The Nazarene gave the perfect law, the only rule that is wholly just, wholly Christian, and that wholly assures success: "Seek ye first the kingdom of God, and his righteousness; and all these things shall be added unto you." [1] None will hold that this rule has been operative in industry on either side. How little have industrialists put the motive of service above profit! How little has labor sought to serve God in the day's work! So far as mortals are able, seeking the Kingdom of God is the seeking of service that is deemed necessary to the welfare of mankind; to the production of something that provides for the necessities of life, the things deemed necessary to the experience of harmonious living. But this purpose of serving God must be first, above mere profit, or even of meeting the urgent needs of the day; to fulfill the law, seek first the Kingdom, it must be paramount.

The truly Christian businessman undertaking to develop an industry, be it large or small, sees as his first purpose, not to make a profit, perhaps not even to make a living for himself and his dependents, but first to serve and glorify God by doing something useful and worthy for mankind. This high purpose established, he will righteously administer his affairs; then

---

[1] Matt. 6:33.

mercy and consideration for his workers, fair wages, comfortable conditions for the labor, and concern for their welfare in general will naturally follow in fulfillment of his righteous desire. Doing by them as he would have them do by himself, were the conditions reversed, is a fair criterion by which to judge his attitude.

The word "righteousness" has an imperative connotation in the fulfillment of the Master's instructions. Righteousness of action stems from right thinking—in fact, is its constituent element. If we think rightly, we shall act righteously; and conversely, wrong thinking—that is, from the basis of selfishness, greed, or indifference to the rights and welfare of others—is the precursor of false standards toward those whose labor is necessary to industry.

Now we are assured in this perfect rule promulgated by the Master that, having met the conditions that may be regarded as preliminary, the results will be satisfactory to all. "And all these things shall be added unto you" is the promise. The meaning plainly is this: when once the conditions laid down are adopted and faithfully carried out, the results will be prosperity; the things needed and righteously sought will become manifest. This is the perfect rule for successful industry—one, however, that must be carried out in spirit and in letter if the desirable results are to be attained. Can one doubt that the provisions here set forth, really accepted and practiced by an employer, could fail to convey to his laborers a deep impression of an earnest desire to deal righteously with them?

This, however, is but one side of the case. What of labor? Does the Master's saying apply only to the employer? By no means. None is excluded from the necessity of obeying it to the full. Righteousness is not for one party to a situation, but for all concerned. When the laborer knows and acknowledges his obligations to God, then will his labor be elevated far above the sense of toil and drudgery. It will be lifted onto the plane of true service, the privilege of serving God through his efforts to produce something needed, something useful to mankind.

This service, it will be seen, precludes labor to produce that which is harmful, which is deleterious and injurious to man's highest status. In other words, it must be service of good, not of that which is evil and harmful. This criterion established, this modus utilized, can there be any doubt as to the peaceful relations that would result between capital and labor?

The laborer is entitled to a just share of the product of his work. Capital, property, has no inherent, sacred quality that lifts it above the status of labor. To be sure, property rights have long been held above all others in the social economy. Possession of property has been deemed of more importance than the protection of human welfare, even of life itself. If it were not now so held, property, wealth, would not escape the same treatment as citizens in time of national emergency. Men and women are commandeered by authority of government. Property—taxed, to be sure, to meet the tremendous expense entailed in the prosecution of modern warfare—is, however, in the Democracies commonly left to the ownership and management of its proprietors. It would seem that definite adjustment is necessary to hold property and life in the right relationship.

Labor has awakened to a deep-seated realization that its rights have in the past been too largely ignored. With this awakening has come the conviction that it is inherently entitled to a larger share in its product. And this increased return should come, not from the generosity of the employer, but as a right inherent in the fact that labor is as essential to industry as capital. Furthermore, labor is the means, the only means, open whereby the workman may gain the necessities of life, the things that are imperative to the provision for himself and his dependents. Here rights and necessity go hand in hand. Realization of this truth has brought about greatly changed conditions both in wages and hours of labor and in the conditions under which labor is carried on.

Much of this improvement has resulted from just legislation; much from awakened consciousness on the part of employers that justice must be done—that the welfare of the laborer and his family is paramount, even more important to the general welfare than profit. The laborer, awakened to a sense of the importance of his work and, in some degree, to the sacred character of true service, is demanding his rights because of the nature of his contribution to his specific industry and to the common welfare as well. He has a new perspective, a new vision. Social justice has become to him a goal of practical attainment.

Some fifteen years ago I had the privilege of writing, under the title "Fellowship," the biography of Mr. Clarence Howard, then the President of the Commonwealth Steel Company of East St. Louis. This company had grown from very small beginnings to occupy a large place in the production of railroad equipment. It developed a locomotive bed that quite revolutionized the method used in the production of steam engines for railroads. In consequence, it attracted the envious eye of the most important builders of locomotives in the country, and a corporation was formed to buy out the Commonwealth Company. The transaction was carried out, and a very large sum paid for its stock. Its shops were closed, its workmen for the most part dismissed, and its activity moved to the East Coast, all of which is pertinent to the subject under discussion.

Mr. Howard was a man of great philanthropic motives, generous to a fault. He instituted welfare activities for his workmen which at that period were scarcely paralleled in the country. He promoted a social center, a company store where all goods were sold at cost, and established a course of education to afford opportunity for the employees to prepare for higher positions. He provided a plan for bonuses based upon years

Labor and Industrial Peace

of service. Representatives of the various departments lunched with the officials of the company weekly, an occasion for the bringing of proposals for improving the conditions of the workers and new ideas to improve the methods of the industry.

Riding through the great buildings in a Ford car, Mr. Howard would be greeted by shouts of approval and appreciation. There was but one strike in many years. A gang of puddlers left one morning for some unknown cause. Immediately fellow workmen familiar with that phase of the work volunteered their services, so that the industry went on without interruption. The son of the leader of the striking gang was at the time attending college through Mr. Howard's generosity.

This recitation is to present a picture of an industry carried on under a management that had deep interest in the welfare of its employees—that, in fact, was constantly looking for opportunities to increase the welfare work. But the point is this: all these beneficences were proffered at the will of the management, especially of Mr. Howard himself. They sprang from a noble generosity, a deep love for his fellows. Splendid! But something was lacking, and that something was recognition of the inherent right of the laborers in the earnings of the industry, expressed in terms of wages that would have enabled the laborers themselves to procure all the advantages provided by a generous management. That the corporation which took over the Commonwealth was actuated by no such motives was apparent in the closing of the mills once possession of the valuable patents was gained.

The remedy for industrial injustice is deeper recognition of the rights of labor and a keener sense that industry, truly to succeed, must have the primary purpose of serving God by serving mankind in some useful way; and true service must of necessity partake of the righteousness that stems from knowledge of God and a primary desire to serve Him.

Labor and Industrial Peace

It is inevitable that this awakening on the part of labor should be characterized and described as class-consciousness. It is based upon a new understanding of the importance of labor to the social welfare. Says the worker, "I raise your food, market and distribute it. I do the world's work in all industries of whatever type—in commerce and in transportation, as well as in all forms of manufactures; in short, I provide the motive power that keeps the wheels of industrial activities revolving. Hence I am indispensable and deserving by right not only of a larger share of the product of my industry, but entitled to a voice in the management and direction of the industry to which I contribute so much. In other words, I am no longer satisfied to receive a wage plus such largess as the employer may see fit to bestow upon me. Since in any industry I am of equal importance with capital, I am entitled to share in the profits accruing from my services. Surely, such sharing is just and economically sound."

That this position is deserving of and is receiving much attention, there is strong evidence. "The Spirit of truth" is at work in the minds of men, and ultimately will bring about the day of social justice. That the movement has become international is of special significance. The International Labor Organization, which functioned so successfully under the able leadership of Mr. John G. Winant, now Ambassador at the Court of St. James's, is but an impelling sign of the awakened interest in the labor problem and of the realization that it is bound to have great weight in the formulation of the plan to establish peace based upon righteousness, when victory by the Allied Nations is won. The I. L. O., fearing invasion of Switzerland by the Nazis, wisely moved its headquarters from Geneva to Montreal, where it is carrying on its affairs in an atmosphere conducive to their effectiveness.

A most encouraging event was the recent meeting of employers and labor in amicable discussion of the tremendous problems involved. Many publicists are convinced that the failure earlier to solve the problems attached to the proper relation between capital and labor has been a large factor in bringing about the present global war. None can deny that it has been a factor. Wise statesmen are now recognizing the situation and, even in the midst of the clash of arms, are undertaking to formulate plans for a just and lasting settlement that shall include this type of social justice. It is bound to follow that when both sides approach the situation in the spirit of the Golden Rule, a just settlement will eventuate. The Christ is no less potent and no less available to furnish the solution for this than for any other problem crying for solution.

That the concept of united action both between groups within a given state and between international groups has ever been in the thought of those accustomed to look to the divine Father for the salvation of all mankind is well known to all students of religion. Nearly fifteen centuries ago, Augustine of Canterbury urged upon his fellow religionists the need for such united action. Said he, "Thou shalt unite the citizens of one place with another, nation with nation, group with group, and in general all men among themselves, and so not only weld this society more secure, but form a universal brotherhood." How manifestly was this great religionist voicing what the Christ had revealed to him as to the necessity of establishing the true sense of brotherhood, not alone among groups within a nation, but between groups of many nations! This was, indeed, a foretelling of what the ancient prophet foresaw, that the nations should flow together.

Thoughtful men in many lands are searching for a formula that will bring into actuality the truth so impressively uttered by the Nazarene, iterated and reiterated upon many occasions. Fair adjustment between capital and labor is of world-wide interest. A single example will illustrate the far-flung interest. Down in Hamilton, New Zealand, I came upon a plan worked out by a public-spirited, retired businessman that possesses great merit. Like all plans, it must be entered upon with the high purpose of using it for a righteous purpose. So interesting did the Brookings Institution regard it that they set it forth *in extenso* as founding a practical solution of the all-important issue of capital and labor. So impressed with its possibilities is its originator, Mr. H. Valder, that he has established a foundation in the University of New Zealand to ensure careful and thorough study and exploration of the plan in order to determine its weaknesses, if any, and, so far as it is found practical, to encourage its introduction in industry.

The plan, as Mr. Valder described it to me a dozen years ago in Hamilton, is essentially this: "In the employees' partnership plan, surplus profits after payment of all production costs, including the agreed-upon cumulative rate of payment for the use of capital, are the property of the laborer share-holders."

Explanation of these "laborers' shares" is necessary. Each laborer entering upon employment in any corporate industry receives an industrial share, or shares, entitling him to participate in the net profits of the industry so long as he continues in its employ. The number of shares a person receives depends upon his value to the business as represented by his wages. The unit of ownership of shares is the lowest wage that is paid for the least important service. This rises in multiples according to the importance of the laborer, as determined by the various scales of wages, reaching ultimately to the management itself. Thus, each employee becomes a sharer in the profits of the business in addition to the wages received. Obviously, this procedure in some measure recognizes the importance of labor to the industry and provides for the practical application of the proposition that the laborer is entitled to a share of the profits.

Since Mr. Valder first explained the plan to me, the rights of labor have been further recognized as carrying "a title to representation on the board of directors." It is contended that

Labor and Industrial Peace

this method brings into play the system of payment by results for the service of labor and supplants the deadening effect of the restrictive wage system.

It should not require statement that for any plan to succeed, it is necessary for both parties concerned to approach its application in the spirit of the Golden Rule, of justice and righteousness, with the avowed purpose of inaugurating its provisions upon a Christian basis. There must be an abandonment of those things that are behind and a looking forward to the establishment of such relations between the two great groups concerned, termed capital and labor, as will bring to each true prosperity. Then the "things" promised will be added to those who seek first the Kingdom and its righteousness; for these conditions, this plan of divine justice, forever prevails in the universe of reality.

Already the awakening of society to the necessity for reform in order that justice may find expression has taken form in plans and resolutions formulated and impressively set forth by thoughtful and prominent men and women. Notably the Conference held at Malvern, England, in January 1941, not only pointed to the failure of the Church to bring forth plans to improve the condition of labor and of the working class as a whole, but presented definite steps to be taken to reform present practices. A summation of the resolutions is this: "The true status of labor independent of economic progress must find expression in managerial framework of industry; the rights of labor must be recognized as in principle equal to those of capital in the control of industry, whatever the means by which this transformation is effected."

In this forthright language did a body of representative citizens of Britain, a group containing some of the most competent men and women, even the new Archbishop, William Temple, declare unequivocally for equality of privilege between capital and labor. Specific resolutions declared for public ownership of natural resources, equality of opportunity to gain and maintain harmonious and adequate living conditions, and equality in the privileges of education and cultural attainment. It was an extremely forward-looking presentation of steps necessary to the attainment of that ideal of social security which springs from the spirit of the Master's teachings.

Injustice is the enemy of the Golden Rule. And the sooner the ruling and privileged classes recognize this and take steps to rectify existent wrongs, the sooner will the basis of just and permanent peace be attained. It profits little to pray, "Thy will be done," [2] and continue in a course wholly representative of self-will and self-seeking. The Word of God is to be motivated—to be introduced into human affairs as the true voice and method of procedure that will lead mankind onward and upward to that mental state where the brotherhood of man approximates the real brotherhood of the children of God. Nowhere will there be greater need to recognize this than at the Peace Table.

Labor unions as constituted have not afforded a complete remedy for social injustice experienced by the underprivileged. While their purpose was primarily a good one, the execution of that purpose has fallen far short of the ideal of justice for all. It must be fully recognized that justice, to be truly just, must be righteous. And righteousness demands fair treatment for all parties involved. It seems but a common tendency of mortals, when the opportunity is offered to gain the status originally desired, to go to extremes, thus often failing to accord to the other party involved the degree of justice that they are demanding for themselves. Selfishness is in the saddle and rides ruthlessly. This tendency has frequently characterized the position and acts of the labor unions, especially in the United States. And it seems that the excessive demands of

---

[2] Matt. 6:10.

Labor and Industrial Peace

labor have often been encouraged and abetted by both the Congress and the executive departments of the national government.

Favoritism toward labor has even been attributed to the highest judicial tribunal of the country, the Supreme Court. This result has evolved, it seems, from the desire to placate labor and thus strengthen politically the position of the dominant party. The remedy for this erroneous situation lies with the people. Since the United States purports to be a true Democracy, the government, at least in theory, expresses the will of the people. Reformation must spring from popular desire. To bring to the electorate adequate understanding of political problems, to render them politically conscious to a degree that will enable them to determine wherein justice and righteousness most nearly are subserved, is a major problem, a necessity, in a successful Democracy. It seems that the proletariat can be prepared for Democracy only through some measure of Christianization.

Designing persons and groups, actuated solely by a desire for self-profit and aggrandizement, have at hand the means to propagate their theories to the point of confusing those whose support they seek. The defense against this barrage of error is attainment of "the Spirit of truth" to the degree that enables the electorate to determine definitely whether a given proposition which they are importuned to support has a divine Source or is merely an expression of human will to accommodate selfish ends. The situation is not insoluble—far from it; and the perfect remedy is found in the gaining of that mental status that can distinguish between good and evil, between right and wrong.

Two conditions have arisen in relation to the labor unions in America that manifestly need to be remedied for their future welfare as well as for public interest. Labor unions are not above the law. To permit any group of citizens or aliens to feel themselves above the law is directly a subversion of the general welfare. For it is inevitable that such a position, once assured, leads to the arrogation by the labor union of power that inheres in the government itself.

The belief long prevailed that labor unions could not be made answerable to the laws of the land: that they were to that degree immune from prosecution for any misdemeanors they might commit. While claiming for themselves the right to seek justice through orderly legal procedure, the opposite theory—that they were in turn answerable for their acts—they denied. This position, however, has been rectified in some measure by recent court decisions that called a labor union to account for evading or breaking the law of the land.

The situation should be clarified and rectified by further legislation. Many believe that the Wagner Labor Act did not hold the balance even as between the employers and the workmen: its promulgators no doubt went too far in the desire to ameliorate certain vexatious conditions to which labor was subjected, conditions reminiscent of the days when profit of the employer was the primary purpose of industry. The public is awakening to the need for corrective legislation to remove special privileges to labor that result in injustice to the employer and the public.

Another unfortunate condition to which the labor unions are subjected is found in the development of a class of agitators who profess an extreme desire to right all the wrongs, real or theoretical, obtaining in the labor situation. These self-seekers often mislead their innocent victims to the point of gaining a position little short of that of dictators—and all in the name of and under the banner of labor's suppressed rights. Not infrequently have these men gained substantial wealth by plundering the treasury of a union under a pretext of using the funds for the advancement of the interests of the union. The news often relates the bringing to justice of these enemies of labor and the public (for it is inevitable that what injures the interests of labor is equally disadvantageous to the people).

It is not irrelevant to discuss the profit motive under the general title of industrial justice: the two, labor and capital—industry and profit—are inextricably interwoven in the social pattern of the day. Many eminent economists defend the profit motive as the dynamic force that creates industry, asserting that without the opportunity for and expectation of establishing and conducting a profitable business, there would be little incentive to invest capital and undergo the mental and physical strain often involved in the planning, developing, and maintaining of industry. This position has its logic. The contention that the laborer is worthy of his hire applies no less to the proprietor than to the laborer. It has recognized merits.

There are, however, some negative considerations in this question. If management and ownership of a business were uniformly actuated by the desire to promote the common welfare, the profit motive would be justified. But when great financial empires result from industry that exploits not only the natural resources of a country but the laborer whose toil is an indispensable factor in the success of the industry, the evil results of the profit motive become manifest.

No more notable example of this fact can be cited than that of the famous steel magnate, Andrew Carnegie. A man of great capability and genius in organization and management, arriving in America at the opportune moment for the development of an industry basic and vital to an era of unprecedented development such as the country was about to embark upon, seized the opportunity and, in consequence of his energy and capability, amassed a fortune that made him a modern Croesus. To be sure, he played a prominent part in the great industrial development of the country. Would the importance of his contribution have been less had he made the Golden Rule the criterion of his business? Was he a consistent promoter of the Christianity to which he adhered when his laborers were forced into the terrible situation that led to the rioting and strike at Homestead? These are questions that must be faced and answered when the blueprint for the New World Order is drawn.

Without the settlement of such questions of and the problems between capital and labor upon a basis of righteousness and justice, any peace plan is merely temporary, and is sure to be followed by further world eruption—and such eruptions are bound to grow more terrible as human ingenuity produces more deadly weapons by which to make dominant the human will. This argument is not to deny that the profit motive *per se* may be sound and based upon justice. It is patent, however, that in a World Order founded upon and undergirded by Christian principles, the first purpose of true service of any kind, whether that of employer and manager or of laborer, must be to glorify God, to establish justice and righteousness in the social order.

And, *per contra,* it must be recognized that merely to serve personal ends, to seek that which merely satisfies one's sense of possession, to gain and secure ease and comfort for one's self and one's dependents, is definitely antisocial. This attitude stems from personal sense and not from divine purpose.

In any fair discussion of the rightness or wrongness of the profit motive, whether it be social or antisocial, a question also arises as to the wage and salary motive. Is it wrong to seek profit from ownership or management of business but altogether right and justifiable to seek higher wages and larger salaries through such means as are at hand—through the strikes of the labor union, or some equivalent means for the salaried worker? Here is posited a truly urgent question.

[180]

Labor and Industrial Peace

L. P. Jacks, eminent publicist and Christian, sometime President of Manchester College, Oxford, and Editor of *Hibberts Journal,* raises the question in a letter to the London *Times.* His argument is that the desire of the proprietor of a business to increase his profit, say, from 4 per cent to 6 per cent, is no less Christian and defensible than the desire on the part of the salary or wage earner to add to his earnings. And he admits that dangers arise when the profits of the captains of industry assume colossal proportions, as in the case of some of the great industrialists of the world, the Carnegies, Rockefellers, Fords, Rothchilds, and so forth.

And the query is raised, Are the employers to be suppressed because they are more greedy, more self-seeking than are the salary and wage earners who desire larger returns for their labor? Of course they are not. But when the businessman out of the profits of his industry is enabled to live in unlimited luxury, having all that makes for comfort, recreation, culture, and education—for satisfying physical desires to the utmost —while many wage earners, on the other hand, as has been true in recent decades, have almost none of these privileges, something is emphatically wrong.

Would society have been less well served, would it have been more antisocial, if there had been a profit-sharing plan in every industry that has created a host of millionaires, so that the laborers who had an all-important part in accumulating the vast profits could have lived more abundantly, could have partaken more generously of what civilization has to offer for the comfort, culture, and well-being of all? There can be but one answer to this query. And the one solution is that presented by the Nazarene. If the primary purpose of both proprietor and wage earner be to seek the Kingdom, the mental state where harmony, righteousness, and justice are forever expressed; if they have gained the understanding of God and His love for all to the degree that develops a full faith in the divinely ordained words of His messenger, then these problems will be perfectly resolved. If they seek this righteousness *first,* the "things" will be added—all that is necessary to a well-ordered, happy, and prosperous human experience.

This state of consciousness, both ideal and practical, may not be attained by humanity at once. But if it be set as the goal, the acme of right desire, a long step will have been taken. The shadows of greed, of self-seeking, will disappear under the light of the Christ-purpose. A beginning may be made at once. Application of the Golden Rule is an immediate step for all who have been quickened by the sense of justice and righteousness that it so impressively sets forth. The Christ will then be chosen as the way to the establishment of permanent peace because its purpose is holy, its method divine. This presence at the Peace Table alone will ensure that for which humanity so poignantly longs, the joy of permanent peace. Just settlement of the relation of capital and labor will be a long step toward bringing human affairs into the alembic of the Kingdom.

XVII

"And all the nations shall flow unto it"

THAT great prophet-statesman, Isaiah, son of Amoz, had a clear vision of the ultimate course of the nations. The mountain of the Lord's house would be established "and all the nations shall flow unto it." [1] The Lord's house manifestly is that state of divine consciousness commonly termed the Kingdom of Heaven. In the present relationship of the nations, engaged as they are in deadly combat, the time seems far distant when they shall literally flow unto the Lord's house, shall come together under any form of agreement that will bring permanent peace, that will make the recurrence of devastating war impossible because they seek to establish the true brotherhood. Yet great is the hope and keen is the expectancy of Christendom that the way may be found.

Vice-President Henry A. Wallace, in a stirring address delivered before the Free World Association on May 8, 1942, said, "The peace must mean a better standard of living for the common man, not merely in the United States and England, but also in India, Russia, China, and Latin America—not merely in the United Nations, but also in Germany, Italy, and Japan. . . . Those who write the peace must think of the whole world."

Here are inspired words that envisage the magnitude and purpose of the urgently sought peace, an agreement between all the nations, including all mankind—the more than two

---
[1] Isa. 2:2.

"And all the nations shall flow unto it"

billion inhabitants of the earth. None are excluded. Thus, on the horizon of human affairs, even daily shedding rays of light upon the dark clouds of destructive warfare, are appearing signs of the approaching day when the prophet's vision may become actual experience in national relationships. Many—and the number is increasing—are convinced that under divine guidance what is most beneficent in international relationships is possible of accomplishment. There are no insoluble problems when Omnipotence is properly invoked.

Two recent events lend encouragement to hope. The signing in Washington by thirty-one nations of an agreement for concerted action in the prosecution of the war is a heartening example that unity of purpose and action is a present possibility among the nations having the fundamental purposes of protecting themselves against destructive aggressors and of promoting the general welfare of all the peoples of the earth—of every nation, regardless of the present state of development.

The second ray of hope, perhaps an even broader gleam of light, springs from the conference held at Rio de Janerio. That nineteen American nations there signed an agreement based upon the common desire to defend human rights against destructive aggression is something more than a sign: it is a tangible proof that the desire for unity of action to ensure the common good is both practical and possible. That two prominent nations of South America declined to join in the common purpose beyond doubt was due to subversive acts of tools of the Axis planted for precisely the purpose of defeating unity of action among the South American countries.[2] That their efforts were no more successful is proof of the soundness of judgment of the signatory nations.

These incidents, carefully examined for their deeper meaning, furnish an impressive example of what may be further

---

[2] Chile has since repudiated the Axis Powers.

"And all the nations shall flow unto it"

accomplished when nations are willing to agree upon a common plan of action even though such a plan may seem to restrict in some measure the soveignty of individual states, may even call for some degree of sacrifice in implementing the common pact. The benefits that may follow from the united action would far outweigh any loss of sovereignty. The possibilities for gain in moving toward the ultimate goal of lasting and just peace are immeasurable.

No argument is required to establish the generally accepted fact among Christian nations that success in establishing unity of action must stem from a righteous desire, that is, from the high purpose of improving the conditions of all humanity, of lifting all peoples out of the ruck of the mean and low—of bringing the underfed and underprivileged into the status of prosperity and well-being that is commonly envisaged as the ideal state. However long the way may seem, however arduous the tasks involved, whatever obstructions may seem to block the way, it is the avowed desire, deep-seated and persistent, of the United Nations to lift the lives of all the peoples of the earth into a higher, happier, even holier atmosphere.

This purpose was excellently and impressively set forth by President Roosevelt in his message to the Congress on January 8, 1942. "We of the United Nations," he declared, "are not making all the sacrifice of human effort and human lives to return to the kind of world we had after the last World War. We are fighting today for security and progress and for peace, not only for ourselves but for all men, not only for one generation but for all generations. We are fighting to cleanse the world of ancient evils, ancient ills."

For this avowed purpose thirty-one nations have signed a solemn pact to pursue their battle plan until victory makes possible the establishment of the conditions that the President so resolutely set forth. It is a noble purpose, nobly conceived, and, it is fondly hoped, to be nobly achieved. The permanence of the results will be precisely in proportion to their recognition and acceptance of divine Authority as the foundation of all that is good, that is real and hence durable.

This plan makes it imperative that the nations flow together for laying the cornerstone of the structure of permanent peace; for gaining a mental state among the nations wherein the vision of the prophet will be brought into realization, when literally they shall beat their swords into plowshares and their spears into pruning hooks—manifestly a mental state from which the war psychosis shall have been wholly extirpated. It is for the achievement of this state that the thirty-one nations signed their solemn pact; it is for this state that all Christians earnestly pray.

How to bring this vital hope into realization, how to make actual all its promises, is the problem that looms so impressively upon the mental horizon today, even in the midst of a terrific struggle. The method may not at present be foretold. How is the splendid idealism of the President's words to be brought into human experience? That is the persistent question. The term chosen to characterize the concerted efforts of the signatory powers was a most felicitous one. "United Nations" bespeaks an element of prophecy that should not be overlooked. It foretells a hope to be made actual. But the question persists: On what basis can the nations unite in a common agreement that will eliminate the possibility of future destructive warfare that would threaten the very foundation of civilization?

Thoughtful persons, looking backward over the period of the last war and measuring the terrific cost of the present struggle in lives and treasure, in misery and suffering, are becoming convinced that the repetition of this holocaust every generation would devastate society, would turn back beyond recovery the upsurge of the influence that makes for social betterment. It is this firmly held conviction that is emphasizing the inescapable necessity of discovering some formula for concerted action that will place the winning of the peace beyond

"And all the nations shall flow unto it"

the pale of doubtful eventuality. So imperative is the need, that there must be no failure, no element of doubt. The situation has developed far beyond the status of theory. The world is faced with a stark, mandatory necessity. The situation is far too complex—too broad, deep, and involved—to be settled out of hand through any mere human planning. The welfare of humanity is at stake. The solution will be found only by invoking all the wisdom available to the leaders of the nations who seek inspiration and guidance from on High; who have learned that righteousness and justice, goodness and mercy, and selfless love for humanity must be the important and perpetual factors in the foundation upon which this Temple of Peace is to be reared.

The failure to preserve international unity in solving the problems of humanity but emphasizes the need to return to the fundamental truths, iterated and reiterated by the Great Teacher: the Fatherhood of God and the brotherhood of man. But these fundamentals must be translated into the present situation to meet the need of the hour. First of all is the need to agree upon a common purpose. This has in broad terms been set forth in the Atlantic Charter and in declarations by President Roosevelt and Prime Minister Churchill. Now remains the taking of such steps as will make practical these noble utterances.

Careful survey of the history of the League of Nations reveals its weakness. Conditions that obviated its functioning to the possibilities of accomplishment envisioned by the founders are uncovered. That some form of union is imperative is beyond doubt. The precise form is yet to be determined. Righteous and consecrated prayer will reveal the best, because the most practical, plan. That the task is enormous, all can see. To bring together peoples so far apart in cultural status, social history, tradition, religious concepts, and economic disparity— to bring peoples of such divergent conditions into a unified

"And all the nations shall flow unto it"

whole is certainly a task to challenge the best in wisdom and practicability that may be won from seeking divine guidance.

Certain conditions to be dealt with are obvious. No nation can expect to win support of lesser privileged peoples except by the utmost degree of genuine friendliness, by manifesting as its paramount purpose the welfare of all: to lift the backward peoples gently upward to a state where self-government is both possible and practical.

The mistake of putting suffrage into the hands of those wholly unprepared to use it has had sad exemplification in the United States. The Negroes, held in slavery, and accordingly wholly devoid of political consciousness, were at one stroke given the same privileges of participation in the choice of administrative officers as the mature and politically wise citizen. It followed that these people, innocent of the meaning of Democracy, became the tools of designing politicians. The result was one of the darkest pages ever written in the history of the Republic. Not only was it a gross injustice to the citizens of the Southern States, but it worked equal injustice on the Negroes themselves, for it stimulated a false sense of government and the view that suffrage was something of little value, to be bought and sold for a mere pittance. Furthermore, it advanced them automatically to a position which they had not mentally attained. In this was an injustice, since it laid them open to the machinations of evil men.

National smugness is no more defensible than personal snobbishness. The individual who does much talking, professing lofty principles that he does not exemplify in daily conduct, soon becomes known as a hypocrite. He fails to impress his neighbors with either his sincerity or his fundamental honesty. The best proof of his sincerity as a Christian lies in his daily contact with his neighbors. Not by his words, but by his works is he known. Works are far more eloquent than words.

If Jesus had not buttressed his precepts by his works of mercy,

"And all the nations shall flow unto it"

it is doubtful if he would have been recognized as the Messiah, the Christ, come to show humanity the way out of its self-imposed labyrinth of material falsities. Emerson voiced the same truth when he declared that he could not hear what you say, your works speak so loudly.

This applies to the situation in the world today, to the wilderness of pain and sorrow out of which a way is sought. To be of help to the lesser privileged peoples, the nations more advanced, large and small, must not only take to them words of peace and comfort, but they must by their attitudes, their genuine interest, show their purpose to be of service in the way of Christian brotherhood. This implies practical means of succor. For any nation to assume a position of superiority and smugness would be fatal to the declared purpose to unite all men in a Grand Unity. The farther advanced any people as a nation has become in terms of wealth, culture, education, and material prosperity, the greater its obligations to the lesser privileged.

The individual who hopes to impress his fellows with the blessing of Christian living is under great obligation to purify his own life, to rise above the sense of self-interest, to demonstrate love for his neighbor, and to justify the spiritual status to which he claims to have attained. Precisely similar are the obligations of the nations that are to take leading parts in the reconstruction of the social order. Pretense, sham, words more than works, will characterize the establishment of a very transitory peace. The antidote is the Golden Rule in its many implications.

Moreover, the process of preparation for the great work ahead necessitates the examination by each nation of its own domestic situation. Are its internal conditions such as would impress the lesser groups with a full faith that Democracy is the very best form of government? That under its banner all are equally privileged, all have the same opportunity for self-expression; that all are enjoying the Four Freedoms that have been so appealingly set forth in recent months? Are we in the United States in a position to take the role of leadership in world reconstruction when within our own borders there are very serious social problems awaiting solution; when so large a proportion of the population is sadly underprivileged, underfed, underhoused, underclothed, and with but meager education facilities?

At the convention of representatives of the Protestants of America, called in March, 1942 by the Federal Council of Churches of Christ in America, Bishop Francis McConnell in the opening address set forth the situation admirably. He told of a friend of his, a professor of economics in a well-known university, who had expressed to him the purpose to write a volume on the success of Democracy in the U. S. A. On meeting the professor some months later, the Bishop had inquired as to the progress of the volume. The friend sadly explained that he had abandoned his purpose. When he came to the Negro problem as it now stands, he could not honestly continue to set forth to the world the United States as an outstanding example of the workings of true Democracy. In his sincerity he could not present as a successful form of government a Democracy in which existed a situation so unjust, so unsolved, as the Negro problem presents in the United States today.

To say that it is unsolvable is a counsel of despair. To say what is the solution is a precarious proposition unless it be placed squarely upon the perfect religious foundation, the Fatherhood of God and the consequent brotherhood of man. And this solution calls for an exhibition of patience, of the true Christian spirit of tolerance, nothing short of that displayed by the Nazarene himself. The Apostle to the Gentiles was convinced of the primary unity of the nations: God "hath made of one blood all nations of men for to dwell on all the face of the earth, and hath determined . . . the bounds of their habitation." [3]

It is wholly impractical to declare that all are created physically equal, are equally endowed with mental and spiritual qualities. Equality is actual, is true, only of God's children, His spiritual children, of whom it may be truly and fearlessly declared that they are equal. In that true and already perfected brotherhood are no inferior races; hence there is no racial inequality, no race problem. All are bound together in one grand brotherhood, governed by the divine Intelligence, the God who is unchanging Love. That is the situation in the Kingdom of God as presented by Christ Jesus.

How and in what measure may this fact be made practical in the formulation of the New World Order? At most, the actual can be only approximated in the material universe. But that approximation, if properly sought and in the highest degree attained, will bring many of the blessings of the true Kingdom into human experience. The method and the manner are the chief concern of the United Nations whose high purpose has been so enthusiastically proclaimed.

The Negro problem will never be solved by clinging to the tradition of social equality as is so often proclaimed among mistaken friends of the colored race. There can be no attainment of social equality through a mere declaration or proclamation. Racial equality can be gained only through adoption and pursuit of the means required for attaining it: education, cultural pursuits, spiritual unfoldment that rises above the emotional into stabilized knowledge of reality—by such means this same underprivileged colored race will be elevated to a position mentally and spiritually comparable with that of the white race.

That this suggestion is a practical possibility is evidenced by the eminence gained by Negro men and women in various walks

---

[3] Acts 17:26.

of life. If these accomplishments have been gained by a few, they are within the possibility of attainment by many more. And as these outstanding personalities devote themselves to raising the level of their own race, progress will be both rapid and substantial. There need not be, there is not, a condition of racial inferiority once the problem is lifted out of the realm of biology into the spiritual atmosphere of true brotherhood. That all of God's children are created equal and so known in the sight of the one Father is a sublime fact that points the way to the only right solution of the so-called race problem. The dignity of the individual cannot be impaired.

Let it be repeated, true Democracy may not be exemplified in a nation that tolerates within its citizenry a substantial proportion of its population held in bonds of poverty, fear, despair. That nation's bounden duty is fearlessly to undertake to solve the problem of the underprivileged citizen on the Christian basis. It is not a one-sided situation. The need for the Negro to remain within his own social status, there to bend his efforts to the demonstration of the true status of man, is his necessity. The path upward will be precipitous so long as there is claimed what has not been attained. Contentment within his own group, there to assist in working out the salvation of his own race, will go far toward the solution of the problem.

Meantime the privileged nations, those that have attained more through many generations, have an inescapable obligation to aid the humbler peoples in their journey toward the light of an abundant life. Helping toward educational facilities, to better conditions of nutrition, sanitation, and housing, to a clearer concept of the rights and duties of citizenship—all these are particulars in which the white race may reasonably assist the black race in the United States.

The problem is urgent. It requires much healing of prejudice on the part of both white and colored, much laying off of bitterness engendered through the decades since the close of the War between the States. The whites of the South who live in close contact with the Negroes are certain that the people of the North know little or nothing of the problem or of the means of its solution. The Northerner is equally certain that the white Southerner has a mistaken concept of the race and of the course to be pursued in order truly to emancipate the colored race.

Both are wrong insofar as the solution is sought in any merely human planning based upon alleged biological disparity. The only solution is in the approximation in the most practical manner of the true status of man. To force an idealism that has not been attained in social relationship would be to court disaster—to accentuate existing difficulties. Better physical surroundings will go far to develop a better type of citizenry, one that in the long siege ahead will become self-supporting and self-respecting because of hard-won attainments. No nation is free from such problems: they vary in the same proportion as the lesser-privileged population to the entire population.

Another phase of the same problem lies in the colonial populations formerly held under imperial control by the larger and more prosperous nations. What shall be done with them will be a major question to be solved in the New World Order. Obviously, if the Churches insist that the sentiment of the Golden Rule shall prevail, a practical means must be developed of lifting these teeming millions above the status of semi-serfdom into a self-respecting body looking toward the day of both economic and political freedom.

Here is demanded a definite and radical change of policy. The stronger nations have too long held these peoples, regarded as inferior, in a kind of bondage that is not to be tolerated in a genuinely Christian New World Order. Exploitation of simple peoples for the aggrandizement of the white race is outmoded. Imperialism must go. Its repercussion upon the white race is in itself a deleterious incubus: its effect upon the

"And all the nations shall flow unto it"

exploited is to perpetuate a status of existence far below the normal level to which all are entitled. Only a revolution in policy will meet the new requirements.

The effect of the imperialistic policy upon the exploited had impressive illustration in the campaign in Malaya when the Japanese overran the peninsula. The natives showed little if any interest in the defense offered by the British, displaying a mental state indicative of a lack of understanding of the meaning of freedom either in government or in way of life. They had lived, as had their forebears, in a state of servitude, taking what was proffered, listlessly submissive to economic conditions far below the normal level of the white race.

What to do with the colonies in the New World Order is a problem that will require prayerful and persistent attention upon the part of the nations undertaking to establish lasting peace. The vast territory involved, much of it with a native population numbered in the millions, gives some idea of its importance. How are these primitive races to be reached and lifted into a state of economic well-being that shall make possible their elevation to a cultural standard comparable to that which the white race believes it has attained?

Surely the problem, though vast, is not impossible of solution. Nothing of good is beyond demonstration through the utilization of the divine All-power available through the Christ, the Comforter, "the Spirit of truth." Surely it would be unchristian and an acknowledgment of defeat to assume that any situation is beyond the reach of this beneficent God, everpresent and ever available.

The crux of the situation is in the approach that will be of most benefit to the peoples in need. How best may Truth be applied? It cannot be done through compulsion. Peoples cannot be forced up the ladder of Christian progress. Rather must they be led, inspired, and convinced that the purpose of their benefactors is to render genuine aid rather than to exploit them for either personal or communal profit. Too long

[194]

"And all the nations shall flow unto it"

has the profit motive characterized the attitude and purpose of the dominant nations toward the unlettered peoples of the world. A Christian motive has no part whatever in such exploitation.

Certain lessons may be learned from the experiences of the mandated territories under the authority of the League of Nations. In some instances, the results were good—excellent, in fact. Despite the trouble that arose between Jew and Arab in Palestine, a situation not yet solved, it cannot be claimed that England's influence there was not beneficial and worthy of a Christian nation. Japan's experiences with the islands placed in her care in the South Pacific were, on the contrary, far from happy for the native population. And, as is well known, wholly contrary to the spirit of the mandate, Japan treacherously carried out a policy of preparing military and naval bases for the war that the military party of the Empire had long foreseen and for which they had long been planning. But this, however, should not be regarded as a fair example of the general results of the mandate policy.

Enough has been learned, it seems, to justify the conclusion that the policy of mandates is not adapted to the primary purpose of improving the native populations, regardless of national benefits to be gained by those nations accepting the mandate. It seems inevitable that the nations that assume the responsibility of establishing the New World Order on a Christian basis shall provide for joint action, the purpose of which shall be service to the peoples involved, a genuine effort to extend the hand of fellowship in improving their living conditions, bringing to them, as rapidly as they are prepared to receive them, the benefits of civilization that have been gained through the centuries by the white race.

When this fundamental purpose is accepted, the way will open for the right steps to be taken. Righteous prayer is a most potent means of securing right direction when the desire is for true service to those less privileged. Divine Love will

"And all the nations shall flow unto it"

guide and direct in answer to the Christian's earnest prayer.

That native populations will respond to the right approach has exemplification in the Philippine Islands, however much remains to be done in order to reach an ideal situation there. It cannot be denied that progress was made in bringing to a submerged native population an improved way of life, approaching in some degree the Christian ideal. The motive established by the Government of the United States was a good one, to prepare the native population for either citizenship in the Republic or self-government.

It is to be regretted that private commercial interests, encouraged by the profit to be made from exploiting native labor in the production of useful crops, entered so largely. The soil and climate were so well adapted to the raising of tropical products that great profits were made. These interests were entered upon by citizens of the United States to such a degree that the welfare of the natives became of little importance in the sight of the exploiters.

Yet that a gleam of hope for greater political freedom and final self-government inspired a large section of the population was proved in the gallant defense made by the native soldiers at Manila and Bataan. It is the hope for independence, the longing for better opportunity to work out individual salvation, that inspires and strengthens the willingness to sacrifice even the material sense of life for the prospect of the fuller life for oneself and for posterity. The upward surge in the human heart of the love for better living is a force to be stirred through Christianly treatment of the underprivileged races.

Health, better economic conditions, education, and, most of all, the introduction of the spirit of Christianity—these are the purposes that must be introduced by such means as will unfold to the leaders in the all-important work ahead. The one fundamental purpose, however, must be the desire to serve those in need regardless of returning profit. To secure the welfare of

"And all the nations shall flow unto it"

all is the object to be attained, for only as all the peoples are raised to a comparable degree of culture will the brotherhood be established.

No longer may the brown, and black, and yellow races be regarded as the means for gaining material wealth by individual groups or nations, for such prosperity is more detrimental to those who win it unjustly than to those who are the victims of the process.

I shall long remember the native workmen on rubber plantations in Ceylon. While living only a dozen miles from Colombo, yet I was informed that not many of these forest dwellers had ever ventured even that far from their native huts. In the harbor of Hong Kong, the many boats, taxi-carriers for the traffic of the ships, were the homes of the families of the workers and from which they seldom if ever departed. These are but solitary examples of the conditions that are to be improved through the introduction of the policies springing from the conviction that only as the true brotherhood is established will permanent peace be won.

A situation is not stable in which a large part of the world's population are submerged in the darkness of ignorance and, because of that submergence, become the victims of designing men and nations. It is precisely these types of injustice that have been prominent factors in bringing to the world the frightful situation known as "global war." The situation should be squarely faced and the answer found in justice, Christianly founded.

If individual self-interest is no longer to be paramount in the affairs of a country or state, surely there is even less reason for its continuance in international relations, when the interest at stake is so much more vital to society. To be sure, these improved motives and means must take root in the smaller groups before they can be utilized in the solution of larger problems. Society is a unit to which must be applied uniform principles of justice and righteousness. What is right and just in California is equally just and right in Ceylon, in central Africa, and in Iceland. For right is a universal quality of the Infinite One, and all have the same privilege to its service, as all who have the consciousness of right have the obligation to share it with their fellowmen.

The utterly false doctrine that might is right has precipitated the present conflict. The Allied Nations are defending at whatever cost the exactly opposite view, that the only right is that which stems from divine justice translated into terms of human experience. And this right includes the Four Freedoms that President Roosevelt so eloquently stated, the right of free speech, the right of worship, freedom from want, and freedom from fear.

XVIII

Good Neighbors

MANY steps are being taken by the government of the United States to cement friendships with the Latin nations to the south. Sums aggregating more than a half-billion dollars have been voted for relief of these countries. In the various conferences held during the last two decades, much has been done to allay suspicions as to the genuineness of the friendly gestures made by the Great Republic of the North. The Pan-American Union is an excellent example of a practical effort to bring peoples of widely divergent races, religions, traditions, and culture together on a common platform of good will. Much more awaits the doing.

All available methods for disseminating the truth should be authorized in order to inform each nation of the best in the cultural and social aspirations and accomplishments of the others. It is a two-way need. The United States needs to learn more of the peoples to the south, to learn intimately of their hopes, desires, aims, purposes, and accomplishments in the development of a Christian social order. This relationship should include exchange of information regarding educational methods and practices and industrial, financial, agricultural, and commercial accomplishments. All this makes for the understanding that leads to lasting friendships. Let the purpose of the United States be to convince her neighbors that the day of exploitation has passed, and that co-operation for mutual welfare is the new order of the day. Neither ignorance nor a patronizing attitude will aid in this effort. Conviction gained

Good Neighbors

by each people concerned that the others are acting in good faith is the platform of success in establishing the status of good neighbors.

Already the interchange of educational and cultural groups is having a salutary effect. In his latest book on South America,[1] Hubert C. Herring proposes that Henry Ford, after the example of Cecil Rhodes, establish a fund to make possible the exchange of students between North and South America. This proposal, judging by the issues of the Rhodes experiment, has great merit. It is proved a practical means of giving that understanding which lessens the chances of enmity, suspicion, and envy to build a wall of separation. The stake is very great. The means are at hand for winning an important bulwark in the grand battle for global amity.

In all efforts toward the winning of a just and lasting peace, it must not be overlooked that the Temple of Peace must be built upon the only firm foundation, the Fatherhood of God and the brotherhood of man. Any other basis will be found to be but shifting sand, which, assailed by the winds and waves of mortal desire, of human selfishness, will, as has ever happened in the past, crumble and fall. For the status of durable peace to be attained, peace must be the goal of human desire. The belief that war is inevitable, that for biological reasons peoples will forever be arrayed against each other in deadly combat, is a counsel of despair. War is no more inevitable than any other form of evil. Education, the desire to serve the lesser privileged, is the way to peace. Peace is gained only as it is desired. Since it is a mental state from which the seeds of strife, selfishness, and lust for power and prestige have been extirpated, it is to be attained through right mental discipline. The Golden Rule is as applicable to national policy as to individual conduct. The principle involved is the same.

---

[1] *Good Neighbors,* Yale University Press.

Good Neighbors

Government of a Democracy is but an aggregation of duly elected officials, acting to express the will of the electorate. It is and should be answerable to the people. Therefore, it follows that the right purpose, the right desire, regarding government must be developed in the minds of the individual electors. There is the beginning of righteous government, the kind that purposes to be a good neighbor. If the electorate is not educated to this point, the country is not ready either for successful self-government or to take part in a unity of all the Nations.

A policy has developed in the Western Hemisphere that partakes of the very essence of the spirit of world unity. Under the promising title of the Good Neighbor, the Administration of the Government of the United States has taken important steps to bring a practical plan into actuality in the affairs of the American nations. In fact, the effort of the United States to promote amity, to engender a greater degree of friendliness and unity, among the nations of the Americas has become a major feature of international policy. The effort is far-reaching in its implications and, if proved to be a successful policy, will become an impressive example before all the nations of earth of the possibility of unity of action in serving one another whereby all the peoples of the earth will be blessed.

Any proposition for unity and more intimate relationship between nations must have its basis in an honest purpose looking to the betterment of all involved, especially of those thought to be somewhat lower on the ladder of culture and civilization. The desire to help the lesser privileged, if honestly conceived and earnestly held, will strengthen also the more advanced nations philanthropically inclined. The Big Brother attitude, however, has within it elements of danger to a noble purpose. If it springs merely from a sense of generosity and if it smacks in the least degree of patronage, it is handicapped in its very beginnings. Accordingly, a first step is to take all possible means to ensure the recipient of the good graces of the well-

Good Neighbors

intentioned nation, that its purpose is good, is in fact a Christianly effort to help in the upward course to which every nation is rightly committed.

A fair question is, What does it mean to be a Good Neighbor? There is obviously a definite analogy between the personal relationship of individuals living in a neighborhood in close or remote proximity and international relationships that have given rise to the "good neighbor" policy. A pertinent symbolism may be drawn from Robert Frost's familiar poem, "Mending Walls." Neighbors with a common stone wall separating their properties, each spring "walk the wall" to replace stones thrown down, perchance, by the frosts of winter. Each walker replaces the stones fallen on his side, with the result that the wall is restored to its original effectiveness as a sturdy partition dividing the properties. And the poet draws the conclusion that the wall is really not needed, evidence being that some unseen force is constantly operating to throw it down.

Here is drawn in homely phrase an important lesson concerning the interrelation of nations. There is in reality, that is, in the ideal conditions to which nations are striving to attain, no need for barriers to separate peoples and nations. "Something there is that does not love a wall" and that "something" is the spirit of brotherhood forever operating to unite men into one grand brotherhood. It is the Comforter promised by Christ Jesus, "the Spirit of truth," which, under the Fatherhood of God, inevitably tends to unite all mankind in a spiritual unity or brotherhood on earth that patterns the divine. This is the basis of true relationship between neighbors, no less of nations than of the residents of a community.

It will be recalled that at the close of the first great war, President Wilson, in Europe to aid in establishing a just peace, addressed a vast audience in the famous Old Guildhall in London. The subject of the address was the unity of nations

[202]

Good Neighbors

through better understanding, more intimate knowledge, each of the other. To illustrate the point, he recalled a statement from Charles Lamb. When one evening, in a party of gentlemen, the name of a man not present was mentioned, Lamb haltingly blurted out, "I hate that man." To the query, "Do you know him?" came the retort, "No, I don't. If I did, I couldn't hate him." In this statement lies a truth fundamental in human nature. It emphasizes the pressing need for the nations to become better acquainted with one another.

The Good Neighbor policy, to become successful in establishing international amity, must be based upon knowledge by each of the hopes, aims, racial habits, traditions, and inherent ambitions of all the others. Also fundamental to any degree of success in promoting this condition must be mutual confidence in the integrity and reliability of governments. It could have been said formerly with assurance that primarily nations and peoples have common aims that are worthy and, in a measure at least, righteous. This, however, more's the pity, now needs modification, for it no longer describes the attitude and purpose of certain great nations, great in numbers but plainly devoid of the qualities which make for greatness in nations no less than in individuals. But notwithstanding the moral madness, springing from false idealism, that has plunged the whole world into a mighty struggle for supremacy, there still exists in the basic purpose and aims of many, even most, nations a keen desire to live at peace and on terms of amity with all the rest of the world. There is more than a modicum of this desire operative in the halls of state.

There are also, however, conditions, common in some measure to all nations, that constitute a barrier, a wall of separation, as it were, between nations and peoples. The analogy of the good neighbor in a community has another side—the bad neighbor, the person who acts only or primarily from selfish motives, who falls short of fulfilling the criterion of good neighborliness. It is the generous, unselfish person, one who seeks and finds enjoyment in helping another, who best subserves his community —not afraid to be kind, seeking the opportunity to meet a neighbor's need, seeing his brother's misfortune and helping to allay it: this is basic in good neighborliness.

This is fulfillment, practically at least, of the spirit of the Good Samaritan. It helps another without surveying the probability of immediate reward accruing to oneself. It is the mental attitude that is rewarded in the satisfaction derived from helping another. It is wholly logical that the same spirit of good will, because it is universal and without limit, that promotes neighborliness and friendly aid in the community should have practical application in national relationships. This spirit flows from an inexhaustible fountain in streams copious enough to meet the needs of great peoples no less than of individuals.

Those not informed of the motives that conceived and gave impulsion to the Good Neighbor policy adopted by the United States and carried out for several years in order to promote unity among the nations of the Americas, are suspicious of the sincerity behind it. It has been increasingly patent that for the Western World to continue in peace and increase in prosperity, to bring to its peoples of various races the opportunities for progress to which they are entitled, there must be established an era of good will based upon mutually better understanding. Genuine love for humanity must supplement purely selfish aims.

Looking back over the history of a generation, one finds unmistakable evidence of deeds done by the Great Republic of the North that have brought questioning and distrust on the part of the lesser nations. These same smaller nations are, however, being gradually convinced that this desire to promote good will is not now motivated by a selfish purpose. Yet the questions, Is this sentiment genuine? and Can we trust her to

Good Neighbors

become the leader of the Americas? are still in some measure unanswered.

The situation is crystal clear. The Latin American countries must be convinced that the desire to help is genuine; that the United States is honestly and earnestly desirous of promoting the well-being of its neighbors; that there is no underlying purpose of promoting the exploitation of the vast natural resources of the countries to the south for the benefit of northern capitalists; that there is in the national policy of the U. S. A. no imperialistic motive—no desire to add to her own territorial holdings or *to dominate* those of less potential powers.

That there is an awareness on the part of the Administration of some lingering measure of doubt among our neighbors is beyond question. Argentina and Chile have openly manifested this in their reluctance to join the general pact of the American republics. The influence of Axis agents harbored in these countries beyond doubt accounts for this position of noncooperation.

Argentina is also convinced that she has had good reason to doubt the sincerity of her Northern neighbor. The long-discussed question of admitting Argentine beef into the United States was one source of her grave doubt. It seemed an extremely selfish policy that kept her chief product from entrance, when in turn she was in great need of the manufactures that the United States was so abundantly producing. It is beyond question that the cattle-raising interests of the United States were able through a bloc in the Congress to secure legislation shutting out the importation of Argentine beef, and that the reason given—danger of introducing a serious cattle disease—was probably a trumped-up reason for bad legislation.

The people of the Argentine, among the most successful cattlemen in the world, deeply resented this imputation. The exigencies of war have brought about a somewhat modified policy on the part of the United States. But the situation is far from composed. It illustrates in a practical way that it is the issues engendered largely by selfish reasons that keep nations apart—that in a definite measure defeat a Good Neighbor policy. The only remedy is for the people to rise above mere personal gain into the great purpose of promoting brotherhood.

It is a cause for gratitude, however, that the good-will policy inaugurated during the administration of President Coolidge and carried on by President Hoover has been given increased impetus by the present administration. In this policy may be found a suggestion of the method of promoting unity of all nations through a good-will policy. It is a beginning in the right direction. Its success will be measured by the degree of its adherence in the future to the Golden Rule and to the firm purpose to establish God's Kingdom on earth.

It may not be asserted that the purposes of the Good Neighbor policy have been wholly outside the role of self-interest. To protect the American Continent from invasion in its entirety has had some place in the policy adopted. The Monroe Doctrine is still a lively stone in the foundation of American policy. To unite all the nations concerned in a pact of defense against invasion by a foreign power has become a pronounced factor in the situation. The need for such provision has been rendered startlingly apparent by the plan for world domination that underlies the Axis campaign. The unfortunate factor in the situation is that, in the case of Argentina at least, there seemed to be some grounds for complaint against the Great Republic of the North.

The success of any league or confederation of nations depends upon the preparedness of the constituent members to carry out the purposes for which the union is created. If the individual nations hold to selfish aims, still primarily seek individual gain or aggrandizement in any direction except that which will accrue from the fact of unity itself, they are scarcely prepared for united action. The necessity then is for each member nation to prepare mentally for the unity of action that alone will make a success of the enterprise. And this preparation must include the willingness to surrender something of the national sovereignty that has been developed through its political history.

This willingness, in itself, is not easy of attainment. People are proud of their nationalism. Their hard-won freedom, merging into self-government, the many internal battles fought and won over the obstructing forces of evil, the consciousness of cultural attainments, all these make for national pride. To surrender to a super-government any vestige of this attainment is a serious matter.

No better illustration of the struggle involved, or of the successful outcome of such struggle, can be cited than in the union of sovereign states into the United States of America. Here, as we have seen, were Thirteen Colonies of widely divergent background—racial, historical, religious, and cultural—each proud of its own accomplishments, united in a formal and closely knit union, with an over-all government that should administer such affairs as pertain to the common welfare. Thus arose a great Republic, a sovereign state, that has survived many storms, has risen measurably to the mental and spiritual heights where, in notable instances, it has reached out the hand of genuine friendship to suffering, benighted people held under the cruel administration of selfish and rapacious governments.

However, although selfishness, the arch-enemy to true brotherhood, has often crept into its policies, it cannot be denied that the purpose to succor and save, to help less privileged peoples up the ladder of freedom and progress, has been an important item in the policy of this government. The injustices that have crept in have resulted in major degree from the greed of corporations and individuals actuated by no motive higher than material gain, even when wrested from a primitive and underprivileged people.

Noble as the aspiration was that prompted the policy toward

Good Neighbors

Porto Rico and the Philippines, it has in a measure been constricted and sometimes defeated by the devastating greed of individuals and favored groups. Yet provision was made in both instances for ultimate freedom, when the people had attained to the status of political consciousness that promised successful self-government. It would be far from Christianly to turn loose a people politically unprepared to govern themselves. Exploitation and self-seeking are always at hand, waiting like hungry vultures watching from the tree tops for weak victims to be pounced upon and utilized to their own purposes. That this was in a degree true in the Philippines is all too patent in the light of recent events. A weak and vacillating policy always pays for its weakness and indecision. If the judgment of those best informed as to the long-held purposes of Japan had been accepted and followed, a sad page in American history might not have been written.

It seems a long way to bring Japan to a realization of the wrongness of her position, the treachery of her attack, the cruelty manifested in her war methods. Viewed by Christian standards, Japan for the most part is a pagan nation, actuated by self-interest, with a national consciousness based upon racial and religious tradition. That she has come to regard herself as a major nation was given support by America and Great Britain in the naval ratio agreed upon. Five-five-three was adjudged justifiably to represent the relative sea strength of these nations. This recognition naturally supported the sense of importance held by the Japanese war party.

That Japan felt deeply her limitation of territory became manifest in her seizure successively of Formosa, Korea, and Manchuria, and in her attempt to overrun China. In Japan in the spring of 1932, I was frankly told that while the other great nations had been seizing the territory they desired for exploitation, Japan had been laggard, but that the war party then gaining in power in the government was determined to right this mistaken policy. Subsequent events have fully proved the accuracy of this assertion and the ability of Japan to acquire temporarily, at least, what she was determined to have.

It should not be concluded, however, that the Japanese people are a unit in the present war policy for the moment completely dominant. There is among her citizens a considerable group, many of whom have accepted the Christian way of life, who woefully deprecate the present situation. They are, however, overridden and voiceless for the moment. This group may become the active leaders of the movement to bring the country back to a position of sanity after she has been conquered in the great struggle. Ambassador Grew gives no hope of winning her back to that position except through a complete victory over her forces at arms. To judge from the present situation, the way will be long and arduous.

The position of America toward Japan has often been far from wise. Grievous mistakes have been made, mistakes that less stubborn administrations could have well avoided. The amity early established between the two countries following the friendly visit of Commodore Perry was intensified by the establishment of commercial relations to the mutual advantage of both countries.

Many Japanese scholars came to America and Europe for the education offered in the best-known universities. There was an awakening among the Nipponese to the conviction that their interests would be most rapidly advanced by ostensibly, at least, taking on Western culture. This conviction led to action. The relationship between the countries became more intimate. Many Americans became deeply interested in the ancient culture of the Nipponese. Japanese immigrants swarmed to American shores. So many came that the inhabitants of the West Coast justifiably raised a loud voice in protest.

The newcomers, accustomed to a much lower standard of life, brought a problem of competition with American laborers, shopkeepers, and, especially, the agriculturists and horticulturists, which became very heavy. National legislation was demanded, but without avail. Then the State of California, convinced of the dangers of this peaceful invasion, passed laws limiting the property privileges of the Japanese. This action rankled in the bosom of a proud and industrious people. A "gentleman's agreement" preserved the status quo but did not heal the wound. The poison of resentment still rankled. Yet America became by far Japan's best customer, purchasing a major part of her silk, toys, and gimcracks, in the making of which Japan developed marked skill.

This attitude of friendly relationship made no impression upon the Japan war lords. Nothing but complete domination of the western Pacific would satisfy their insensate ambition. They were bound to fight. Ten years before Pearl Harbor, I was told plainly in Yokohama that Japan would have to fight America. There seemed to be no other way in which to satisfy her growing sense of importance and of her ability to take what she wanted. There is no doubt that her experiences with weak China and the much more formidable Russian Bear had convinced the war party of her invincibility. That she was fully capable of getting what she went after was firmly planted in the mentality of the war party membership—and their strength was such as to overpower any peace motives. War became the policy of Japan. The Emperor was merely the rubber stamp of the war party.

The policy of the United States adopted by the Administration seemed both vacillating and weak. Division in the Congress regarding the whole Pacific situation did not strengthen the hands of the Administration: rather did it weaken it. The future of the Philippines became a football in Congress, buffeted about by opinion varying all the way from complete abandonment to the conviction that strong fortifications should be provided there and in the island groups important to their defense. A halfway policy was adopted. Compromise had its innings, with the result that a military force was developed at Manila, and several of the Pacific Islands thought to be important in a defense plan were partially but inadequately fortified against attack. When the storm broke, the weakness of this policy was appallingly apparent.

Meantime the Administration had done little to prevent the flow to Japan of oil and iron, the two basic objects in its preparation and prosecution of modern warfare. Against the earnest protest of hosts of citizens, trade in these essentials was allowed to function. The result! Many an American service man has lost his life from wounds inflicted by the materials sold to the enemy. Appeasement, as always, cost a very high price for a mistaken policy.

The Administration, be it said, was way out in front of Congress in its desire for better preparation to meet the storm so manifestly rising above the Western horizon. But appeasers, isolationists, were numerous enough to stay the hand of the Administration. And when finally the stream of commerce was gradually reduced, Japan had acquired a sufficient supply of necessary materials from her most favorable commercial neighbor to enable her to undertake a war of aggression second in magnitude only to that prosecuted by Hitler himself. Vacillation is no more a successful factor of Democratic government than is mild pusillanimity.

The sneers that the Dictator hurled at Democracy have had some measure of justification. Weakness on the part of the Democratic nations encouraged the tyrants step by step to conclude that Democracy is impotent, unable to maintain itself in opposition to authority that assumes entire command of its people. It is up to the Democratic nations now to disprove this calumny; to prove once for all time that the Democratic way of life, while loving peace and domesticity, yet when aroused in defense of its principles is unconquerable by any unholy aggression. Peace-loving nations, like the United States and England, do not make preparation for aggressive warfare their highest purpose. They fight only when attacked directly or when they see a conflict arising that threatens the very foundations of the Democratic way of life.

The national policy of Democracies has not in the past provided for the invention and construction of great war machines against the day when the invader would be at their borders. This policy seems to leave them in a precarious position when attacked by a ruthless foe. But the spirit of Democracy, of a people defending their greatest possession, the spirit of Free Peoples, will soon rise to meet the invader, and victory will ultimately perch on the banners of righteous purpose.

The difficulties arising from failure to maintain a military force adequate for immediate defense are somewhat balanced by freedom from the enormous expense necessary to maintain such forces. Now that the air force, a third arm, has been added to the war machine, the expense may be even greater. But many are contending that so efficient is the air force becoming that it alone, if properly maintained, would be equal to keeping the aggressor at bay. An aggressor nation on plunder bent will think twice before attacking strongly prepared countries backed by the inviolable and invincible spirit of free men.

In the peace to be won after the military victory, the Democracies of necessity will have a large part to play. Their success in this great enterprise will, as has been pointed out, depend in major degree upon the spirit in which the situation is approached. Pride of power, pride of material possession, pride of accomplishment, will but defeat its grand purpose. Only true humility, only the desire to extend the helping hand to those in distress, only a willingness to sacrifice whatever appears necessary for winning the peace and making secure the position of the smaller nations; only as these mental attitudes characterize the approach to the needs will there be a successful outcome to the world's most direful struggle. The devastated nations, stricken and stripped of manpower, populations scattered to the four winds, productive capacity transferred to Germany or completely destroyed, can do little toward rehabilitation without assistance. There will arise the need for the Good Neighbor. The Samaritan will find a most urgent demand for his services.

America, with her great facilities for recuperation from any loss to which she may be subjected, will be in better condition to help the stricken peoples than will any other nation. She will have suffered less under devastation. Even England, with her resources drained to an unprecedented degree, will need to conserve much of her resources for her own recovery. Yet her previous history encourages the belief that her traditional spirit of helpfulness, her deep Christianly desire to have part in the work of the Good Samaritan, will find ample means to instrument her desire to play her part in the work of improving the world situation. The type of relief work carried on so successfully by former President Hoover in Belgium after the last war will be in urgent demand, but multiplied by a large factor.

To the visualization, in some measure, of the extent and character of the work of rehabilitation—which will demand the earnest effort of every Christian impulse—and to the means of establishing a lasting peace, the Church is now giving its attention. The extent of this work is seen in the number of organizations in America and England that are taking it up as a "must" part of Christian ministry. And the determination that characterizes the purpose of the ecumenical movement to make impossible a repetition of the present calamity can scarcely fail to make a deep impression upon those who will have the tremendously important task of formulating the peace terms.

The mission of the Church is to impress these peacemakers with the inescapable necessity of building the structure upon the firm foundation of the Fatherhood of God and the brotherhood of man. Upon this base alone can a lasting and just structure be created. Human means have failed; else the present tragedy would not have been thrust upon the world. What more proof could be adduced that the old way of self-interest, national pride, and the spirit of imperialism have egregiously failed than the present condition of the world? There must be a better way, and that way is "the way of holiness." [2] It seems highly improbable that the victorious nations will be fully inspired by the Christ-spirit. It is likely that there will be at most only a gradual reception of the divine purpose, the Christ-Comforter. But the foundation stones must be laid in the cement of brotherly love and of righteous purpose.

Formidable difficulties will be encountered—no great purpose has escaped them. But nothing is unconquerable before the omnipotence of infinite Spirit, Father of all. All will agree that the desire for revenge must have no seat at the Peace Table. However great the temptation to punish in kind the atrocious crimes of the aggressors, the spirit of forgiveness is the only healing agency. To be sure, the guilty must be restrained, placed beyond the possibility of again using their influence for world domination at incalculable expenditure of human lives. The property loss, huge as it is, will not be weighed in the balance with the destruction of millions of noncombatants as well as of those directly engaged in the combat.

It will be the bounden duty of the peace formulators to provide for the establishment by the victorious nations of two arms of service—the one, as we have seen, a military power of whatever type deemed most effective such as an international police force to hold surveillance over the aggressor nations; the other an international Court of Justice before which the guilty may be brought for trial. This Court also should look to the

---

[2] Isa. 35:8.

Good Neighbors

international police power to enforce its decrees of every type. These two departments will be necessary adjuncts of an adequate peace plan. They represent a practical assessment of the means of enforcing the plans for permanent peace.

If the victorious nations immediately begin to jockey for individual advantages, the situation will be appalling. The lesson of true service will not have been learned. The way to the establishment of the Kingdom on earth will have been missed. The punishment suffered from the unprecedented conflict now sweeping over the world, terrible as it will be, will not have been adequate to enforce acceptance of the lesson of true brotherhood. The precepts of the Great Galilean will not have been accepted as the true Way of Life.

Such a situation is even more depressing to contemplate than the forcing upon society of the present conflict. For it would bring the inescapable conclusion that all the sacrifice had been in vain: that the world was not ready for establishment of a peace, lasting because righteous and just. The tragedy would have to be repeated over and over until the lesson of brotherhood had been learned. And doubt not that every succeeding tragedy would be more costly in lives and treasure than any that had gone before. The number of Lidices would be multiplied until the world had become bathed in the blood of selfishness and cruelty.

The contemplation of such a situation should so impress the peacemakers that the way of righteousness will be made the chief cornerstone of the Temple of Peace which they are to erect. The ancient prophet foresaw the succession of tragedies that humanity would undergo. But he saw a just God manifest in human affairs, who through His righteous prophet declared, "I will overturn, overturn, overturn, it: and it shall be no more, until he come whose right it is; and I will give it him." [3]

---

[3] Eze. 21:27.

Good Neighbors

The process of overturning has long been exemplified in the history of the nations. It will continue until the nations of earth unite to establish a Policy of Peace based upon divine power.

XIX

Peace and the Atlantic Charter

FOR a nation or a group of nations to persist in the prosecution of successful warfare, it becomes increasingly necessary for those in authority to declare their motives, to state in terms that may be understood by the masses the purposes that they are called upon to defend, the ideologies that they are fighting to promote. What are we fighting for? is an insistent cry. It was recognition of this fact that led President Roosevelt and Prime Minister Churchill to meet in August, 1941, and to draw up a statement of purposes of the nations opposed to the Axis now known as the Atlantic Charter. This statement is a broad declaration of the objects for which the Allied Nations were carrying on what was to become an all-out, or total, war.

In *The Christian Science Monitor* of August 14, 1942, Roscoe Drummond characterized this document thus: "The Atlantic Charter is a promissory note. There is a lot back of it but it still remains to be redeemed. The Atlantic Charter is expectation, not fulfillment; it is pledge, not performance; it is an earnest, not a guarantee, of things to come." And he defines the kind of peace it proposes as (1) affording "to all nations the means to live in peace and safety within their own borders," and (2) as assuring "to all peoples the opportunity to choose their own government and to live out their lives in freedom from fear and want."

Here are set forth noble aims with which all Christian peoples will agree and for the attainment of which all will pray. To understand the Charter, however—to grasp the meaning of what it promises and to discover what it lacks—it should be analyzed step by step. What did these eminent leaders of the two great Democracies declare? *First,* that their countries, that is, the United States and Great Britain, seek no aggrandizement, territorial or otherwise. In the light of the issues at stake, this was necessary. Their opponents, Germany, Italy, and Japan, both by declaration and, more convincingly, by their acts, were bent upon a campaign of plunder, of robbery, and of slaughter, the magnitude of which had never before been equaled. Their propaganda carried over the world had falsely and, it seems, maliciously, declared a purpose wholly contrary to the common welfare, wholly devoid of the faintest semblance of Christian motives. Their goal was an out-and-out purpose of plunder, piracy, and world domination. What they wanted they would take by the force of the war machine they had surreptitiously, but determinedly, built. To draw a clear distinction between this wholly cruel and unprincipled program, it became the bounden duty of the opponents to this unholy state to declare the position of the Allied Nations. They sought no new territory, and no privileges not accorded to all nations and peoples.

Such territorial changes as might follow the victory should be made in accord with the wishes of the peoples; that is, each ethnic group or groups of divergent races united for governmental purposes should have the right to choose and establish the type of government they desire without interference. This would exclude the possibility of a strong nation seizing territory by force and setting up puppet governments, as Japan has done in Korea, Manchuria, and China, and as she is doing elsewhere as fast as her conquests make such action possible.

The right of self-government is the essence of declarations *Two* and *Three.* There is no provision, however, whereby this is to be carried out. Each nation or people is free to adopt its own type of government, each in its own method or procedure.

The *Fourth* Article becomes more specific in that it makes definite promises as to what shall be the attitude of the two nations toward freedom of trade and access to the material resources of the world commonly termed "raw materials." It is so important as to justify quotation: "They will endeavor, with due respect for their existing obligations, to further the enjoyment by all States, great or small, victor or vanquished, of access, on equal terms, to the trade and to the raw materials of the world which are needed for their economic prosperity." Here is a Big Brother policy, broad in its scope and yet specific in its provisions. The welfare of their own nations, the U. S. A. and Great Britain, is not overlooked. Policies declared must not be inconsistent with the preservation of their own economic welfare. Surely a just provision. And the promise of equality extends not alone to the Allied Nations but even to those now undertaking to wrest from them both national sovereignty and economic prosperity. Obviously an outstanding example of magnanimity and Christianly brotherhood.

Wisdom, far-sighted and practical, is manifest in this phase of the declaration. It must be patent to all endowed with ability to look into the future that great peoples like Germany, Italy, and Japan cannot be reduced to poverty and ineptitude without repercussions upon the whole world. So closely interrelated have the nations become, so dependent for their welfare each upon the others, that a poverty-stricken people retards the progress of all. Material prosperity is a condition necessary to the common welfare of nations no less than within the national boundaries.

That lack of territory for expansion of population, "Lebensraum," as the Germans term it, no less than the right and ability to acquire such of the raw materials as were deemed necessary to the industrial welfare of a people, had beyond question much to do in the development of the war psychosis that plunged Germany into her career of plunder and sanguinariness. That this situation is realized to the extent of including it in this Declaration of Principles is a most hopeful sign. It indicates an awakening to the obligations devolving upon the "have" nations to share their natural resources with peoples less blessed.

The *Fifth* Article is likewise important and far-reaching. It declares, "They desire to bring about the fullest collaboration between all nations in the economic field with the object of securing, for all, improved labor standards, economic adjustment, and social security." The fullest collaboration between nations, obviously, can be secured only through some sort of international unity, some form of organization that makes such collaboration possible and practical. The mere statement does not provide the machinery for such unity. The desire must have motivation to become in any degree useful. The recognition of this necessity foretells an effort for the formation of some type of interrelation that will provide for the mutual consideration and aid necessary to the common welfare.

The larger aspect of these declarations lies in the recognition that no nation or people can live to itself alone; that there is a bond, an obligation, on the part of each to co-operate for the welfare of all. This recognition in itself is a long step away from the national self-interest and smugness that have all too long characterized the Great Powers. These signs, it seems, pertain only to material prosperity and well-being, yet they stem from an awakening to the Christianly need, recognition and application of which constitute the only path to permanent peace. It is a most encouraging sign of the times. It is only a sign, however; for all these promises, both stated and implied, are to be incorporated in national policies and then carried into the realm of practice.

The *Sixth* Article is general but impressive. After the Nazi

Peace and the Atlantic Charter

threat is removed, that is, after victory is won by the Allied Nations, they hope to see established "a peace which will afford to all nations the means of dwelling in safety within their own boundaries and which will afford assurance that all men in all the lands may live out their lives in freedom from fear and want." A brave hope, and a worthy one. All persons of brotherly instincts would fully subscribe to such a hope. Recent events have instilled in the lesser nations an intense fear of losing all semblance of national sovereignty, all hope of independent existence and of right to self-determination. None can doubt the justice of such a desire; none can wonder at the rising fear, in the light of recent events. For the great Democracies to declare so prominently their purposes in this direction inspires hope among the fearful. But it scarcely needs explication that to state the need is far from its accomplishment.

Again, it becomes apparent that there must be established some type of organization of nations that will bring this hope into actuality, and that there must be provided some organized force to see that the common desire is not again overwhelmed by a belligerent and cruel nation. Even the most ardent advocate of Christianly forbearance can scarcely deny the necessity of enforcing the means of protection. As a police force in every community is a necessity to ensure local order, so in the international community its duplicate must be provided.

The last phase of this provision is important: "freedom from want." Here is one of the most acute problems facing the nations. Not one is free from it as a condition in large measure due to national hard-heartedness and lack of brotherly sympathy with the so-called underprivileged—those who are forced to live below a reasonable subsistence line. It is a situation that demands improvement, for no nation can prosper while it tolerates within its border a group, large or small, that, because of economic conditions forced upon them, are living far below the common level of comfort and well-being. No nation is free from this incubus, although some have the problem in larger measure than others.

It is doubtful whether any other so-called rich and prosperous country has within its own borders a larger underfed, underhoused, and underclothed population than is found in the United States. It is an anomaly almost beyond understanding that a nation that calls itself Christian, wherein wealth and prosperity have been developed in unprecedented degree, should have tolerated and often abetted a situation so appalling. The nearly 13,000,000 Negroes, a great number of poor whites, in both North and South, the sharecroppers and generally indigent, constitute a grave problem that shames every person in any degree motivated by Christianly desires. It is a situation to be remedied, and that in the not-distant future if the country is to abide in economic peace. The need is great, and time presses.

Article *Seven* of the Atlantic Charter states that the peace it foresees "should enable all men to traverse the high seas and oceans without hindrance." This but restates, albeit in definite terms, the doctrine popularly known as "freedom of the seas." It conceives that the ships and craft of any nation shall have all the rights that any nation may claim in going and coming at will. No nation can assume control of the seas; none can forbid traffic by any other. This of necessity foresees a peace from which all exigencies of war have disappeared. It provides for the same degree of freedom on the ocean for all nations that obtains on the inland waters of any nation for traffic by any citizen or group. In other words, it internationalizes the waterways of the world. It is an excellent, righteous hope to be motivated and applied through some unity of purpose and action agreed upon, established, and enforced by the common will.

The opening sentence of Article *Eight* makes the first reference to a reason other than moral or definitely material. It reads, "They believe that all of the nations of the world, for realistic as well as spiritual reasons, must come to the abandonment of the use of force." "Realistic": here is a word that demands attention. As it is used in contradistinction to the next word "spiritual," it must appertain wholly to material reasons, the "reasons" that have so long obtained in ruling potency in the affairs of men and nations. In other words, "realistic," or "realism," as so often used in the parlance of the day, connotes things as they are, or better, as they seem to be, and this use invariably implies that the realistic is the real, and hence must be dealt with on that basis.

If this be true—if materiality, as met and dealt with in the complexity of human experience, is the real—what of the spiritual, the things of Spirit, that is, the Kingdom of God? Surely both cannot be real. Two conditions so completely opposite and antagonistic cannot partake of the same degree of reality. This situation turns us back to the teachings of the Nazarene. Can there be any doubt of what to him was real? It was invariably the Kingdom of his Father, the realm of Spirit, in contradistinction to the universe of matter, the laws and conditions of which he so often changed and nullified because they were unreal.

Does it not seem beyond possibility of doubt, that if the serious problems now facing humanity, touched upon however lightly in the Atlantic Charter, are to be resolved, it must be from understanding God and His universe? In other words, from seeing realism as pertaining solely to the Kingdom of God, and *per contra,* from dealing with all else as temporal, and hence ephemeral. When once this is understood and acknowledged, a beginning will have been made in the right direction. And more people who are deeply concerned about healing the world of its wounds are arriving at this conclusion, are seeking the means to put their desires into actual experience.

Realizing the necessity of finding means to prevent the use

of force by any aggressor nation, a declaration follows that looks to the disarmament of those nations that are now aggressors in the gigantic effort to conquer all peoples apart from the Axis. The statement goes even further. In recognition of the tremendous burden imposed upon peace-loving nations by the aggressors, the hope is expressed that a means may be found to lift such burdens. And surely when aggression is no longer tolerated, automatically all nations will escape from the necessity of maintaining expensive armaments. Since the weapons of modern warfare have increased by leaps and bounds, it seems that this relief may in many instances provide the way to escape national bankruptcy.

The Atlantic Charter as a whole is a useful document. As at the time of its formulation the United States was not in the war as an actual combatant, it tended to encourage the struggling nations in believing that she was their friend and ally. It seemed to line her up with Great Britain, thus strengthening courage and stimulating hope. Its extreme breadth is both a strength and a weakness. It is but a blueprint of the hopes that, to meet the situation, have to be worked out in minutest detail. It was probably all that could be wisely stated at the time, since the President could make no binding agreements apart from the action and sanction of the Congress.

An oft-repeated criticism is directed to the lack of utilizing the experience gained in the past twenty-five years. Absolute national sovereignty has not made for peace; in many nations, the result has been quite the opposite. Can nations be safely left to determine their own methods and practices in government, when under such freedom, they may prepare for future aggression with all the malevolence exhibited by Germany and Japan? Or must there be an overlord, a supersovereignty, that would make impossible such a recurrence? There, too, is a problem that will await solution by the peacemaking authorities and in the ultimate will be resolved only in proportion to reliance upon the introduction of divine power in the solution of the problems of humanity, national and international no less than personal. There is no other way—and the peace will be lasting and just precisely in proportion to the laying down of national pride and selfishness and the supplanting of these fatally dominant factors with the rule of the divine Will, the sovereignty of God.

Could there be adduced greater evidence to prove the futility of material means than the drama of world events enacted on the stage of human experience during the years since Versailles? Fear of loss of national prestige, greed, jealousy, commercial interests, and other destructive qualities so weakened the covenant of the League of Nations in practice that what might, if properly administered, have saved the world from the present calamity lost much power and prestige. A magnificent idealism, divinely conceived but ignobly carried out, failed to prevent a situation that it might have averted.

In fact, the policy adopted contributed by its very weakness to the conviction of Japan, of Italy, and finally of Germany that there was not the slightest likelihood of any effective interference from the League with their nefarious plans. On the contrary, they were encouraged by the signs of supineness that, as it eventuated, they so accurately assessed. The skirts of the United States were by no means clear of blame. A nobly conceived plan for uniting the nations was offered to the peace-making body and was in substance accepted, only to be abandoned to the despair of its parent and chief promoter.

It is notable that the strongest and most vociferous antagonists in America to the adoption of the covenant of the League are immersed in a dense silence. While none may state with certainty what might have been the results to the world if the United States had accepted its responsibility, none can conceive of a worse situation than that with which the nations are now engrossed.

XX

Religious Revolution

IT HAS been wisely remarked that revolution is but evolution hurried up. The processes of revolution are but the short cut to the results of evolutionary development, slow, ponderous, and, as commonly regarded, inexorable. The prime necessity is to make sure that what seems to be progress through the revolutionary process does not in fact become the opposite in effect: a devolutionary process, a retrogression.

If one carefully examines the animus, method, and success of the early Christians in making practical application of the spirit of the Master's teachings, the question arises, Has there been the progress in the process of evangelization of humanity that the Master anticipated and the early Christians expected? Of the tremendous consecration of the early martyrs there can be no doubt. They did often, indeed, surrender their human, material sense of life and gain the divine understanding of Life, the spiritual concept.

As the Church grew in membership and material wealth, it became denominationalized and internationalized. It lost something of its ability to utilize the Christ-Comforter in the solving of the urgent problems of the individual, of the masses, and of the nations. None can doubt the deep conviction and earnest effort of the Protestant Church today to have an ever larger part in the forming of a pattern for the new world order that will render impossible the recurrence of a situation similar to that in which the world is at present immersed. Many reflective persons express the conviction that Christian civilization, or that stemming from any of the great religious groups, could not endure another such calamity. Be that as it may, certain it is that every means should be called into play to prevent the repetition of such a devastating occurrence.

Reviewing the situation, certain queries are inescapable. Have the teachings of the Nazarene been understood and applied to humanity's problems? To be sure, they have regenerated untold millions, leading them to more successful, because more purposeful, lives; have lifted a great section of humanity out of the depths of material living into a concept of Life that has brought peace, joy, and a goodly measure of happiness. "But," says the inquirer, "if Christianity has been applied, if the teachings of the Master have been grasped and applied, why this terrible chaos into which the world is at present plunged?" Was Jesus the true teacher? Was he the greatest evangelist that has ever appeared on earth, or was he a charlatan, an impostor, who misled the people and whose precepts were lacking in the potency necessary to the solution of humanity's problems? And if his teachings were true, why has their potency not been manifested to the degree of making such a calamity impossible? Christians are convinced beyond possibility of doubt that his teachings were true, absolutely true in both letter and spirit; that, if properly applied, not only would they heal the individual of every phase of evil to which he might be personally subjected, but they would be equally potent in solving the problems of humanity collectively in all social relations, national and international alike. That it hasn't been done is all too obvious. What then, is the reason? And is there a remedy?

It cannot be denied that the Christian Church through the centuries has traveled in a direction that has not increased its spirituality and, hence, its potency. The formal doctrine, the crystallized creed, highly materialized forms of worship, and the strife for popularity have lessened greatly its spiritual power.

Religious Revolution

This is seen and acknowledged by many thoughtful persons, capable and earnest men and women, devout Christians. The process that should have developed even greater potency and spiritual power has, on the contrary, been rather of a retrogressive character, a devolution, as it were. Spirituality has been buried under a burden of materialism in worship and practice that has hidden the infinite possibilities that the Nazarene revealed as wholly practical of accomplishment. The spiritual animus of his precepts is neglected—almost forgotten, it seems—by the body of the Christian Church. This does not mean that Christianity has not been of immeasurable value in lifting humanity out of the depths of materialism.

But, looking about, the evidences are inescapable. The world is ablaze. Evil is rampant and seemingly tremendously devastating in its potency. Has Christianity done its work? Has it accomplished what was possible of accomplishment, had its precepts been faithfully applied? The obvious answer is, No! It has egregiously failed. Why? Because it has not understood, accepted, and applied the teachings of the Founder. It has drifted far from the moorings that the Master so effectively set in the sea of human misery. A false concept of Deity, plus a false concept of His Christ, plus a false concept of man: these in their unity have been the primary cause of its failure.

It is never too late to reform. There may be an instant revolution. It is not necessary to wait upon evolution in thought or method. The time is now. If we have traversed a course found to be wrong, a course that takes us nowhere, or along a dangerous and unhappy way, we can change that course once its character is understood. To be sure, the wrong way is often the easier to travel. The Master well knew that the wrong way is broad while the right way is, in a material sense, both straight and narrow. But it is the way of life and leads to the Kingdom.

Religious Revolution

I recall an experience in the long ago that well illustrates the point under discussion. With a guide I was climbing a mountain in the densely wooded section of Maine—our goal, an isolated hunter's cabin near the summit. A spotted trail showed us the course. After a time, I told the guide I would enjoy taking the lead to try my skill in following the spots. This he readily agreed to; and, confidently going ahead, I presently came upon a well-defined path running across the general direction of the spotted line. Assured that at last we had found a path that would lead to our goal, I struck out boldly in the well-trod path. Almost at once I was halted by the guide, who sharply interrogated, "Where are you going?" My query, "Is not this the way?" brought the assurance that that path came from nowhere and led nowhere. It was a deer's runway. The lesson has been of great value in bringing me up sharply when tempted to follow a trail unfamiliar, leading from nowhere to nowhere, however well-trod, however broad and alluring it may have seemed to be.

Is it not indisputably true, then, that the all-important work confronting mankind is to learn of the true God, of His Christ, and of man, in order to find the right way; and, having found it, to keep it?

Could there be by any possible reasoning a greater need to change our course than now confronts a world engaged in an all-out global conflict, so grim that it justifiably may be said to dominate—even vitally to affect—every human being in the world? It is a struggle to determine the kind of society of which we are to be a part: a people free, or a people enslaved. So great is the issue, so much is involved, that the situation should be approached with deep humility, with a genuine desire to know the truth, even though this calls upon us to cut off the right hand and pluck out the right eye—that is, to surrender our most cherished, our longest-held beliefs. The problem, then, resolves itself into one of education; of learning the most important truths, truths that are priceless beyond words, beyond the realm of material evaluation.

To know God is certainly the Christian's first necessity. Knowledge of God leads to the understanding of His Christ and of man made in God's likeness—the likeness of Spirit, not of matter. Again, Christ Jesus becomes the most effective teacher. Study of the New Testament and of the Old Testament in the illumination shed upon it by the Nazarene leaves one in no doubt as to the character of Deity, of His immanence and availability through the Christ, the divine Messenger, to solve every problem that ever has or ever can confront humanity. An infinite Intelligence that is Life and Love, that is Spirit and divine power, is available to every mortal everywhere through the Christ.

If it be possible to select one brief saying as the universal rule for the solving of the world's problems, for healing every type of discord, it would perhaps be this, "Seek ye first the kingdom of God, and his righteousness; and all these things shall be added unto you." [1] Here is the perfect rule. To become effective, it must be applied. Has it been? How many nations have had this holy purpose? None! And yet we speak of Christian nations. Then, is not the fundamental need, the *sine qua non* of human welfare, to learn and accept this perfect rule, to adopt it as the way to the goal and follow it, whatsoever temptation may arise to lead us astray?

This need very clearly points to some system and method of education that will lead into the understanding of this primary rule, the need to practice it, and to the necessity of keeping assiduously to the task. This way alone leads to the Kingdom. Moreover, it is only by this true type of education that righteous Democracy, the true government, is possible of

---

[1] Matt. 6:33.

establishment. To find the means for this education is the immediate necessity.

Agreement reached as to the underlying necessity that a new and better type of religious education be developed upon which will rest the structure of permanent peace, the problem of determining the plan and means of such education presents itself. A brief survey of the situation in America will aid in visualizing the problem. A glance at the early history of the country reveals that religion was a prominent factor in urging various groups of adventurous people to find in the American wilderness opportunity to establish and promote their specific type of religion and worship. These religious zealots often followed adventures actuated by the less worthy purpose of trading with the natives for material gain. And often this trading was accompanied by wicked and shameful procedure.

In the southern and central regions, these bold missionaries were constantly faced with dangers from wild beasts and frequently from savage Indians as well. This did not stop or greatly hinder the primary purpose, to establish schools to instruct the native population in their specific religious doctrines.

On the Eastern coast the situation was somewhat different. The spirit of commercialism sent traders up the Hudson and Delaware rivers and many other lesser streams, lured by the prospect of profitable traffic with the Indians. To the settlements founded by these early comers presently came religionists of various denominations to establish churches. The Dutch in New York, the Calverts in Maryland, the English Cavaliers in Virginia, Penn and the Quakers in Pennsylvania, all opened the way for the establishment of churches and religious teachings, each in accord with their specific beliefs. And these religious teachings were prominent factors in the civic and social development that followed.

The beginnings in New England were in general after the

same pattern. First came adventurers to the rivers of Maine, for trade with the natives. These were followed by stern religionists who, harried in the mother country for daring to become dissenters from the doctrine of the established church, set out across an uncharted sea to face the rigors of a New World wilderness in winter, for conscience' sake, for freedom to worship God according to their deep-seated convictions.

The purpose and expectancy of the Pilgrim group in Massachusetts was to establish a community that should be divinely planted and divinely directed, a pure theocracy, each member of which should be bound to all in a truly Christian brotherhood. The Mayflower pact set this forth in specific terms. And these early comers and those who soon followed were actuated by a high purpose: the purpose to worship God, to lead religious lives under divine guidance and with fervent desire to share their blessings with others.

It was logical, even inevitable, it seems, that the education established should have been primarily for the advancement of religion. The Bible was the constant textbook. To be sure, the rudiments of secular education were taught, but the central instruction was religious. The surroundings of the early settlers were wholly unlike what they had left behind in the Old World. There, civilized conditions and methods were far advanced. Here was an untamed region from which were to be wrested, through the most strenuous labor, homesteads, farms, villages, and cities. The wilderness was to be overcome and wild nature brought under cultivation.

It seems inevitable that their physical surroundings should have influenced the religious situation. As they became absorbed in their strenuous labors, the fervor for their doctrinal beliefs and worship somewhat lessened. The material prosperity that developed gradually darkened their spiritual vision. As the physical sciences grew in popularity in the academies and colleges in answer to the demand of industry and commerce, education in the things of the spirit—the unseen and, to the physical senses, less tangible—lessened in interest and promotion.

Education became secularized, and the people lost much of the vision of the early comers. As prosperity increased, as vested interests became dominant in the civic life, so their influence crept into the Churches. Religious doctrine gradually became modified, less strict, more adaptable to the ways of the flesh. Religious education, weakened in character, lessened in its popularity as material wealth and the physical became more dominant in the demands for their satisfaction. As this trend continued, it slowly but surely undermined the religious stamina that characterized the founders of the country.

The result is what one beholds today: the influence of the Church greatly weakened, its spiritual animus drained off to a degree that scarcely distinguishes the spiritual and vital in education from the merely ethical and moral—even from the physical and temporary. Religious seminaries are no longer attracting, in numbers, the type of young men and women who formerly came to prepare for the sacred ministry. Something serious has happened, with results that have changed the direction of the civilization of the Western World.

What is the remedy? To overhaul the curriculum of schools and colleges, of all our institutions of learning, placing definite religious education as the very basis; this is but the first round of the ladder. It is immediately objected by the incredulous and fearful that this would in America run counter to the provisions of fundamental law, the Constitution—that State and Church would come into conflict. This is mere excuse for not doing the necessary things. There is no word in the Constitution of the United States or in its amendments that forbids religious education. In fact, by implication it assumes that there shall be such education.

Then the objection is raised that the teachings will become

denominational, thus promotive of a specific brand of doctrine. This is completely and adequately met by basing this primary education upon the teachings of the Master, setting forth his simple instructions in their primary meaning as they fell from his lips. This is by no means an insurmountable task: by no means is there sufficient reason for not undertaking it when once the people are agreed that only by increasing the spiritual purpose of society will the longed-for peace be brought into realization. The necessity is great. The remedy is at hand.

How long will humanity hold to its old moorings, to its faith in the things that are seen, when passing events hourly are proving that such things are but temporal, are fleeting and unworthy when measured by things of the Spirit that are eternal? Humanity must awaken to the necessity for a change of purpose, for putting the desire for spiritual gain in the place of the zest to win material possessions. The man who built bigger barns to contain his increased possessions did not live to enjoy them.

It is the commonly accepted belief of society that childhood is the proper period for education. That when the mind is unfolding or being led through some process of education, the opportunity to direct it rightly is too obvious to need discussion. The child mentality is most susceptible, is most plastic and responsive to instruction. Then inevitably it follows that a profound obligation devolves upon those responsible to see that the child thought is turned to the eternal, to God and the true way of life. The home has great responsibilities in this education. And it seems that many conditions have conspired to so change the character of the home and its impact upon the child as to lead directly away from the most important type of education. Until there is an awakening to parental responsibility as to the proper education, there will be no radical change in the direction in which the child grown to maturity will walk. Any other effort made to remedy the situation can be only partially successful. Nothing can take the place of a mother's influence upon the child thought.

The release of children from public schools one hour a week for religious instruction is a worthy effort, but one, it seems, that offers but faint possibility of furnishing the remedy for the present almost complete secularization of education. With its possibilities fully evaluated, there remains the problem of meeting the situation before the children will have arrived at the state of adulthood, when they shall have assumed the duties of government and social relations in general. The need is for a present awakening. The Assembly of the Church of England has adopted a five-point program providing for the introduction and development of religious education in British schools. The subject is not an obligatory part of the curriculum, but it is definitely provided for.

The Churches are organized and now have great influence in the right direction. Do they see the need? Do they recognize that the rules of the Master laid down so effectually must be made operative *now* in order to ensure against another world-wrecking calamity? Even a few of the Master's precepts made practical in the lives of church members would accomplish untold good. The Golden Rule actually motivated in affairs of government, in business, in all international relations, would surely be the perfect preventive against a recurrence of this world-wide tragedy.

The Churches have the means. They have the teachings of the Founder of Christianity in their practical simplicity. If the clergy should now undertake to inspire their flocks of whatsoever specific denomination with the essence of the sayings of the Master, willing to lay aside doctrinal beliefs and learn anew the simplest precepts, wonderful results would follow. The age of miracles has not passed, and the time is *now*. But the miracles must be earned. How? Return to the simple words of the Master and their application to the needs at hand.

Develop a full faith in God and His availability to meet every human need, social as well as individual. The Churches can do much if they understand the method. "Seek ye first the kingdom of God, and his righteousness" is not an admonition impossible of accomplishment. But to become effective, it must be put into practice. "Do unto others as you would have them do to you" contains no mystery. It is as plain as words can set forth the righteous way.

Education is the highway to the peace the world is seeking. But it must be lifted above the secular into the realm of reality, into the Kingdom of Spirit, for only there abides the eternal truth, the truth that Jesus assured his disciples would make them free. And there can be no reasonable doubt that what he promised, the true freedom, is liberation from all that restricts and disturbs the human experience—freedom from want, discord in whatever form, strife, warfare. But this blessed state is found only as mortals think rightly, seek truth instead of falsity—in short, know God and His universe. This is the true education.

Meantime, knowledge of many phases of the material situation is necessary. Science, art, language, mathematics, economics, history—in fact, the curriculum of education as generally accepted—are from the standpoint of human need, a necessary equipment. But when carried on to the exclusion of true education, knowledge of God, there result conditions like what is now threatening the whole world with devastation and disaster. First things will be put first when the right perspective is gained.

The Protestant Church is making a vigorous and highly effective effort through a union of various denominations, both in America and in England, to ensure a prominent place at the Peace Table when victory has perched on the banners of the United Nations. None can gainsay that the effort is a most worthy one, both in purpose and method. There is

Religious Revolution

strength in unity; but only when that unity is based upon the infinite One is success assured.

Does the Church realize its mistakes? Is it awake to the fundamental fact that only through the true concept of the Master's teachings can there be obtained the understanding and knowledge of God that must underlie any peace that may become permanent? It is a situation that requires humility, willingness to surrender preconceived notions of doctrines and policy as well, and a return to the simple precepts upon which primitive Christianity was founded.

This by no means requires the Church to enter upon war, that is, to engage in the actual conflict. The fact is, since the Church is a spiritual concept, it can never be engaged in a human or material conflict. It is above all materiality, all human strife. It has its counterpart in the human institution called the Church, which is but the instrument or vehicle having the holy aim of evangelizing humanity: to lift struggling mortals out of the mire of materiality into the realm of peace and good will in which the children of God forever abide. Never have the demands upon the Church been so great, so imperative, as now. Now is the opportunity for it to prove itself the instrument of the Almighty to lift the peoples of earth out of deadly combat into that state where perpetual peace is found. It is indeed the testing time.

But the way has been charted. Christ Jesus has done all that could be done to inspire his followers, not only to seek the way of salvation, but, once it is found, to remain in it. A mere glance at history carries full conviction that strife—destructive warfare—has been humanity's heaviest burden. It is not inevitable, it is not a condition necessary to human experience. The Nazarene opened the way to permanent peace.

In the work of regenerating humanity, of establishing lasting peace, the Church has two functions. The one is to evangelize individuals—its own membership, and all whom it may reach —with its transforming message. Imbued with the spirit of the Christ, these regenerated ones become instruments to teach and influence all with whom they come in contact. They become missionaries of "the Spirit of truth." In the Democracies, they make their way into the halls of State, serving in many capacities, not only aiding to bring the Christian's point of view into government, but by their Christian example becoming exemplars of the Christian way of life.

When this type of ministry becomes a specific purpose of the Church, the work of Christianizing governments will grow apace. Always the ultimate purpose of the Church is to establish on earth that brotherhood which symbolizes the true brotherhood of God's children. This spiritual brotherhood is in fact the true Church, of which the Christ is the head. Paul states this very clearly in his message to the Ephesians.

The process of evangelization of the individual carried on by the Church is its direct method of reforming the social order, of bringing it into conformity with the teachings of the Master. This process brings to the disciple a vision of true brotherhood so comprehensive as to include all mankind, regardless of race or cultural condition. This has been the spirit of the grand missionary work carried on by the Church so effectively through the centuries. It is this same spirit that will become the herald and promoter of global and lasting peace.

Another prominent function of the Church is to utilize its influence as a body upon the course of world events. The determined action of the Federal Council of Churches of Christ in America, and now in an international Ecumenical Movement for permanent peace, if brought to bear, can scarcely fail to wield an impressive influence upon the framers of the New World Order to follow victory of the United Nations. When the Church through its righteous prayers invokes the omnipotence of the Almighty, the results can be nothing less than complete success. This conviction by the Church will necessitate insistence that its representatives shall have their place at the Peace Table, and that their proposals shall be given due recognition.

These efforts will be successful precisely in proportion to the righteousness of their prayers, prayers based upon understanding of the Christ-presence and upon absolute faith in the availability of the greatest of all peacemakers. The God who is infinite and everpresent good, will, through His Messenger, Christ, support every righteous effort for the establishment of just and permanent peace.

In accomplishing this task of peacemaking, the Church has a responsibility in proportion to the tremendous need confronting society—nothing less than saving what we are pleased to term Christian civilization; and not alone to save it in its present inchoate form, but to remodel and rebuild it into a structure after the pattern seen in the Mount.

XXI

Citizens of the World

THIS chapter is in a minor degree autobiographical. The reason will be obvious. It outlines briefly the processes whereby I became a citizen of the world. I was reared in the deeply rural section of northern New England. Our home was in a prosperous farming community where truly "the richest was poor and the poorest lived in abundance." As there was little to vary the round of daily experience, the Town Meeting held annually early in March was an event of compelling interest. As a mere lad, I was permitted to accompany my father to this annual gathering of the citizens of the town, and early became intensely interested in this perfect example of true democracy in operation.

These bearded and hard-handed farmers, practically every one a toiler who knew the long day made necessary by his vocation, came together to elect the administrative officers of the town, to lay the self-imposed taxes, and to discuss all questions pertaining to the general welfare of the townspeople. It was a most impressive experience to a youth just looking out upon the world of affairs with something both of curiosity and of wonderment.

Sentiments bordering on animosity held over from the strenuous days of the Civil War often flashed out in the heated debates on some question regarded as of major importance. "Copperheads," as the Democrats were termed who opposed the war, was sometimes hurled by the Republicans who had upheld the war. But in general the meetings were calm and orderly, good examples of people governing themselves.

Citizens of the World

First was the election of a moderator to preside over the meeting. Then followed the election of the officers of the town, who were to administer the will of the people. Three selectmen were chosen by ballot and a town clerk, treasurer, tax collector, superintendent of schools, and minor officers, after the fashion of earlier times. Then followed determination of taxes to meet various expenses of the town. These covered highway expense, care of the poor, support of schools, salaries of the town officers, and any other necessary expenses that might arise. These matters settled, all departed, usually in the best of humor, to meet again to repeat the experience a year later.

Here I early learned my first lesson in Democratic government. Very soon, however, my horizon lifted. In September of each year was another election. Other officers were needed for broader purposes than those considered at the Town Meeting. Our town was one of thirteen united into a county for the purpose of providing for other needs not met by the Town Meeting. Courts were necessary to adjudicate problems rising among the citizens of the towns and to give hearing to violators of the law who should be apprehended, tried, and penalized.

There were also inter-town relations to be settled. These called for county officers, a court and a sheriff to enforce its decrees and to administer the law in general; also county commissioners, whose duty was to settle problems involving the rights and interests of the constituent towns. Here was a type of government above the authority of the town, elected by the voters of the several towns, administrative in character but with no power to lay taxes.

Thus I found that I was a citizen also of the county. But I soon learned that not all the needs of society were met by the town and county officers. There were other and important needs to be cared for by a government above both of these local governments. The State comprised sixteen counties. To administer their general affairs, a State government was needed. Following the pattern of the United States Government, this State government consisted of three departments, legislative, executive, and judicial, constituted of persons chosen at the September election.

I had become a citizen of the State as well as of the town and county. But I learned, as my political horizon was further lifted, that something more was needed. Even these three forms of government, well conceived and righteously carried out, did not meet all the needs of the citizen. The individual States in the long past had found that certain necessary relations could not be satisfactorily met without a super-government, to be brought into actuality only by agreement of the sovereign States to unite in a common federation, a veritable Union which should determine the general needs, pass laws to meet them, and provide for the enforcement of those laws through administrative and judicial departments. Moreover, this government should have sole charge of the relations of the United States to all other nations; that is, it should determine and motivate our foreign policy.

Then it dawned upon me that I was a citizen of this great union of States, known as the Republic of the United States of America. How my horizon as a citizen had expanded! How great were my privileges as a citizen of four civil groups —town, county, State, Nation! But these privileges also entailed serious duties, the duties of good citizenship. Since the character of each of these four governments was determined by the quality of the constituent citizens, there appeared a conviction of the need for honest, clear understanding of the obligation that this citizenship imposes.

Government can rise no higher in its ideals and execution of those ideals than the mental qualities of those who bring it into existence. When this relationship is clearly visualized, the duties attaching to citizenship in the Democratic form of government can scarcely fail to be realized by every reflective citizen.

It is generally agreed that the poets are the seers who strike through to the heart of humanity's problems. It was Lowell who wrote lines pertinent to this discussion:

> "New occasions teach new duties; time makes ancient good uncouth;
> They must upward still, and onward, who would keep abreast of truth; . . ." [1]

The "new occasions" that have come upon the world since the turn of the century are too many and too obvious to need examination or explication. It is a vastly changed world that we are looking out upon since I gained my first lesson in Democracy in that primitive Town Meeting.

There are, however, certain underlying truths that have not changed; nor will they change, for since they emanate from the divine Source, they belong to universal man. In that rustic neighborhood there was manifest among its denizens something that was true and beautiful. It was the genuine spirit of friendliness. It was, in fact, the exemplification of the Christ-presence, although it was not so recognized. However much of warmth was engendered in the debates at those March meetings, when they were adjourned the heat died out. These were neighbors and friends engaged in friendly intercourse in the daily round.

If a farmer became ill and his affairs suffered, the neighbors milked his cows, harvested his crops, and cut his hay; in fact, they did whatever was needed to carry out his humble plans. If a new barn was to be raised, the whole countryside turned out, making a sort of fiesta of the occasion. The women prepared hearty food for the men, and all rejoiced. When sick-

---

[1] James Russell Lowell, "The Present Crisis."

ness came, kindly neighbors watched at the bedside, nursed the sick one, happy in the privilege of Christian ministry.

Now the whole world is gravely in need of the entry into the communal consciousness of that same spirit of friendly service of the ministering angel of peace that brings good will to all men. This is "the Spirit of truth" for which Jesus promised he would pray. The urgency is great that our political horizon be lifted far beyond the limits of mere national boundaries, until there is envisioned the great fact that all men are brothers and must in the end be looked upon with the same sense of compassion and friendliness that was manifested in that rustic community of my youth.

The need is great—the demand imperative. The whole world is now a neighborhood. It took Andrew Jackson as long to travel from his home in Tennessee to Washington to be inaugurated President of the United States as it recently took Mr. Wendell Willkie to traverse the entire globe, including visits at several of the world's important capitals. In the New World Order that will be built at the close of the present conflict, the foundation must be laid in the cement of friendship inherent in the Golden Rule, of genuine interest on the part of the more privileged groups in the less advanced people. The Christ must be accepted as the guide and rule. We are, willy-nilly, citizens of the world. To perform our part in this expanded sense of citizenship, we need to rise above self-interest into the mental state that recognizes that humanity cannot proceed to its ultimate destiny part free and part submerged within the limits of ignorance and want.

It is not what we in a personal sense may wish to do. It is what is forced upon the more enlightened peoples, not alone by pressure of circumstances, but by the operation of that spiritual law that is ever at work in human consciousness, lifting humanity to higher levels exactly in proportion to the extent of its reception. We are thus of necessity forced to recognize that in the fulfillment of divine purpose we become citizens of the world, with obligations in conformity with this enlarged sense of citizenship.

The United States had one great opportunity for promoting world unity and peace, and missed it ignominiously. Woodrow Wilson caught a vision of a union of nations that, if properly effected, would make a future conflict unlikely, if not impossible. Nobly he strove to have his ideal accepted, and after much discussion he won the major part of his program: acceptance by the Nations at Versailles of his plan for a League of Nations. The war to end wars was to become more than a slogan. It was gaining actuality. As all the world knows, he brought his covenant for a League of Nations back to Washington in the spirit of a great victory won; and he looked for a ready ratification by the Senate, as provided in the Constitution. But he did not measure the depth and determination of the political opposition, which was not able to rise above party interests, even when the peace of the world was at stake.

Valiantly did the President labor for the realization of his great vision. Day and night he strove for the peace victory. But in vain: the opposition was too strong. Idealism was not sufficiently backed by understanding of that Omnipotence that is always at hand and available to forward any just cause, any cause that leads to the Kingdom of righteousness and peace. The Christ was not present in the deliberations that defeated the righteous purpose. The covenant was rejected by the Senate by a vote so small that the presence of a small group of absent Senators who were said to be favorable could have turned the tables completely. The promise for a permanent and just peace passed.

President Wilson, stricken in the midst of his great struggle, weakened and passed on, a discouraged and defeated man. It may be, probably is, true that had he possessed more of the breadth of great statesmen, he would have placated the opposition by taking them into his inner councils and sending their representatives to the peace conference. This possibility by no means lessens the value of his vision or diminishes it as a prospective means of bringing to the world a stable peace, just and therefore durable.

When President Wilson passed on, *The New York Times* cabled Jan Smuts at Capetown, asking him to characterize his accomplishment in a message of three hundred words. Smuts replied in substance: Somewhere along the line of human progress, the nations will develop some type of unity of action. When that day comes, be it far or near, the credit will belong to Woodrow Wilson.

Speculation may seem useless. But as the situation is reviewed and the awful calamity now engulfing the world is faced, the query is inescapable: What would have been the result had the United States supported its child, had entered the League and taken its place in all the deliberations that followed? Would Germany have been permitted to engage in a propaganda that convinced her own people and many others that she was not the aggressor and had not begun the war, but was in fact a nation much maltreated and sinned against, surrounded by a ring of steel poised for her destruction? She might not have been permitted to embark upon and carry through a program of rearmament that has produced her appalling military machine. She might not have been permitted to reoccupy the Ruhr.

There might not have been a momentous incident developing into Japan's wicked assault upon China; there might have been no Italian onslaught upon Abyssinia, a benighted and primitive people, innocent of recent aggressive or unseemly effort against Italy or her people. There might not have arisen the disgraceful situation in Spain where an effort to establish a Democratic way of life was not only beset by a Spanish Fascist party supported by Italy and Germany, but which had in some measure even the support of the British government.

Surely much of distress and turmoil might have been avoided had that group of absent Senators been present at the roll call. All the disaster now harassing humanity might logically have been avoided, and the nations now engaged in gigantic effort to destroy each other might now be fully occupied in the arts of peace. Contemplation of what might have been and what might be in place of the world tragedy now being so bloodily played out can scarcely fail to characterize the failure of the Senate for political reasons to ratify the covenant of the League of Nations as one of the world's greatest calamities.

To be sure, nearly all of the chief actors in that terrific tragedy have passed from the scene. But there still threatens the danger that a concerted and powerful effort may be made, in the peace settlement that is sure to eventuate, to duplicate the incidents of the last peacemaking. If the presence of the Christ at the peace table is ignored and "the Spirit of truth" does not become dominant, no just and permanent peace will be negotiated.

It may be asserted that had the Christ-Comforter been acknowledged and accepted as the directive agency at Versailles and in the Senate, the world might now be enjoying that state of peace and prosperity for which the Democracies of the world so keenly long. If ever there were need to gain wisdom from past experience, that time is now. All earnest Christians and all who pray to a supreme Ruler of the universe should pray that there may never be a repetition of the present frightful holocaust.

To ensure the answer to these earnest prayers, the Christ, forever knocking at the door of human consciousness, must be admitted, be placed in command, in order that the peace to be arranged shall be based upon that divine Purpose, that perfect and infinite Love which the Christ reveals. If this policy be adopted, there will be no repetition of the results that followed the Versailles Treaty, no backing out of a moral and spiritual obligation that the United States owes to all humanity.

Another position of isolation, another refusal to unite with the nations of the world to form the necessary union to promote peace, would be pretty sure to plant the seeds for further conflicts, each to grow more terrible before the increasing destructiveness of material invention. It is poor logic that reasons that the United States has no obligations to co-operate politically, since it is sure to seek international relations in trade, commerce, and other interests. The fact is that isolationism is a purely selfish doctrine: it cares only for its own welfare. And with the close and ever closer relationship of all the nations, it is, moreover, a short-sighted policy, for it is plainly patent that the safety and well-being of each nation is inextricably involved with the safety of all the others.

It is little wonder that certain of the Great Nations now united in the supreme effort to win the war are deeply concerned with what will be the position of the Great Republic after the war is won. From past experience they have reason for their concern. They remember that the Senate of the United States alone of all legislative bodies of the world not only requires a two-thirds vote to ratify a treaty, but also has the power to amend the body of the covenant. This power, if held to, contains the possibility of great difficulties in arriving at a definite policy of world unity. It is clear that modification of this provision might be an important step toward ensuring that the United States will take a new place in the vital work ahead.

XXII

The Christ at the Peace Table

IN GREAT crises in history, men have frequently declared their faith in God and have sought divine intervention in behalf of their causes. It seems that, to support a cause with valor and persistence, men must have some faith in the right of that for which they are contending. Even Hitler in recent months has talked of God as an ally of the Nazi party, absurd as this seems to the sane portion of humanity. But when victory shall have been won, will there become manifest in formulating peace plans for the freedom of mankind the degree of sincerity that has been so commonly proclaimed by the United Nations? Then will be the testing time. Then will be revealed the degree of progress that has been made toward bringing the Christ, "the Spirit of truth," into active operation in the settlement of these affairs so vital to the welfare of all peoples.

Will this "Spirit of truth" be the guiding star illuming the thoughts of the peacemakers with its ineffable light of love and mercy? If these makers of peace be receptive to this divine visitor, all will be well. And it is indubitably true that the peace terms agreed upon will be just and lasting precisely in the degree of their accord with this "Spirit of truth." As self-interest is merged in the general welfare, as national interests are subordinated to the international, the universal needs, the peace will be won.

Peace is a mental state. It is the atmosphere of Good Will, the mental state in which individuals and nations develop toward the goal of completeness the privilege of self-expression that makes for the highest status attainable to mortals. It is this atmosphere that is native in true Democracy. In Lincoln's Second Inaugural Address the great Emancipator uttered words that may well be pondered for their pertinence to the situation that will face the peacemakers: "With malice toward none, with charity for all, with firmness in the right, as God gives us to see the right, let us strive on to finish the work we are in, to bind up the nation's wounds, to care for him who shall have borne the battle, and for his widow, and his orphans—to do all which may achieve and cherish a just and lasting peace among ourselves and with all nations."

With such noble words did Lincoln plead that the Christ, "the Spirit of truth," be the guide and rule of the government toward those who had striven to undo the nation. And he forespoke a condition of peace with all the peoples of earth. If the situation that the Nations will face at the next peace conference be visualized, the prayer of immortal Lincoln is a ray of divine light. The charity devoid of malice that he sought will be a mental state necessary to ensure lasting peace.

This "Spirit of truth" also found voice in Woodrow Wilson's second inaugural spoken prior to the close of World War I. Visualizing the unity of peoples, he declared, "We are provincials no longer. The tragic events of the thirty months of vital turmoil through which we have just passed have made us citizens of the world. There can be no turning back. Our own fortunes as a nation are involved, whether we would have it so or not." And he saw that the principles that underlay the American social and political structure were "not the principles of a province or of a single continent." They were world-wide in their application and must be so recognized.

And among the principles he declared were: "That all nations are equally interested in the peace of the world and in the

The Christ at the Peace Table

political stability of free peoples, and equally responsible for their maintenance; That the essential principle of peace is the actual equality of nations in all matters of right or privilege." [1] Clearly did the first World War President visualize the conditions preliminary to a just and durable peace. A condition of free nations with equality of opportunity is the only political atmosphere in which the dove of peace may prosper.

Little has been said as to the personnel of the peacemakers who in the near or remote future will be called upon to engage in making some of the most urgent and far-reaching decisions that have demanded the attention of mankind. Upon its decisions rest the welfare of future generations. It will forecast the future—whether there will be established the conditions under which men and nations attain their highest degree of development; or whether the earth will periodically be bathed in blood until what is termed Christian civilization shall perish and the darkness of chaos again overshadow the earth, blacking out the last vestige of the light of Love and Good Will.

Preliminary to the coming of this momentous event, there must be an awakening among the citizens of all countries as to the importance of the decisions at stake. It may be too early to discuss the personalities to undertake this great work, but there are certain general observations that may well be made.

One aspect of the situation may be introduced by words of James Bryce, appearing in his "American Commonwealth." In commenting upon the great progress made in the recognition of the work of women in the Americas, he writes, "When one compares nomad man with settled man, heathen man with Christian man, the ancient world with the modern, the eastern world with the western, it is plain that in every case the advance in public order, in material comfort, in wealth, in decency and refinement

---

[1] "The Principles of a Liberated Mankind."

The Christ at the Peace Table

of manners among the whole population of a country—for in these matters one must not look merely at the upper class—has been accompanied by a greater respect for women, by a greater freedom accorded to them, by a fuller participation on their part in the best work of the world." [2]

In these words, written more than thirty years ago, did the British Ambassador favorably note the progress of women in the development of society in America. In the intervening decades the progress has gone on with a rapidity that leaves no least doubt, either as to the capability of women to play a major part in the world's work, or as to the general recognition of this fact.

Earnest and widespread efforts are now being made to determine the best method of establishing a just and lasting peace after the war shall have been won. What type of persons shall be selected by the various Governments to carry on the peace deliberations? is an urgent question. In both the near and distant past, such deliberations have been conducted wholly by men. In the role of peacemakers, women have been excluded, neglected. Analysis of the mental attitude regarding this fact discloses some very important phases of what is termed "psychology." It has commonly been held that women have not developed the mental qualities, the wisdom, political acumen, and stability of purpose, that go to make up the successful peacemaker.

It must not be overlooked that at every Peace Table in history self-interest has been in the saddle. And it has been held that only men were capable of defending the rights and interests of the Governments engaged in the important work of framing peace treaties. Unfortunate and inadequate as the Versailles Treaty has turned out to be, yet it may be safely asserted that a noble effort was made to rise above the interest of the states

---

[2] Vol. ii, 1910 edition, chapter on "The Position of Women."

The Christ at the Peace Table

individually into the common welfare of all nations and peoples involved.

The query naturally arises, Would the conclusions arrived at have been more just, would they have contained in larger measure the elements that constitute the basis of permanent peace, had representative women engaged in the general deliberation? While the answer to this query can be but a matter of conjecture, of personal opinion, yet there are events and circumstances in the long range of human affairs that could be drawn upon in the search for a logical answer.

In both sacred and secular history, women have exercised an unmistakable influence upon the course of human events. Women of the Bible—Sarah, Rebekah, Deborah, Ruth, Mary, mother of Jesus, Mary and Martha of Bethany are notable names in the galaxy of womanhood who played no small part in shaping the events of their times. Looking down the pages of history, the names of Helena, mother of Constantine, of Catherine II of Russia, of Elizabeth of England, and, in later times, of good Queen Victoria stand out in bold letters.

These women, characterized by mental qualities of strength and wisdom, made substantial contributions in directing the course of events of their times. Political wisdom, coupled with the intuitive something that so commonly characterizes the feminine mind, plus the strength and courage of honest convictions, enabled these, each in her own way, to aid in solving the problems of their day that demanded public attention and definite solution. The qualities generally attributed to women —compassion, tenderness, mercy, and patience—are manifestations of the Christ, "the Spirit of truth," the true Peacemaker.

The basic situation has not changed during the long annals of the race. Crises have successively arisen, sometimes even threatening the course of civilization, that have demanded the very best that mortals could demonstrate in the way of wisdom and justice, of righteousness and mercy. We are now, it seems, in the midst of a cataclysm, extrication from which will require the right thinking and righteous prayers of all good citizens—of women no less than of men.

In two major aspects has the position of women in the social order undergone marked changes in recent decades. A degree of liberation has come to womanhood, resulting in the admission of women into many walks of life formerly closed to them. Not only in intellectual pursuits, as teachers, professors, scientists, lawyers, and preachers, but, in short, in every type of the so-called learned professions have women succeeded. In several of them women have made outstanding contributions —have, in fact, gained the top of the ladder in their chosen work. In the business administration field women have been equally successful. The conclusion is inevitable that with enhanced opportunities opened to them, women have displayed the capability, the courage, enterprise and wisdom, to enable them to become worthy coadjutors of men, wherever these qualities are needed in the solution of important problems.

The hard-won battle for equal rights of suffrage, fought out for the most part by women in England and America, developed a type of political acumen and persistence that brought victory in a just and righteous cause. The oft-repeated statement that women were not politically conscious, and hence would be but an added incubus in the determination of political problems, has been gloriously disproved. In Parliament, in the Congress, in executive positions in both countries, women have taken their places with honor and credit to their posts and to their sex.

To be sure, when the right of suffrage had been gained, a period of education was necessary, for without the franchise women as a body had not developed a knowledge of or active interest in the political problems of their states and countries. But once they had gained a voice in the government of the Democracies, immediately there began a process of education that has left nothing unattained in political science. Thus have women in the last half-century gained a place in the conduct of affairs that entitles them to a voice in the determination of questions involving every phase of the public welfare.

Another aspect of the present problem calls for careful consideration. In the tremendous war effort into which the peace-loving nations have been hurled, women are contributing priceless aid. In many forms of mechanical work involved in the production of the matériel of modern warfare, women are nobly responding. At first voluntarily and later under the increasing demands entailed in the prosecution of the war, women in England have willingly responded with a spirit nothing short of the utmost determination to do their full part in winning a complete victory over the inhuman aggressors.

Likewise in the United States, as the demand for men in the armed services has increased, women have gladly sprung to the places made vacant at the bench, at the lathe, and at the assembly line; and they have been found extremely efficient in the prosecution of many varieties of mechanical labor. In other words, it may be boldly asserted that women have responded gallantly, even nobly, to the demands for the huge production necessary to the prosecution of global warfare. They have won their way to a position that can no longer be characterized as less worthy, less capable, or less patriotic than the position that throughout the ages has been assumed by the masculine portion of society.

No longer can it be said that the feminine thought is less entitled to its rightful place in the councils of government, even in the discussions and deliberations concerning international relations. For it has been proved beyond cavil that no mental qualities usually attributed to men may not be justifiably attributed to women also. They have proved their equality. It is now to be recognized and honored in the great events that lie ahead.

The Christ at the Peace Table

Still another aspect of the peace problem is so acute, so poignant, so intimate to women, that it may not be overlooked or denied. Who are most interested in peace—men or women? Who suffer most from the terrible ravages of war? Whose sons, husbands, fathers, and brothers make up the ranks that march off to war, many of them never to return? It is sometimes said that those at the battle front who are engaged in actual combat suffer less than those who remain behind, hoping, longing, praying for the welfare of their loved ones. Can there be any denial of the assertion that women have even more at stake in the holocaust of war than the men who actually fight the battle? The long nights of sleepless vigil, the long days of prayer, are not to be disregarded in counting the cost of war and in allocating the roll of honor.

Does it not follow, then, that womanhood, which is called upon for such tremendous sacrifices incident to warfare, should have a voice, yes, a prominent voice, in the efforts to establish a peace so just, so completely based upon divine justice, upon righteousness and truth, that it will never again be broken by the harsh clash of arms? It is a demand that will not down. Many of the treaties made exclusively by men have not been successful. Something more is needed in the councils where the fate of humanity is at stake.

There is no dearth of capable women. Madame Chiang Kai-shek, Pearl Buck, members of the Parliament and of the present Government in England, women in the Congress and Administration of the United States, and many others possess the qualities and capabilities required of successful representatives at the Peace Table.

So vital is the need, so great beyond the possibility of measurement, that no least possibility should be disregarded. Let the women of the world have their hard-won place in the joint deliberations that will determine the course of events for all humanity!

The Christ at the Peace Table

It is generally recognized that in the work of rehabilitating the ravaged countries and of rescuing primitive peoples from their lowly state, the United States will of necessity play a major part. Her geographical position, her great resources, and her spirit of the Good Neighbor will enable her to engage in a degree of usefulness that perhaps no other nation is prepared to exercise. America, still youthful, will have the opportunity out of her largess to repay something of the debt she owes to the older civilization of Europe. For it is from these sources that she has drawn much of her inspiration and in great measure the culture that she has attained in her comparatively brief career. It is, in a sense, a return of the child to the parent from whom has been drawn her life blood and so much of the mental, spiritual, and cultural values possessed by the parent.

Walt Whitman, "the good gray poet," in his incisive vision saw this situation and voiced the obligation resting upon the young youth of the West in these words:

"Have the elder races halted?
Do they droop and end their lesson, wearied over there
    beyond the seas?
We take up the task eternal, and the burden and the
    lesson,
    Pioneers! O pioneers!" [3]

"The Spirit of truth" finds expression in human affairs in terms of humanitarianism. And when the guns shall have been silenced, it, in turn, will be the work of the Good Samaritan to bind up the wounds of both friends and enemies, to feed all who are hungry, to clothe all who are unclothed, regardless of race or color, whether classed as friend or foe in the great con-

---

[3] From *Leaves of Grass*, by Walt Whitman. Copyright, 1924, by Doubleday, Doran & Company, Inc.

The Christ at the Peace Table

flict. This is the humanitarian work with which the United Nations will be faced.

And the manner in which the task is done will in a large measure determine the value of the lessons learned from the terrible experience in which the world is now involved. Have the mental states that led to the conflict been sufficiently transformed to admit the Christ, the holy visitant ever-ready to enter the door of consciousness when once it is opened? This will be the test of the lessons learned. If the old mental states —persistent nationalism, greed, competition in place of co-operation—be the dominant and determining factors, then will the lesson be of little value, and humanity will go on to other wars and other forms of turmoil.

To provide every Hottentot daily with a quart of milk is good, but not good enough. Better, vastly better, would it be to help him to provide his own quart of milk through lifting him up to a state of independence and self-support. If the prosperous nations cease to exploit him, but fairly exchange the products of their industry for his coconuts and bananas and sisal on just terms, the native population, under Christian tutelage and encouragement, will advance to a position of independence and self-support. They will become factors in the general prosperity of the world, rather than remain dependent and exploited peoples. Adjustment of the commercial relations of the nations and peoples will be secondary only to the political problems to be settled at the Peace Table. "The Spirit of truth" alone will guide the settlement into the channels that make for lasting peace.

"The Spirit of truth," the Christ, at the Peace Table will ensure the success of its great endeavor: nothing less than to provide a peace in which all nations and all peoples can work out their destinies in safety, unplagued by the terrible curse of war. That the people of the United Nations yearn for it is beyond question. That it is possible of realization is equally assured. If there be the same determination to win the peace that is now manifested in winning the war, the peace desired will result. But to base it upon "the Spirit of truth" alone will determine its permanence. "Blessed are the peacemakers: for they shall be called the children of God." [4]

There is no nobler purpose: none is more deeply imbued with the spirit of Christianity than the desire to aid the lowly toward mental, spiritual, and economic freedom. The Great Teacher was definite in his characterization of this type of service: "Verily I say unto you, Inasmuch as ye have done it unto one of the least of these my brethren, ye have done it unto me." [5]

---
[4] Matt. 5:9.
[5] Matt. 25:40.

Index

Abyssinia, 246
Airplanes, use of, 81
Alexandria, 23
Allied Nations, 111, 122 ff., 143
Allied Nations at Versailles, 160
America, early history of, 231
Americas, unity of, 201
Anointed One, 4
Appeasement, 211
Aramaic language, 28
Argentina, 205 ff.
Atlantic Charter, 187, 217 ff.
Augustine of Canterbury, 173
Axis Nations, purpose of, 125, 193
Axis Powers, 120

Babe of Bethlehem, 4
Baptist, John, 21, 76
Beatitudes, 89 ff.
Belgian Congo, 115
Beveridge report, 146 f.
Bible For Today, The, 84 ff.
Big Brother policy, 29
Brotherhood, true, 118
Bryce, James, quoted, 251
Buck, Pearl, 256
Burmese, the, 115

Caesars, 20
Caesars, authority of, 25
Calcutta, 162
California, 210, 219
Calverts in Maryland, 231
Carnegie, Andrew, 179
Catherine II of Russia, 253
Chemistry, benefits of, 82, 112, 128
Chiang Kai-shek, 159, 256
Chile, 205
China, 151, 208, 218
Christ, as the Comforter, 109 ff., 129, 214
Christ, as the Redeemer, 46
Christ at the door, 50
Christ everpresent, 3
Christ, the, expressed by Jesus, 7
Christ, the healing mission of, 54

Christ, the universal truth, 69
Christian Advocate, the, quoted, 115
Christian Brotherhood, 189, 219
Church, Christian, 6
Church, Christian, and Golden Rule, 193
Church, failure of, 46 ff., 228
Church, freedom of, 125
Church, mission of, 213
Churchill, Prime Minister, 187, 217
Citizens of the World, 240 ff.
Colombo, experience at, 197
Colonial population, 193
Confederation of Colonies, 153 f.
Congress, division of the, 210 f.
Coolidge, President, 206
County government, 241 f.
Court of Justice, 214

Darwinian theory, 14
David, reign of, 18
Dead Sea, 116
Decapolis, 22
Deity, true concept of, 13
Democracy, citizens of, 132
Democracy, government by, 201
Democracy made safe, 113
Democracy, obligations of, 141
Democracy on trial, 139
Democracy, preparation of, 177
Democracy proved, 137
Democracy, spirit of, 158, 212
Democracy, true, 16, 114, 117
Democracy, type of, 147
Democracy, weakness of, 211
Department of Peace, 124
Dictators, sneers of, 211
Divine Will, the, 110, 114, 132, 225
Dogmas, divergent, 15 f.
Drummond, Henry, quoted, 14
Drummond, J. Roscoe, quoted, 217
Dutch in New York, 231

East Indies, 115, 121
Economic unity, 220
Eddington, Sir Arthur, quoted, 40

[261]

Index

Education for Democracy, 139 ff.
Education, religious, 233 ff.
Education, secularized, 233
Egypt, 22
Elisha, 130
Elizabeth, Queen, 253
England and India, 162 ff.
England, weakness of, 213
English Cavaliers, 231
Eschatologists, the, 64
Esdraelon, plain of, 22
Ethiopia, 135
Evil, resistance to, 92

Faith, effectiveness of, 71 ff., 133
False prophets, 100
Fascism, 164
Fatherhood of God, 187
Federal Council of Churches, 190
"Fellowship," 170
Ford, Henry, 181, 200
Forgiveness, 61 f.
Forgiveness, Jesus' words, 93
Formosa, 208
Freedom of expression, 145
Freedom of the seas, 222
Freedom of worship, 145
Freedom from fear, 145
Freedom from lack, 146
Freedom from want, 221
Freedoms, The Four, 144 ff.
French possessions, 115
French Republic, 138
Frost, Robert, quoted, 202

Gardara, healing at, 55
Garfield, James A., quoted, 148 ff.
Garment, the whole, 79
Germany, aim of, 218
Germany, an aggressor, 246
Germany and the League, 225
Germany, economic collapse, 112
Germany, claims to superiority, 157
Germany, conquered, 616
Germany, control of, 213
Germany, policy toward, 219
Germany, purpose of, 160 f.
God a Spirit, 12
God, Jehovah, 12
God, the only Creator, 13, 96
Golden Rule, 99 ff., 118, 131, 151, 173, 175, 182
Good Neighbors, 199 ff.

Good Neighbors, policy of, 203
Good Samaritan, 163, 203 f.
Gospels, The Four, 13
Great Britain, 121
Great Britain, at Peace Table, 151
Great Britain, social aids, 142
Greece, Democracy of, 20
Greek culture, 24
Grew, Ambassador, 209

Hamilton, N. Z., 173
Heavenly City, 51
Helena, mother of Constantine, 253
Herodians, 24
Herring, Hubert C., quoted, 200
Hitler, Adolf, 211
Holy Ghost, 7
Holy Spirit, 110
Homestead strike, 180
Hong Kong, 197
Hoover, President, 206, 213
Howard, Clarence, 170 f.

Ideologies of government, 136
I.L.O., The, 172
Immigration, Japanese, 209 ff.
India, 22, 158, 162
Isaiah, 183
Italy, 161, 218, 219, 225

Jacks, L. P., quoted, 181
Jackson, Andrew, 244
Jairus' daughter, 56
Japan, aim of, 218
Japan and the Islands, 195
Japan and the League, 225
Japan, attitude toward, 159, 219
Japan defeated, 161
Japan, difficulties with, 159
Japan, pagan nation, 208
Jefferson, Thomas, 147
Jesus, as the Christ, 8
Jesus, as evangelist and reformer, 34, 227
Jesus, as teacher, 32
Jesus as the way, 9
Jesus, bearer of good news, 20
Jesus crucified, 4
Jesus, the Great Physician, 16
Jesus, healing a sick man, 37
Jesus, healing mission of, 54 ff.
Jesus, Master Metaphysician, 48
Jesus, resurrection of, 58 ff.

[262]

Index

Jesus, Revelator of God, 19, 67
Jesus, specific teachings of, 37
Jesus, Source of authority, 35 ff.
Jesus, unity with God, 49
Jesus, wisdom of, 75 ff.
John's Gospel, 85, 118
Joppa, City of, 22

Kingdom of God, 63, 233
Kingdom of God, glories of, 33
Kingdom, safety of, 64
Kingdom, What, Whence, Where, 63 ff.
Korea, 208
Korea seized, 218

Labor and Industrial Peace, 165 ff.
Labor, attitude of, 167
Labor, Jesus' teachings and, 168 f.
Labor, rights of, 171 f.
Labor Unions, 166 f.
"Laborers' shares," 174
Lamb, Charles, 187
Law, divine, 19, 143
Lazarus, story of, 48
League of Nations, 126, 135
League of Nations, opponents of, 225, 245
League of Nations, weakness of, 187
Lepers, healing of, 55
Life, Eternal, 38, 40
Life, the perfect, 60
Lincoln, Abraham, quoted, 250
Love, its effectiveness, 73 ff.
Luke, interest in place, 84 f.

Macaulay, quoted, 147 ff.
Malvern Conference, 175
Mammon, god of, 99
Manchuria, 135, 208, 218
Mark, Gospel of, 85
Mary, mother of Jesus, 4
Materiality discussed, 39 ff.
McConnell, Bishop Francis, quoted, 190
McKinley, President, 117
Mein Kampf, 9
Merchants, Roman, 25
Mesopotamia, 22
Messiah, The, 4
Messianic Mission, 57
Military power, 212
Millikan, Robert A., 40

Mt. Gerizim, 47
Moving pictures, 80 f., 206

National government, 242
National socialism, 112, 164
Nationalism, spirit of, 113
Native soldiers at Manila, 196
Naval ratio, 208
Negro and sharecroppers, 221
Negro problem, 144 ff.
Negroes, treatment of, 143, 188
Netherlands and East Indies, 162
New England, beginning of, 231 f.
New World Order, Pattern of the, 150 ff.
New York Times, The, quoted, 246
Nicene Creed, 46
Nicodemus, 35, 40
Nipponese, claims of, 157

Palestine, 19, 116
Pan-American Union, 199
Parables, use of, 52
Parker, Theodore, 136 f.
Paul, sayings of, 25
Paul, Roman citizen, 20
Peace, lasting, 110
Pearl Harbor, 121, 159
Penn, Wm., 231
Pentecost, Day of, 69
Perfect Rule, a, 102 ff.
Perry, Commodore, 209
Peter, Sermon of, 70
Pharisees, lack of understanding, 36
Philip rebuked, 7
Philippines and United States, 117
Pilate, Pontius, 23, 713 f.
Pilgrims, 132, 232
Political unity, 153
Profit motive, 179
Property exemption, 169
Protestant Church, 226
Protestant Church, obligation of, 235 ff.
Puerto Rico, 144, 208

Quakers, 132

Racial equality, 191 f.
Racial poverty, 192 f.
Raw materials, 219
Reason, realistic and spiritual, 223
Redemption, how won, 51
Religious unity, 156 f.

[263]

Index

Revolution, religious, 226 ff.
Rhodes, Cecil, 200
Rich young man, the, 39
Rio de Janeiro, Conference at, 184
Rome, authority of, 25
Rome, Imperial City, 19
Roman Eagles, 23, 25
Roosevelt, President, 31, 185, 187, 217
Ruler, the, 135
Russia in Peace Council, 151 ff.

Sadducees, 24
Safety of Nations, 221
Salvation, universal, 38
Sanhedrin, 20, 25
Science and Christianity, 80 ff.
Senate, U. S., adverse to League, 245
Sepphoris, city of, 23
Septuagint, 24
Sermon on the Mount, 84 ff.
Shepherd, The Good, 51
Sinai, Law of, 90
Slavery in United States, 142
Smoot-Hawley tariff, 113
Smuts, Jan, 246
Solomon, reign of, 18
"Spirit of truth," 249
State, government of, 242
Sterling, John, quoted, 84
Super Nation, a, 155
Supreme Court and labor, 177
Syria, 22, 116

Temple, desecration of, 44
Temple, teaching in, 42
Temple of Peace, 215
Temple, Archbishop William, 175
Thirteen Colonies, the, 207
Times, London, 181
Times, The New York, quoted, 246
Tolstoy, quoted, 78
Total peace, 123

Total war, 121
Totalitarian countries, 140
Totalitarianism, 137
Town Meeting, 240 ff.
Truth, nature of, 17

United States and American Republics, 199
United States and Labor, 160
United States and League of Nations, 126
United States and Palestine, 160
United States and peace, 160
United States at Peace Table, 151
United States, responsibility of, 160
Unity of Nations, 173 ff.

Valder, H., 174
Versailles, Treaty of, 112
Versailles Treaty, lessons from, 151
Virginia, early settlers of, 231

Wagner Act, 178
Wallace, Henry A., quoted, 183
War, global, 127
Way, the joy of the, 60
Whitman, Walt, quoted, 257
Willkie, Wendell, 244
Wilson, President, 126, 202, 245, 250, 256
Winant, John G., 172
Wise building, 101 ff.
Women at Peace Table, 252 ff.
Women of the Bible, 253
Women, struggle of, 253
World Association, 183
World League, 153
World War I, 250
Worship, true, 47

Zaccheus, 43